There Goes the 'Hood

# There Goes the 'Hood

Views of Gentrification from the Ground Up

LANCE FREEMAN

TEMPLE UNIVERSITY PRESS
Philadelphia

**Temple University Press**
1601 North Broad Street
Philadelphia PA 19122
*www.temple.edu/tempress*

☉ The paper used in this publication meets the requirements of the American National Standard for Information Sciences—Permanence of Paper for Printed Library Materials, ANSI Z39.48-1992

Library of Congress Cataloging-in-Publication Data

Freeman, Lance.
    There goes the 'hood : views of gentrification from the ground up /
Lance Freeman.
        p.   cm.
    Includes bibliographical references and index.
    Contents: Introduction—The evolution of Clinton Hill and Harlem—There
goes the 'hood—Making sense of gentrification—Neighborhood effects
in a changing 'hood—Implications for planning and policy—Conclusion.
    ISBN 1-59213-436-X (cloth : alk. paper) — ISBN 1-59213-437-8
(pbk. : alk. paper)
        1. Urban renewal—New York (State)—New York—Case studies.
    2. Gentrification—New York (State)—New York—Case studies.
    3. Gentrification—Social aspects.   I. Title.

HT177.N5F74   2006
307.3'41609747—dc22                                        2005056054

        6   8   9   7   5

ISBN 13: 978-1-59213-437-3  (pbk. : alk. paper)

# Contents

Acknowledgments     vii

1   Introduction     1

2   The Evolution of Clinton Hill and Harlem     17

3   There Goes the 'Hood     59

4   Making Sense of Gentrification     95

5   Neighborhood Effects in a Changing 'Hood     125

6   Implications for Planning and Policy     157

7   Conclusion     188

Appendix: Methodology     211

References     219

Index     231

# Acknowledgments

I OWE A DEBT OF GRATITUDE to many people who, in being a part of my life, helped me write this book. Frank Braconi at the Citizens Housing and Planning Council in New York collaborated with me on my first foray in researching gentrification and was instrumental in getting me to tackle this thorny topic. The idea for this book grew out of our attempts to explain some of the counterintuitive results we found in that research.

The Institute for Social and Economic Research and Policy and the Center for Urban Research and Policy at Columbia University provided funds to support much of the research conducted here. These funds enabled me to hire research assistants, purchase software, and record and transcribe the interviews I conducted. Radhika Patel conducted a pilot study and wrote a master's thesis that informed some of my ideas, and Moriah McGrath provided excellent research assistance. Without their support, this book would not have been possible.

Darrick Hamilton, a professor at the New School University, Lionel McIntyre and Cindy Walters, colleagues at Columbia University, and Kenney Robinson are owed thanks for connecting me to numerous people in Harlem and Clinton Hill who provided the raw material for this book. Darrick has also served as a sounding board for many of my ideas and has challenged me to rethink many of my assumptions. His insight has been invaluable.

I have presented portions of the research conducted in this book to a number of audiences, including the Neighborhood Reinvestment Corporation symposium on gentrification, the National Historic Trust's Preservation Development Symposium, the National Preservation Conference, the Annual Congressional Black Caucus Foundation Convention, the annual meetings of the Urban Affairs Association, the annual meetings of the American Sociological Association, the Robert F. Wagner School for Public Service at New York University, the Smart Growth Center at the University of Maryland, and a brown bag lunch seminar series at the Urban Planning program at Columbia University. The audiences at these presentations forced me to clarify my arguments and rethink some of my conclusions. I am very thankful for the opportunity to present and hone my ideas before so many thoughtful people.

The book also benefited from the thoughtful comments of Kathe Newman and several anonymous reviewers. Their critiques forced me to stretch my thinking and resulted in a much better book.

Finally, my family has always stood beside me and been a pillar of support for anything that I do. Chrishana, my wife, has provided not only emotional support but also intellectual support, always pointing out events and occurrences that were relevant to what I was writing about. My sister, Michele, has always been there for me. I also thank my mother, Eleanor, without whom none of this would be possible and whose perseverance and strength have always been an inspiration to me.

# There Goes the 'Hood

PHOTO 1. Vacant storefront in Harlem. Being primed for gentrification? (All photos by author.)

# 1 Introduction

THE GHETTO, the inner city, the 'hood—these terms have been applied as monikers for black neighborhoods and conjure up images of places that are off-limits to outsiders, places to be avoided after sundown, and paragons of pathology. Portrayed as isolated pockets of deviance and despair, these neighborhoods have captured the imagination of journalists and social scientists who have chronicled the challenges and risks of living in such neighborhoods (Anderson 1999; Bourgois 1995; Wilson 1987). But what happens when commerce, the middle class, globalization, if you will, comes to these forlorn neighborhoods? When whites who were a rare sighting are suddenly neighbors? We are accustomed to focusing on the social pathologies, government neglect, and the causes of the inner city's inexorable decline. We thus know how people feel about the crime, the lack of opportunity, and feelings of being left behind or looked over. But we know less about how people feel when the fortunes of their neighborhoods brighten. How do people feel when gentrification comes to the 'hood?

This book addresses these questions by examining the experience of gentrification from the perspective of residents of two black inner-city neighborhoods. Despite the voluminous literature that has developed on gentrification in the past few decades, this is a vantage point that has been overlooked so far. To the extent that others have analyzed gentrification from the perspective of indigenous residents, displacement, and to a lesser extent concerns about political influence have drawn nearly all the attention. But as this book will show, these are hardly the only forces coloring indigenous residents' perceptions of gentrification.

This book argues that indigenous residents do not necessarily react to gentrification according to some of the preconceived notions generally attributed to residents of these neighborhoods. Their reactions are both more receptive and optimistic, yet at the same time more pessimistic and distrustful than the literature on gentrification might lead us to believe. Residents of the 'hood are sometimes more receptive because gentrification brings their neighborhoods into the mainstream of American commercial life with concomitant amenities and services that others might take for granted. It also represents the possibility of achieving upward mobility without having to escape to the suburbs or predominantly white neighborhoods. These are benefits of gentrification typically not recognized in the scholarly literature.

Yet the long history of disenfranchisement, red lining, and discrimination also inspires a cynicism toward gentrification that might not be evidenced elsewhere. Though appreciative of neighborhood improvements associated with gentrification, many see this as evidence that such amenities and services are only provided when whites move into their neighborhoods. Moreover, many see these improvements as the result of active collaboration between public officials, commercial interests, and white residents. Though much has been written about displacement and somewhat less about the political consequences of gentrification for indigenous residents, this dimension of cynicism toward gentrification has not been explored.

The influx of the gentry into previously decaying neighborhoods also poses the possibility of enhancing the indigenous residents' opportunities for upward mobility through the much heralded poverty deconcentration posited by scholars as a possible elixir for the ills of the inner city and manifested in housing programs like HOPE VI and Moving to Opportunity (MTO). Both of these housing programs are premised on the notion that introducing the poor to more affluent neighbors either by moving them to the suburbs (MTO) or bringing the middle class to the 'hood (HOPE VI) is beneficial to poorer residents. Yet the gentrification literature is virtually silent on whether the promise of poverty deconcentration works in the case of gentrification as well. This book shows that the gentry do indeed hold forth the promise to bring benefits to indigenous residents, but in ways more limited than the poverty deconcentration thesis would suggest. In addition, the income mixing concomitant with gentrification is no guarantee for upward mobility. Thus this book also makes clear that the connection between gentrification and neighborhood effects is one that we overlook at our own peril if we wish to have a complete picture of neighborhood dynamics.

Prior writings on gentrification have tended to treat residents who are indigenous to these neighborhoods as bystanders who are victimized by the gentrification process. For example, Wilson and Grammenos (2005) describe how real estate interests and the media demonize a choicely located Puerto Rican neighborhood in Chicago to prime it for gentrification. Here the residents of this neighborhood are potential victims unless they are able to recognize and counter the threat that this demonizing poses.

Those who sought to explain gentrification by looking at the supply side focused on developers, landlords, and capital (Smith 1979), whereas those seeking to explain gentrification from the demand side focused on the forces that created the gentry and led to gentrification (Ley 1996). In these narratives capital and the middle or upper classes assume the leading roles, and indigenous residents are background characters at best.

Hence, gentrification has been depicted as the manifestation of changing cultural, demographic, and economic circumstances among the new middle class, and elsewhere it has been described as representing the bourgeoisie's revenge on the underclass of the inner city (Ley 1996; Smith 1996). This is not to say that these depictions are wrong or inaccurate, but they only tell part of the story. The cultural changes that may have contributed to the onset of gentrification in the 1990s shed little light on how gentrification changes our understanding of life in the gentrifying black inner city. Likewise, Smith (1996), though sympathetic to the indigenous residents of the Lower East Side, nevertheless did not make them central to his interpretations much beyond the class antagonisms that his Marxist reading stresses. I argue that indigenous residents' experience with gentrification, particularly in black inner-city neighborhoods, is worthy of a starring role itself.

That significant gaps in our understanding of gentrification persists despite a voluminous literature developed over several decades that perhaps reflects the chaotic nature of gentrification as a concept (Beauregard 1986). As such it means different things, under different circumstances, to different people. This chaos results from the differing manifestations of gentrification and its differing ways of impacting people in its wake. Therefore gentrification must be examined from a multitude of angles and perspectives if we wish to understand this dynamic.

The black inner city of America is surely a singular and unique phenomenon that demands its own perspective when considering gentrification. Here I am referring to the countless central city neighborhoods that were transformed from white to black as a result of the great migration of blacks from the rural South to urban centers across America. These are neighborhoods that almost invariably also experienced a withdrawal of resources and subsequent decline. This history is unique in urban America, reflecting the importance of race, or more specifically black race, as a master trait that trumps other categories in social life. This is especially true in the realm of neighborhoods where the history of the black inner city has been a class apart. Unlike no other group in American history the majority of blacks were confined to racially homogenous neighborhoods throughout much of the twentieth century. Although European immigrants of the late nineteenth and early twentieth centuries also clustered in ethnic enclaves, these enclaves were seldom homogenous even if associated with one particular group (Massey and Denton 1993). Moreover, the majority of the immigrant group typically lived outside of the enclave. Likewise, today recent immigrants from Asia and Latin America live in neighborhoods that are much less racially isolated than those resided in by the typical black. As Massey and Denton conclude, "when it comes to housing and residential patterns race is the dominant organizing principle" (Massey and Denton 1993, p. 114). Thus, the black inner city is unique and set apart from the rest of the metropolis.

This unique experience sets the stage for a unique vantage point on gentrification. It is a viewpoint colored by decades of red lining, spatial isolation, and urban renewal. As the book illustrates in graphic detail, it is also a history that breeds cynicism about gentrification. But it is also one that breeds hope and relief about the opportunities that come with gentrification, opportunities that might seem mundane elsewhere in urban America. But this viewpoint is also a part of the story of gentrification. This book therefore adds another angle to the still evolving picture of gentrification.

The significance of this alternative perspective became clear while conducting the research presented here. This volume grew out of a desire to explore how gentrification was experienced by the indigenous residents of affected neighborhoods. For reasons I discuss in more detail later, two predominantly black neighborhoods served as the setting for this research. This unwittingly (and perhaps naively) colored the focus of this project to one considering the unique ecology of the black inner city. The book hence became an argument about the experience of gentrification under the unique circumstances of the black inner city.

## MOTIVATION FOR THE BOOK

This book was originally motivated by a desire to answer questions raised by a research project that aimed to empirically document the amount of displacement due to gentrification in New York City. Despite years of writing on gentrification and a popular wisdom that equated it with displacement, there was very little sound empirical evidence that demonstrated the magnitude of the relationship between gentrification and displacement. It was this relationship that Frank Braconi and I hoped to document (Freeman and Braconi 2004).

Much to my surprise, our research findings did not show evidence of a causal relationship between gentrification and displacement. Poor residents and those without a college education were actually less likely to move if they resided in gentrifying neighborhoods. That similar results were found in a study in Boston (Vigdor 2002) served to suggest further that perhaps we were onto something. These surprising results generally sparked three types of responses: unquestioned acceptance from those with an ax to grind against community activists and the left, incredulity, and curiosity. Those with an ax to grind interpreted these findings as proof that community activists were liberal ideologues without valid arguments against gentrification (Cravatts 2004; Tierney 2002). A second type of response was skepticism. Many people were skeptical because the results were not consistent with their personal observations of change in gentrifying neighborhoods. Perhaps the most common response, however, was curiosity.

I include myself among this last group who wanted an explanation for the surprising results. While disseminating our findings, we hypothesized various reasons for these counterintuitive results. We suggested that gentrification might be associated with greater residential satisfaction and hence less motivation to move. Or perhaps rent regulation was effective in dampening displacement. Truth be told, this was all speculation. We really did not know why gentrification appeared to lower mobility rates. Beyond the possibility of displacement, we did not have a sense of how gentrification impacted or was perceived by indigenous residents.

The voluminous literature on gentrification offered an obvious place to look in an attempt to explain these counterintuitive findings. This literature, however, offered an incomplete picture on how gentrification impacted indigenous residents or how they perceived this type of neighborhood change. Although the advent of gentrification in the 1970s did spark scholarly interest in gentrification and its impact on indigenous residents, much of the initial writing focused on identifying and measuring the extent of displacement. Despite the focus on quantifying displacement, these early efforts for the most part did not yield credible estimates of the relationship between gentrification and displacement. These studies almost uniformly failed to include a counterfactual or simply considered all moves to be displacement. Without knowing how much displacement would occur in the absence of gentrification, one cannot assume that any observed displacement is due to gentrification. Highlighting this point, an early summary of the literature concluded that "the major conclusion from this survey of studies of displacement in revitalizing areas is that very little reliable information exists" (Sumka 1979, p. 486). The methodological shortcomings of these earlier studies were the impetus for the displacement study conducted by Frank Braconi and me (Freeman and Braconi 2004). Nevertheless, the notion that gentrification impacted indigenous residents primarily by displacing them was etched in both the public's and much of the scholarly community's imagination, as summed up here by two of the most respected writers on gentrification:

> It is often argued that the benefits of gentrification are far greater than the costs (Schill and Nathan 1983). Whether this is true is doubtful, but more important it is beside the point. The benefits and costs are so unevenly distributed that one has to look not at some overall equation but at different segments of the population. There are distinct losers as well as winners, and the consistent losers are the poor and working class who will be displaced as

gentrification proceeds, and who will confront higher housing costs in tight markets. (Williams and Smith 1986, p. 220)

Likewise, in seeking to provide an empirical assessment of the experience of gentrification in North American cities, Slater (2004) deliberately focused on displaced residents. Although such a focus is appropriate for highlighting the hardships associated with displacement, it perforce obscures insight on other ways that gentrification might impact residents.

There were exceptions to this displacement-centric literature. Notably, several authors chronicled the political conflicts that arose in the wake of gentrification. Auger (1979) described how in South End, Boston, long-term residents' desire to see affordable housing built in the neighborhood conflicted with the gentry's aims to maximize property values by making their neighborhood an exclusive one. The Queens Village section of Philadelphia was described as one where residents were initially ambivalent about gentrification but grew increasingly bitter about rising housing inflation (Levy and Cybriwsky 1980). This bitterness galvanized some long-term residents into acts of vandalism toward the gentry. Henig (1982) chronicled the increasing pragmatism of formerly radical community groups as newcomers to the neighborhood devoted their concerns to more pedestrian matters. In one of the more multifaceted analyses of gentrification in a specific neighborhood, Abu-Lughod (1994) detailed the many ways that gentrification led to battles over the use of public space, provision of affordable housing, and disposition of vacant buildings and land owned by the city on the Lower East Side of Manhattan. The story that Abu-Lughod tells is one of long-term residents battling to maintain the affordability, diversity, and anarchic and bohemian nature of the Lower East Side. More recently, Wilson, Wouters, and Grammenos (2004) describe how community-based coalitions struggled to resist gentrification by painting developers as "greedy capitalists" and Pilsen as a cohesive and supportive community for indigenous residents but a space of danger for would-be gentrifiers.

When coupled with the displacement studies and concerns about displacement, what emerges from the literature is a picture of gentrification acting to displace indigenous residents and/or sparking political conflict between these residents and the gentry over competing visions of the neighborhood's future. Neither of these conclusions explains why we found lower turnover rates in gentrifying neighborhoods. Nor do these conclusions satisfactorily answer the more global question of how gentrification affects indigenous residents. As Slater, Curran, and Lees (2004, p. 1142) write:

Yet the true nature of the consequences of gentrification for people living in the neighborhoods experiencing it is an issue on which there has been almost total silence. In short, academic inquiry into neighborhood change has looked at the role of urban policy in harnessing the aspirations of middle class professionals at the expense of looking at the role of urban policy in causing immense hardship for people with nowhere to go in booming property markets reshaped by neoliberal regulatory regimes. A focus on the practices of the middle class gentrifiers and how their practices are facilitated by urban policy does not tell us anything about what policy driven gentrification does to communities that fear widely acknowledged disruptions brought about by public and/or private reinvestment. Middle class gentrifiers are only one part of a much larger story.

Slater points out the need for scholars to explore how gentrification impacts the residents living there, but he also assumes that displacement and other hardships will be the primary experience for the residents of gentrifying neighborhoods. But the experience of gentrification might be more nuanced than that.

Indeed, the stories of political contestation hint at gentrification being more complex than was typically portrayed. For example, writers on gentrification in various communities including the Lower East Side (Abu-Lughod 1994), Adams Morgan (Henig 1982), and Pilsen (Wilson, Wouters, and Grammenos 2004) illustrated the many competing interests in these neighborhoods that did not always neatly cleave between long-term residents and the gentry, allowing one to infer that not all of the residents were necessarily opposed to gentrification. By focusing on the political contestations, however, the experiences of everyday residents in gentrifying neighborhoods was muffled by the din of political conflict. This is not to say that a focus on the political conflict stemming from gentrification is wrong, only that it does not provide a complete picture of how residents are impacted or experience the changes taking place in their neighborhoods. For one thing, the most active and vocal residents are not necessarily representative of the entire neighborhood and are likely different, perhaps being most concerned about the changes taking place—hence their activism. Moreover, political combat does not lend itself to nuanced positions. Rather the protagonists must stake out a position and fight for it. In this way the characters in many of these stories appear one-dimensional, singularly focused on stopping gentrification or maximizing property values. As will be shown later in this book, such narrow depictions may not do justice to the complex ways residents experience gentrification.

I concluded that we needed a far better understanding of gentrification from the vantage point of residents living in these neighborhoods. Such an approach could perhaps shed light on why residents of these neighborhoods appeared to be less likely to move in New York City during the 1990s. Moreover, given the increasing attraction in housing and community development circles toward mixing incomes, it seemed plausible that this approach might shed light on the wisdom of the poverty deconcentration thesis.

This volume grew out of my efforts to better understand gentrification from the viewpoint of poor persons indigenous to these neighborhoods. To really get a sense of what was happening in the neighborhoods, I began talking with residents. Who would better know their motivations for staying or the struggles they went through to be able to stay? I chose Harlem as a case study because its rich history as the symbolic capital of black America proved irresistible. It is also a neighborhood I have come to know intimately, living and working on its boundaries. Harlem is a neighborhood where the initial stages of gentrification were readily apparent with trendy restaurants, new housing, and surprise of surprises— whites moving into the neighborhood. I also chose to study Clinton Hill in Brooklyn, New York, another predominantly black neighborhood experiencing gentrification. Choosing two mostly black neighborhoods enabled my analysis to make comparisons across neighborhoods without the confounding influence of race.

Choosing two predominantly black neighborhoods, however, injected race into the thesis of this book in an unanticipated yet overwhelming way. Through the course of my research, the topic of race repeatedly reared its head in a manner more compelling than my original focus on residential mobility and displacements. The book hence became a story about how residents of black neighborhoods view gentrification as much or more so than a story about displacement and mobility in gentrifying neighborhoods. Taylor (2002) and Patillo (2003) have examined the issue of gentrification in two predominantly black neighborhoods. They are sociologists, however, and their work focuses on how the black gentry and other black residents relate to one another in the context of the gentrification process. Taylor and Patillo illustrate the role that middle-class blacks' desires to connect with their blackness plays in spurring gentrification, as well as the way their class differences sometimes puts them at odds with other black residents of gentrifying neighborhoods.

In contrast, my motivation to understand how gentrification impacts people in addition to my pragmatic concerns about how planning and policy can create better cities drove the focus of this book to be more about how residents experience the process of gentrification. This is a necessary first step toward understanding how gentrification impacts residents.

Although I initially set out to see how gentrification is perceived through the eyes of the poor, my interviews suggested that class was not necessarily the all-important lens that I thought it would be in shaping how people viewed and made sense of gentrification. Folks with no more than a high school education told similar stories to those with advanced degrees in their perspectives on gentrification. Through the course of my interviews I also learned that as much as the loss of the black middle class in the inner city has been lamented (see Wilson 1987), there were still plenty of longtime black middle-class residents in inner-city communities like Clinton Hill and Harlem. Because the black middle class was very much part of the fabric of Clinton Hill and Harlem and because class was not proving to be a central organizing theme in my initial interviews, I thought it wise not to exclude them from my research. I therefore expanded my sample to include both college graduates and the nonpoor.

Nevertheless, despite the intrusion of race into my central thesis, this book still meets one of its original objectives: providing a perspective on gentrification that heretofore had been taken for granted if not ignored. The indigenous residents of gentrifying neighborhoods, excepting perhaps middle-class homeowners, were assumed to be displaced or concerned about the ensuing cultural and political shifts resulting from gentrification. In this book I paint a richer and more nuanced picture of gentrification as seen from the eyes of these residents.

## RESEARCH STRATEGY

The counterintuitive findings on displacement and the dearth of literature that might explain these findings convinced me that our understanding of gentrification from the viewpoint of indigenous residents was poor indeed, so poor that an exploratory approach rather than one with preconceived hypotheses would be more likely to yield fruitful insights about the perception of gentrification by indigenous residents. Although I had some preconceived ideas and questions I wanted to answer, I wanted to frame my research in such a way to allow previously unanticipated questions and answers to emerge. In these unanticipated themes especially compelling stories might emerge. Indeed, the importance of race in coloring how residents perceived gentrification is an example of an unanticipated topic of significance emerging.

An exploratory approach with these motivations pointed toward an inductive approach that allows the research to influence both the questions and answers. Such an approach is better suited to a qualitative interpretive inquiry rather than a positivist deductive approach. The latter approach assumes well-developed maxims that can be quantified and empirically verified. Although there certainly are some aspects of gentrification that would fit these criteria, the counterintuitive findings of my earlier research (and as I show in detail in the next chapter) and lack of research from the vantage point of indigenous residents all convinced me that a more open-ended qualitative approach was desirable. The research reported here should thus be viewed as the first phase of a research project that will help us understand the myriad ways that gentrification affects residents and is viewed by them. Using an inductive approach, the book likely raises as many if not more questions than it answers. This also means that the ultimate objective here is to conceptualize how gentrification might impact and is perceived by indigenous residents, rather than making definitive claims about the exact relationship of gentrification to specific variables. Systematically verifying the relationships conceptualized here will be left to a later date.

The qualitative methods employed in the research include primarily in-depth interviews and to a lesser extent participant observation and content analysis of newspapers and other media. One-on-one interviews were the best way to give residents the opportunity to express their feelings and perceptions in a detailed and nuanced way. It was also the best way to establish the type of rapport necessary to encourage the study participants to express their views freely. Because most of my respondents were African American, my being African African probably facilitated this rapport.

The conversations I had with residents of Clinton Hill and Harlem serve as the raw data for the analyses presented in this book. Residents' descriptions of how they see their neighborhood changing and how they feel about this can be taken as straightforward accounts of their perceptions of how gentrification impacts them. Who better than they to relate their day-to-day experiences with gentrification? Our conversations also yielded residents' beliefs about why gentrification was manifesting itself the way it was—something I also discuss and analyze in great detail. Here, I not only report the residents' thoughts but also interpret the meaning of these perceptions. Because residing in a gentrifying neighborhood does not necessarily grant one additional insight into the complex forces that drive the gentrification process, this is a place where merely taking the residents' comments at face value would overlook the context that generates their beliefs.

Purposive and snowball sampling techniques were used to identify participants for in-depth interviews. Initial contacts were made through community groups and my own interactions in these communities. Anyone at least eighteen years of age who had been living in the neighborhood for at least three years was eligible to participate in the study. These criteria ensured that respondents had at least some experience with the changes under way in their neighborhood.

The interviews sought to elicit from respondents their perceptions about how the neighborhood was changing and how those changes were affecting them. Particular focus was given to changes in amenities, services, demographics, and neighborhood social interaction. The interviews also sought information about respondents' housing situations and their

TABLE 1.1. Sample Characteristics of Study Participants

|  | Total | Clinton Hill | Harlem |
|---|---|---|---|
| Percentage black | 85% | 100% | 81% |
| Percentage Latino | 15% | 0% | 19% |
| Aged 18–30 | 22% | 10% | 23% |
| 31–45 | 47% | 40% | 46% |
| 46–65 | 19% | 40% | 19% |
| 65 and over | 12% | 10% | 8% |
| Education |  |  |  |
| High school graduate or less | 43% | 25% | 45% |
| Some college | 13% | 20% | 13% |
| College graduate | 37% | 55% | 33% |
| Resides in Harlem | 66% |  |  |
| Owns home | 19% | 50% | 10% |
| Rent regulated or subsidized |  |  |  |
| (among renters) | 50% | 50% | 51% |
| Median length of tenure |  |  |  |
| (years) | 17 | 19 | 14 |
| Sample size | 65 | 22 | 43 |

future mobility plans. Aside from that, participants were encouraged to discuss whatever they wanted related to their neighborhood and how it was changing. A conversational style where the interviewer establishes a rapport with the respondents was used to encourage the revealing of feelings and emotions and to enable the participants to volunteer their own impressions about topics not introduced by the interviewer. I conducted a total of fifty-one interviews (thirty in Harlem and twenty-one in Clinton Hill). A research assistant conducted an additional twenty-one interviews in Harlem, which she taped, transcribed, and analyzed separately (Patel 2003). This facilitated comparisons between my findings and those of the research assistant's and the dependability of the analysis or the extent to which my findings were not purely dependent on my sole perspective. Table 1.1 illustrates the socioeconomic characteristics of the study participants.

Table 1.1 shows that many of the residents I spoke with had been residing in their neighborhood for a considerable length of time with the median length being seventeen years. My sample is more highly educated than the general population of these communities and slightly older as well. Several of the respondents were highly educated and recently moved into the neighborhood and consequently might be thought of as the black gentry. Although only five or so individuals fit this profile, their inclusion in this study did lend additional insight into social relations between those who might be thought of as gentrifiers and long-term residents—a point I explore in chapter 5. Taken together, table 1.1 suggests the sample includes people from a broad range of backgrounds and circumstances.

In addition to interviewing, I also attended several conferences, workshops, and community meetings, some that were designed to specifically address the issue of gentrification. I even served as a panelist at a conference on gentrification in Harlem. These forums proved to be invaluable as sources of additional insight on residents' perspectives toward gentrification. These forums are places where people had a chance to express their feeling about the changes taking place in their community. I also used these forums to recruit participants for in-depth interviews.

Moreover, as someone who lives on the edge of Harlem (or in Harlem, depending on the definition), I experience this neighborhood as part of my everyday existence. I shop in Harlem, go to movies in Harlem, and eat in Harlem. Sometimes the topic of gentrification came up in everyday conversations, as was the case of one of my visits to my barbershop as the dialogue below attests:

COLLEGE STUDENT: Have y'all heard about gentrification?

[Some nods, puzzled expressions, a few uh-huhs.]

COLLEGE STUDENT: That's where they're taking these burnt out brownstones, fixing them up, and then selling them for half a million dollars. But this is people coming in from outside of Harlem.

BARBER: Word?

COLLEGE STUDENT: No doubt. If we keep sleepin' in a few years won't be none of us livin' in Harlem. What we need to do is start buying some of these properties for ourselves.

This is a conversation I stumbled across while getting my haircut. It is illustrative of one of the perceptions of gentrification, that it is a process whereby the original black residents and blacks in general will no longer be part of the community. This conversation undoubtedly played some role in shaping how I think residents perceive gentrification, even though my observations of it were not planned.

I also experienced firsthand many of the changes in the neighborhood, the new restaurants and stores that made life more convenient, but also the downside of gentrification when my barbershop had to relocate because of rising rents. (My loss of a convenient place to get a haircut is of course minor compared to those whose livelihoods or homes were threatened by gentrification.)

Likewise, although I don't live or work in Clinton Hill, I have several friends that do. Consequently, I often socialized in the neighborhood, taking advantage of the new shops, restaurants, and cultural attractions that were dotting the area. My friends also related to me their everyday experiences, some of which were affected by gentrification. They described the new types of stores that were opening up and the public spaces that were off-limits to whites a few years ago but now had a white presence. They described neighborhoods that formerly invoked fear but were now trendy. In this way my personal experiences in Clinton Hill and Harlem almost led to me becoming something of an accidental ethnographer. Although I did not set out to use ethnography as a major tool in my research, my day-to-day living made this unavoidable. Thus this accidental ethnography came to shape this book along with my interviews and participant observation.

## PLAN OF THE BOOK

The next chapter describes the sites of the analyses that inform the book. Two neighborhoods served as settings for in-depth case studies on gentrification in New York City, Harlem and Clinton Hill. The second chapter provides a brief history of each of these neighborhoods. The bulk of the second chapter, however, will focus on describing recent changes in these neighborhoods that make them suitable candidates for studying gentrification. Data from the decennial census will be used to describe demographic, economic, and social trends in these neighborhoods. Home Mortgage Disclosure Act data will be used to describe trends in housing investment. In addition, semi-structured interviews with key informants in these neighborhoods, including community leaders, planners, and politicians, will be used to further flesh out the contours of the changes taking place in these neighborhoods. This chapter will also set the stage for a better understanding of how residents in these neighborhoods view the changes taking place around them—the subject of the following chapters.

The third chapter describes indigenous residents' perceptions of the changes taking place around them and how they felt about these changes. Gentrification was not a subtle change in the case study neighborhoods. It was a force that everyone appeared to be aware of, that people talked about and reacted to. This chapter explores some of the residents' reactions to gentrification. Sometimes these reactions were negative, as the following quote attests: "I don't have mixed feelings about the gentrification process. I see what it does; I see the difficulty that people face. That's my concern. I love the neighborhood. I love the people. When I see something steam-rolling them, I don't have mixed feelings . . . Community organizer/Resident of Harlem" (as quoted in Chamberlain 2003).

Negative sentiments such as these are consistent with a pejorative view of gentrification that pervades much of the writing on this topic. The impression one gets from typical complaints about gentrification is that it is an unwelcome threat to current residents. These negative sentiments have motivated some to mobilize against gentrification. Although negative reactions were certainly an important theme, many residents welcomed the changes taking place in their community due to gentrification.

This chapter thus also explores in detail an often ignored facet of the gentrification process—the perceived benefits flowing to current residents. This chapter describes the facets of gentrification that residents were appreciative of. The findings described serve as a corrective to the prevailing view of gentrification solely as a disastrous occasion for current residents. A more balanced view that takes account of both the good and the bad of gentrification will result from this chapter and the book in general.

Chapter 4 describes how indigenous residents interpreted the gentrification in their neighborhoods. The dramatic change that gentrification represents—reversing decades of white flight and disinvestment—cries out for explanation. Scholars have been eager to offer theories that explain why and how gentrification occurs. The residents of affected neighborhoods have also crafted explanations for the dramatic changes swirling around them. This chapter describes the way that residents interpret the change. This includes their explanations for why gentrification was occurring and the meaning of whites moving into their neighborhoods. The role of race as a marker of socioeconomic status and as a determinant of who gets what is a recurring theme in this discussion. More specifically, the perceptions that whites command and obtain better services and amenities wherever they live is a source of appreciation, resentment, and resignation. These feelings and their meanings are discussed in this chapter.

The mixing of the gentry with long-term residents has the potential to be both combustible and complementary. By mixing residents from different classes, ethnicities, and races, gentrification can create a potentially explosive scenario as residents negotiate suspicions and differing expectations and norms. But the process also has the potential to enrich neighborhoods by creating more diverse communities. Moreover, the literature on neighborhood effects suggests that such neighborhood-level relationships are important in determining one's life chances. Chapter 5 explores how residents of gentrifying neighborhoods view their interactions with the newcomers in their midst. How are localized relationships affected by an influx of residents of a different class and sometimes race?

My findings show that social ties rarely cross class and racial lines. Gentrification is increasing the socioeconomic diversity of the Clinton and Hill and Harlem, but the social networks within these neighborhoods seem impervious to the changes taking place around them. This chapter discusses the lack of social interaction between gentrifiers and others in the community and the implications of this finding for theories about neighborhood effects and policies that promote socioeconomic integration.

My research also shows that by introducing individuals from a different class and sometimes racial background, gentrification was found to spark clashes that center on differing norms and expectations. Norms are established collectively in a neighborhood. Through the actions of individuals acting in concert, such norms come to take hold. People who have lived in the neighborhood or one with a similar culture and therefore norms will know what type of behavior is deemed acceptable and appropriate. Gentrifiers, however, often come from backgrounds where different types of norms are deemed acceptable. Chapter 5 describes some of the clashes that stem from differing sets of norms between gentrifiers and long-term residents. The sources of these clashes and the means that communities used to mediate these clashes are explored.

Chapter 6 describes the planning and policy implications of the research presented in this book. As a planner, I aim more for more than a clearer understanding of the gentrification process in the context of the black inner city. Rather, the desire for praxis drives the effort to broaden our understanding of gentrification. I begin chapter 6 by summarizing my findings and describing the applicability of them to other people and settings. Although my findings are not based on a systematic survey drawn from a probability sample, I can nevertheless use judgment, logic, and prior research to infer beyond the people and settings on which this book is based. Put another way, although I cannot describe the experiences, perceptions, or relationships detailed later in this book with any degree of statistical precision, that does not mean the findings are irrelevant to other settings. The beginning of chapter 6 describes which findings are likely to be relevant elsewhere and the types of settings in which these findings may or may not be relevant.

The remainder of chapter 6 addresses the planning/policy implications of the themes discussed earlier in the book. Prefacing my discussion with stated concerns for the most disadvantaged among us and a desire for a more equitable metropolis, I describe planning/policy initiatives that will foster equity in the face of gentrification. Despite my stated bias toward equity and the redistribution of resources, I do not ignore the political obstacles that such redistributive policies confront. I therefore attempt to craft policies that would seem possible to overcome likely political objections.

The final chapter will discuss the theoretical implications of this work. I focus on three themes. The first theme I discuss in chapter 7 is the meaning of the ghetto in the face of gentrification. The term *ghetto* originally described walled-off sections of cities where Jews were confined in European cities during the Middle Ages. *Ghetto* also aptly described the black experience in urban America, for although there were no physical walls to confine blacks, the economic, political, and social forces were able to achieve virtually the same effect. The civil rights era was supposed to change everything. Although ghetto walls may have weakened somewhat, making it easier to escape, they seemed as strong as ever in keeping others out. The middle class, capital, and certainly whites avoided the ghetto as always and perhaps in some ways more than before. Thus, the conceptualization of the ghetto persisted as a place of isolation, metaphorically on another planet.

Gentrification, however, changes this equation. Walls that were formerly solid seem porous now, at least from the perspective of who is moving into the ghetto. Does our conceptualization of the ghetto need to change in the face of gentrification? Or is gentrification merely a temporary interlude that will reshuffle the location of the ghetto but do nothing to change its relation to the larger society? The final section of this book addresses these questions concluding that gentrification does indeed change the relationship between black inner-city neighborhoods and the larger society, but for all the changes fundamental inequities for ghetto residents seem likely to persist.

The second theme centers on prior conceptualizations of gentrification in the scholarly literature. As mentioned earlier, these conceptualizations tended to place indigenous residents, particularly black inner-city residents, in support roles at best. Here I reconsider the meaning of gentrification in light of the findings described herein. This reconsideration intends to give indigenous residents a starring role in our narratives on gentrification beyond the story of displacement.

The last theme discussed in chapter 7 is what the research presented here suggests about ongoing debates over neoliberal urban policy. Policies that emphasize the private sector role as well as a retraction or reforming of the welfare state to revitalize the inner city are usually thought to fall under this rubric. To the extent that this neoliberal policy regime encourages gentrification, the reactions of residents to the gentrification process are germane to this debate. Here I discuss how the research presented in this book can help inform this debate.

Thus, this book provides a more complete understanding of the gentrification process as it relates to indigenous households and will inform both the scholarly debate on the process of gentrification and the actions of planners, policy makers, and community-based organizations who are currently struggling to address the ramifications of gentrification in many neighborhoods.

# 2    The Evolution of Clinton Hill and Harlem

To FULLY UNDERSTAND how residents perceive the neighborhood changes associated with gentrification, an understanding of the context within which these changes are occurring is necessary. This chapter provides a brief overview of the evolution of Clinton Hill and Harlem from homes for the upper middle class, to depressed inner-city neighborhoods, and finally through the beginnings of gentrification. This study is based on my field research of these two New York City neighborhoods.

The exact boundaries of Harlem are somewhat amorphous; my mother, a native of Harlem, used to say, "It's where the black people live." For the purposes of this study, I spoke with residents of central and what some might consider to be western Harlem. This section of the island of Manhattan is overwhelmingly black, although the western fringe is becoming increasingly Dominican. For the statistical analyses presented later in this chapter I used the boundaries of Manhattan Community Board 10. Clinton Hill's boundaries are perhaps less straightforward than those of Harlem. My focus here was on the northern section of Clinton Hill that abuts Myrtle Avenue and on the eastern fringes that were once considered part of Bedford-Stuyvesant. These sections of Clinton Hill have experienced gentrification later than others. The maps in the appendix illustrate the boundaries of the neighborhoods that defined the demographic analyses presented later in this chapter.

## HARLEM'S HISTORY

Harlem, perhaps the most famous black neighborhood in the world, has been renowned for being a mecca for black culture and the black intelligentsia, especially during the first few decades of the twentieth century. In its heyday, Harlem was among the most affluent black neighborhoods in the United States and held forth as an example of what blacks could achieve. It drew praise from black and white observers alike.

Harlem's fame stemmed from a confluence of several factors. One is the origin of the area as an upscale suburban community. In the early and mid-1800s Harlem, which is located in the northern part of the island of

Manhattan, was relatively undeveloped. Owing to onerous transportation costs, those that settled there treated it more as a retreat or summer getaway than a primary home. Commutes to the commercial section of Manhattan would have been too long and too expensive to do on a regular basis (Osofsky 1971).

With the expansion of rapid transit to the northern reaches of the island, however, Harlem became a short commute from the business district of Manhattan and was ripe for development. From the 1870s to the early 1900s there was much real estate activity as developers targeted the affluent households with housing that contained luxuries such as elevators and maids' rooms that only the relatively well-to-do of that time could afford. Developers marketed Harlem as having the advantages of country living and the convenience of city life. Years later, a reporter noted that one block's reputation for attractiveness and exclusivity was hardly matched anywhere else in the city (*New York Times* 1920). As a result, much of Harlem's physical appearance was and continues to be appealing. Harlem's originally being intended for upscale residents planted the seed for gentrification a century later.

The nature of much of the real estate investment in the late 1800s was speculative, however, and this had dramatic consequences for the future of Harlem. As with most speculative frenzies, the bubble eventually burst, in this case in the early part of the first decade of the twentieth century. Speculators overestimated the demand for housing in this section of Manhattan. As a result, many landlords found themselves with vacant properties that scarcely began to return their investment. Rather than lose investments, a few landlords turned to another market that was perpetually in search of housing—blacks. Because blacks' housing options were limited, landlords could charge them more, and some preferred them to whites (*New York Times* 1904). Under these circumstances blacks came to enter Harlem in great numbers.

In New York, as in other cities prior to the great migration, blacks were scattered about in a few small concentrations that were almost universally undesirable (Massey and Denton 1993). Although no such large-scale community such as Harlem existed, there were a few identifiable areas, such as the Tenderloin or San Juan Hill. Prior to the great migration, blacks endured antagonistic race relations in the urban North. Although race relations were more fluid than in the South, discrimination in jobs, housing, and public arenas was rampant. Moreover, these antagonisms often boiled over into violent riots whereupon mobs of whites set upon any random black. Indeed, San Juan Hill was so named because the interracial battles that occurred there drew parallels to the battles that had occurred in the just ended Spanish-American War. During a riot in 1900, blacks were actually dragged from streetcars and beaten (Osofsky

1971). Needless to say, such actions and attitudes on the part of whites did little to endear many blacks to the notion of residential integration. But because blacks lived interspersed with whites, the notion of retreating to a safe quarter was implausible.

Thus Harlem, a community originally intended for upscale whites, provided the pull with landlords willing to rent to blacks to recoup their investment, and terrible living conditions in other parts of the city provided the push for African Americans. When offered the opportunity to move into improved conditions in Harlem, many blacks jumped at the chance. This trend was amplified by an enterprising black realtor named Philip A. Payton Jr., who offered to provide black tenants to some of the struggling landlords of Harlem. Their consent provided a path for blacks to move into Harlem and enriched Payton, who shortly thereafter formed the Afro-American Realty Company, which bought, managed, and sold properties, including many that were leased to black tenants. Payton played on the notion of race pride to build his enterprise, selling to prospective black investors not only the promise of a handsome return but also the opportunity to advance the race by contributing to the success of a black-owned business. By investing in a black company that aimed to establish a black community in Harlem, African Americans were a driving force behind the establishment of Harlem as a black mecca (Osofsky 1971).

In this way, Harlem's origins differed from many of the other "black belts" that were forming in cities across the North in the early part of the twentieth century. Rather than being funneled to the least desirable sections of town, as was in the case in the development of many black belts, Harlem owed its origins in large part to the conscious decisions of African Americans to develop a community in Harlem. In 1904, when white landlords organized and attempted to evict blacks from some of the buildings in Harlem, blacks organized to resist and Payton retaliated by buying several buildings on the same street and evicting the whites from those buildings (*New York Times* 1904; Osofsky 1971). In most other cities prior to the great migration, blacks also lived in small clusters as described. Owing to their low incomes, these were typically low-rent districts that they shared with other low-income, often immigrant families (Weaver 1948). When the black population grew, blacks generally filled in existing neighborhoods where other blacks were clustered, making these formerly mixed communities solidly black, and expanded into areas adjacent to the pre–great migration black clusters. In Chicago, for example,

From the beginning of Chicago's history, most Negroes had lived on Chicago's South Side.... The famous South Side black belt was emerging.... The development of a physical ghetto in Chicago, then, was not the results chiefly of poverty; nor did Negroes cluster out of choice. The ghetto was primarily the product of white hostility. (Spear 1967, p. 25)

Likewise, Kusmer describes the burgeoning black ghetto in Cleveland: "In the late nineteenth century, most black new comers settled in the Central Avenue district, one of the oldest areas of the city and a district in which some blacks had lived since the Civil War.... This area, then, constituted the nucleus of what would become Cleveland's first black ghetto" (Kusmer 1978, p. 41). And describing the origins of Milwaukee's ghetto, Trotter states that "Afro-Americans...concentrated in the poorest neighborhood with increasing symptoms of ghetto formation" (Trotter 1985, p. 67).

In contrast, the pre–great migration black settlements in New York, such as the Tenderloin and San Juan Hill, were rapidly superseded by Harlem, a physically more desirable community several miles north. Thus rather than expanding or concentrating in existing slum areas, blacks in New York chose to move to a neighborhood with many desirable amenities. This is not to say that blacks did not exercise a degree of agency in the formation of black belts across the country. The great migration of blacks from the South, which provided the critical mass to develop these black belts, was a crucial act of agency. But in choosing the site of the burgeoning black community, Harlem was in some ways unique.

Thus it came to be that African Americans occupied one of the choicest sections of New York City. Harlem was a physically desirable community, especially compared to other places where blacks lived in New York, or any place else in the country for that matter. These physical assets undoubtedly played a role in the positive perceptions of Harlem and the view that it was a model city that offered hope that all blacks would one day be afforded the opportunity for such "Clean living and civic development" (Dycoff 1914, p. 954). Harlem's physical condition in the early part of the twentieth century contributed to the perception that it was not a slum and inspired pride among its black residents. The quotes that follow from contemporary publications give a flavor of the high regard with which Harlem was held: "The houses are in good repair; windows, entrances, halls, sidewalks and streets are clean, and the houses comfortable to a degree not often found in a workingman's locality" (Dycoff 1914, p. 949); "[where] virtually all the houses are well constructed; none are of wood. Among them are many brownstone fronts. It is by no means a ramshackle quarter of the city" (Crowell 1925, p. 8); "[a place where] from [135th Street and Lenox Avenue] you get an impression of spaciousness, of cleanliness, of prosperity, of success—of brilliance, almost.... Besides Little Italy and the Ghetto, Harlem shines" (Hartt 1921,

p. 334); "a place not of dilapidated tenements, but made up of new-law apartments and handsome dwellings, with well-paved and well-lighted streets" (Johnson 1925); "conveniently and beautifully located, with broad asphalt avenues and streets, modern apartment and private houses, schools and hospitals, and admirable transportation facilities to all parts of the city" (National League on Urban Conditions among Negroes 1915).

Perhaps just as important, however, was that Harlem was the physical manifestation of the "new Negro." Among blacks the new Negro represented a new way of thinking and relating to the nonblack world. Rather than relying on whites, the new Negro would blaze his own trails and knock down barriers before him. Rather than being kept down, held back, or helped up, the new Negro acted to improve his condition and that of his race. In the words of one contemporary observer:

> As it matures we begin to see its effects; at first, negative, iconoclastic, and then positive and constructive. In this new group psychology we note the lapse of sentimental appeal, then the development of a more positive self-respect and self reliance;...the rise from social disillusionment to race pride. (Locke 1925, p. 632)

In sum, there was a new attitude among black Americans, an attitude that said blacks were proud, as good as the white man, and had and would continue to achieve great things.

This new attitude among blacks stemmed from the very act of migrating itself and the experience of World War I. The migration was to date perhaps the largest widespread action on the part of blacks to better their condition. Migration, particularly one that is not forced, requires a leap of faith, a view that things will be better at the destination. This served to heighten one's expectations and realization of the importance of self for determining improvements in blacks' conditions. World War I exposed blacks to the rhetoric of "fighting for democracy" and to conditions overseas. If blacks could fight in Europe for democracy, why not at home? If democracy was the ideal for the French, Poles, and others, why not the Negro? These forces coalesced to create greater race pride and militancy among blacks who migrated to the North.

Although it is easy to exaggerate the importance of this new Negro mentality in explaining demographic trends, the black of the post–World War I era was undoubtedly a more militant and proud one. The red summer of 1919, where blacks fought back against whites with surprising intensity and the popularity of the Garvey movement, with its glorifying of all things black, attest to that.

This new attitude had profound implications, one being the Harlem Renaissance, an artistic movement whereby black art was used to trumpet the humanity of the race and expose the absurdity of Jim Crow and other racialist ideas. By producing great works of art the black race would not only learn more about itself but also demonstrate for all the world to see that blacks were the equal of any race and deserved all the rights and privileges therein. Perhaps even more than the initial physical desirability of Harlem, it was this artistic movement of the 1920s that made the neighborhood famous. Although it is doubtful that the Harlem Renaissance accomplished its stated objective of diminishing racism, the art, literature, music, and theater associated with this movement did make Harlem a household name.

Some additional evidence on the condition of the area can be gleaned from comparing the socioeconomic status of Harlem to the socioeconomic status of black America prior to the Great Depression. Socioeconomic characteristics on blacks residing in Harlem prior to 1940 are difficult to obtain because the Census Bureau rarely tabulated characteristics of racial groups below the county level before 1940. Nevertheless, because Harlem blacks accounted for about 84 percent of Manhattan's black population in 1930, a sense of the overall characteristics of Harlem's blacks can be gained by looking at socioeconomic characteristics of blacks residing in Manhattan.

The illiteracy rate for Manhattan was lower than that for the rest of the city and lower than any of the ten cities with the largest black populations in 1930. Indeed, among the eighty cities with at least 10,000 blacks in 1930, none had a black illiteracy rate lower than Manhattan's in 1930, and only two, Boston and Atlantic City, had rates that low (U.S. Census Bureau 1935, p. 239). Table 2.1 illustrates illiteracy rates for selected areas.

Likewise, by another indicator of socioeconomic status, gainful employment among males, among cities with at least 10,000 blacks, Manhattan had the highest rate of employment among black males. Moreover, the rate was higher in Manhattan than in the other boroughs of New York City.

For the most part, then, Harlem prior to the Great Depression was a mecca for blacks from around the world, had a socioeconomic profile and physical character that compared favorably to other black belts, and was the center for an artistic movement aimed at destroying the myth of black inferiority a well as the center of Garvey's back to Africa movement that preached the glory of things black (Watkins-Owens 1996).

Harlem thus came to represent the aspirations for what blacks could achieve. For a downtrodden race only a few generations out of slavery and still in the clutches of serfdom in much of the South, this was an enormous source of pride. Harlem was not just another ghetto; it truly was a physical and spatial manifestation of the new Negro. Harlem's

TABLE 2.1. Illiteracy Rates in Selected Cities

|  | 1920 | 1930 |
|---|---|---|
| Manhattan | 1.8% | 1.9% |
| Rest of New York City | 2.6% | 2.5% |
| Baltimore | 12.9% | 7% |
| Birmingham | 20.8% | 14.7% |
| Chicago | 4%* | 2.2% |
| Washington, DC | 8.6% | 4.1% |
| Detroit | 3.9% | 2.7% |
| Atlanta (Fulton) | 18.2% | 11% |
| New Orleans | 15.7% | 13.4% |
| Philadelphia | 4.6% | 3% |
| St. Louis | 8.2% | 5.2% |
| Urban areas of the north |  | 4.1% |
| Urban areas of the United States |  | 9.2% |
| Entire United States | 22.9% | 16.3% |

*Cook County, Detroit—Wayne County, Birmingham—Jefferson County

Source: U.S. Census Bureau (1935, pp. 777–79) and author's calculations.

storied and unique beginning is intentionally detailed because of the important role this history played as the seeds for gentrification decades later. The legacy of Harlem's origins not only proved part of the impetus for gentrification, as Taylor (2002) describes, but also colored indigenous residents' reaction to the potential of gentrification as well. As I discuss later in this chapter, this legacy weighed heavily in shaping how people interpreted gentrification.

## From Zenith to Nadir

Although Harlem had an auspicious beginning, the forces that led to its long decay were actually taking root concurrently with the Harlem Renaissance. The housing discrimination that blacks faced slowed the growth of the physical boundaries of black Harlem, and it shut blacks out of most other neighborhoods in the city. Consequently, black housing demand was restricted to a smaller section of upper Manhattan than their numbers warranted and led to severe overcrowding (*New York Age* 1923). Housing discrimination was not the only factor that contributed to this overcrowding. As described, Harlem was in many ways a community designed for the elite or at least the upper middle class. The broad boulevards and luxurious homes attest to this. But the masses of blacks moving into Harlem hardly fit this profile. To be sure, there were members of the black elite who had the means to afford the type of housing available in Harlem, but most did not. Moreover, Harlem was designed not only as primarily an upscale community but as one for families with a husband, wife, and children. Its denizens were a community of migrants, however, and the typical migrant is a young adult who was single or had left their family in their homelands. Thus, housing built for families hardly fit their needs.

Taking in lodgers became one of the means by which Harlem residents resolved the mismatch between the housing stock and their need and means and overcame the onerous housing burdens caused by discrimination. A report by the Urban League suggested "95% of [the residents] are unable to live in these houses without commercializing their homes" (National League on Urban Conditions among Negroes 1915), that is, taking in boarders. The combination of these forces was severe overcrowding and overuse of the housing stock—conditions that bode ill for a neighborhood that suffered from decades of disinvestment and neglect in the future.

If housing discrimination, a mismatched housing stock, and the resultant overcrowding were the seeds of Harlem's future despair, the Great Depression was the sun, air, and water that allowed these seeds to spring forth and recast Harlem from the city on a hill for blacks to a slum community. Before the Depression the color line that restricted blacks to menial occupations and an educational system that infrequently prepared them for more than that meant that Harlem was a community of mostly meager incomes. The Great Depression thus took an underemployed population with few work opportunities and turned it into one where joblessness and the attendant crises were rampant (Greenberg 1991). Housing discrimination and the resultant residential segregation also create a concentration of a poor, oppressed people within a small geographic area and thereby concentrated all the attendant social problems associated with poverty as well.

World War II and the economic boom that followed provided some relief to the residents of Harlem by opening up new employment opportunities. For Harlem as a community, however, the post–World War II era was one of continued decline. The forces that spawned suburbanization across metropolitan America were also felt in Harlem. With the suburban-like outer boroughs and suburbs of Long Island, upstate New York, and New Jersey beckoning, whites fled the cramped, dingy, and older inner-city neighborhoods of New York. The exodus of whites to suburbia opened other parts of New York to blacks. No longer confined to Harlem, upwardly mobile blacks sought greener pastures in Brooklyn, the Bronx, and southeast Queens. Blacks migrating from the South often skipped Harlem altogether, settling in other ghettos like Bedford-Stuyvesant. Indicative of this trend is Harlem's population peaking in 1950 and declining dramatically thereafter (New York City Department of City Planning 1969), whereas New York City's black population continued to grow for another five decades (Infoshare 2005).

Thus, there were two major forces conspiring to transform Harlem into a poor slum. One was the color line that limited blacks' employment opportunities to poorly paid jobs in personal services, retail, and manufacturing. Consequently, most Harlem residents were poor. The second force was the opening of superior housing options in the other parts of New York that lured many of the more upwardly mobile Harlemites.

Limited employment opportunities and racism combined to create the well-known social problems afflicting many ghetto communities (Clark 1965; Sugrue 1996). Crime, health problems, and family instability had long been higher in Harlem and continued to be so in the postwar period (Clark 1965; New York Department of City Planning 1969; Nichols 1939). There was perhaps no greater symptom of the social malaise afflicting Harlem than the heroin epidemic that began in the 1950s. Widespread drug abuse might be a symptom of social marginalization and restricted opportunities. That is, many young men in Harlem abused drugs because it was part of an alternative value system that thumbed its nose at the straight world and because aspirations for the American dream were blocked (Currie 1993). But in this case the symptom may have been worse than the disease. Claude Brown eloquently describes the devastating impact heroin had on Harlem in the 1950s:

> Heroin had just about taken over Harlem. It seemed like some kind of plague. Every time I went uptown, somebody else was hooked, somebody else was strung out. People talked about them as if they were dead. You'd ask about an old friend, and they'd say. "Oh well, he's strung out." It wasn't just a comment or an answer to a question. It was a eulogy for someone. . . . I was afraid to ask about somebody I hadn't seen in a while. There was always a chance somebody would say, "Well, he died. The cat took an O.D." [overdose]; or he was pushed out of a window trying to rob somebody's apartment, or shot five times trying to stick up a place to get some money for drugs. Drugs were killing just about everybody one way or another. It had taken over the neighborhood, the entire community. I didn't know of one family in Harlem with three or more kids between the ages of 14 and 19 in which at least one of them wasn't on drugs. People were more afraid than they'd ever been before. They were afraid to go out of their houses with just one lock on the door. The junkies were committing almost all the crimes in Harlem. They were snatching pocketbooks. If a cat took out a twenty-dollar bill on Eighth Avenue in broad daylight, he could be killed. Harlem was a community that could not take the pressure of this thing. (Brown 1965, p. 187–90)

On the physical side, there was virtually no private investment in Harlem in the postwar period, and this translated into a steadily deteriorating and aging housing stock. By 1969 only 9 percent of Harlem's housing stock had had been built since 1940, and the bulk of this housing was likely to be public housing that served to further concentrate poor and disadvantaged households. The disinvestment in the existing stock left a community with nearly half of its housing dilapidated or substandard at the end of the 1960s (New York Department of City Planning 1969).

This pattern of the middle-class exodus or avoiding Harlem altogether continued for decades in the post–World War II era, reaching its zenith during the 1970s. Faced with ever rising maintenance costs and taxes but only the poorest of tenants, to many Harlem landlords it made more economic sense to either walk away from or set fire to their property to collect the insurance. Thus Harlem, like the south Bronx and parts of Brooklyn, experienced widespread abandonment and arson from the late 1960s into the 1980s. Although not as dramatic as the depopulation of the south Bronx, Harlem nevertheless experienced a 29 percent drop in population in the space only ten years between 1970 and 1980; if one goes back to 1950, Harlem lost 60 percent of its population over that thirty-year period. Such a precipitous decline in population left a neighborhood

PHOTO 2. Abandoned building in Harlem that is about to be renovated. Many abandoned buildings like this one have been renovated, and such renovations contribute to the notion that Harlem is experiencing a rebirth.

pockmarked by abandoned buildings and vacant storefronts as merchants saw their customer base shrivel.

By 1980 the poverty rate for central Harlem reached a staggering 40 percent and hovered near there for the next two decades (see figure 2.1). This 40 percent threshold, although arbitrary, has become the demarcation line in social science for distinguishing ghetto neighborhoods from others. Neighborhoods broaching the 40 percent thresholds were the ones that motivated Wilson (1987) to develop his theory of an isolated and 'truly disadvantaged underclass' and a library's worth of writing on ghetto poverty by other scholars. According to Jargowsky (1997) these neighborhoods "tended to have a threatening appearance, marked by dilapidated housing, vacant units with broken or boarded-up windows, abandoned and burned-out cars and men 'hanging out' on street corners" (Jargowsky 1997, p. 11).

To an outsider, this surely described Harlem to a T. For example, an article in the *New York Times*, described one block in Harlem as "Look[ing] like a city after a war, with its vacant lots, and abandoned buildings" (Lee 1994). Even the lyrics of many hip-hop stars, the modern-day chroniclers of urban life, depicted Harlem as a dangerous, forbidding and forlorn place.

Social conditions in Harlem were so poor by the 1980s that a black man born at that time actually had a lower life expectancy than his counterparts in the developing country of Bangladesh (McCord and Freeman 1990). The crack epidemic of the mid- to late 1980s was another blow to a community that had experienced virtually no private investment for decades, the dumping of the poorest of the poor through city and federal housing

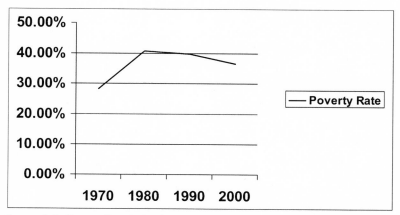

FIGURE 2.1. Poverty Rate in Harlem
*Source:* U.S. Census of Population and Housing

policies, the heroin epidemic of the 1960s and 1970s, and widespread abandonment.

Thus Harlem had went from being a city on the hill for the black race, a beacon of hope and a symbol of what blacks could achieve, to just another 'hood where rappers described a struggling and hardscrabble existence.

## A Phoenix Rising or Gentrification?

Although abandoned buildings, boarded-up storefronts, and menacing streets were symbols of Harlem to the outside world by the 1980s, in the space of only ten years this image began to change as people spoke of a second Harlem Renaissance by the late 1990s. Construction activity abounded as townhouses and apartment buildings were being developed throughout the neighborhood. The vacant buildings and lots that dotted the landscape began to disappear, replaced by renovated housing and gleaming new rowhouses and apartment buildings. Restaurants of the type to be reviewed in the *New York Times*, serving upscale Southern and Caribbean cuisine, began to appear, so much so the Food Network could devote a TV special to the eateries of Harlem. Chain stores that were unheard of above 110th Street were now opening uptown. A Marriott hotel is under construction. Even Starbucks forayed into Harlem, opening a store on 125th Street. The popular media was quick to note these changes, producing headlines like "Uptown Boomtown" (Smith 2000), "Harlem on the Rise" (Robertson 2005), and "From red-line to renaissance" (Moore 1999). And perhaps in the strongest symbol that change was under way was that whites became an increasing presnence as residents or visitors. These anecdotal changes all point to the process of gentrification.

Ironically, the changes were most stark in some of the sections of Harlem that had declined the most. These are sections where swaths of housing had been abandoned and often demolished, leaving vacant lots ripe for redevelopment. On these vacant lots virtually new neighborhoods could be created from scratch. Throughout Harlem vacant buildings and lots are being redeveloped for affordable and increasingly moderate and market-rate housing. Many of the major thoroughfares, such as 125th Street and 145th Street, have also witnessed major reinvestment activity as chain stores increasingly make their presence felt in Harlem. The historic districts in Harlem around Mt. Morris Park and in Hamilton Heights have also been a locus of gentrification because the historically significant architecture of these neighborhoods attracts this kind of activity. Thus, although gentrification is concentrated in certain sections of Harlem, the entire community can be said to be proximate to at least some gentrification activity. Moreover, because the greater

Harlem community has a singular identity as a black space, as the capital of black America, and more colloquially as "uptown," the gentrification of any part of Harlem is interpreted as a change for the larger community.

Despite all of the changes, however, one could also point to conditions that symbolized anything but gentrification. Public housing projects are still major features of the landscape, and abandoned buildings and vacant lots have not yet completely disappeared. Bodegas still appear to be the most prevalent type of store, and despite the steep declines in crime it is not uncommon for store owners to operate behind Plexiglas, presumably out of fear of crime. Whites, though no longer completely absent, are still a relatively minuscule part of the population. Young men with pants hanging down and doo-rags are a much more common sight than yuppie gentrifiers. Although national chain stores have encroached on 125th Street, stores selling hip-hop gear targeted to young black and Latino youth are still ubiquitous. Despite all the talk of gentrification, one would not confuse Harlem with Park Slope or the Upper West Side, two other New York neighborhoods with a history of gentrification. As a visitor from Australia remarked to me, "Harlem seems to be resisting gentrification pretty well."

Is Harlem gentrifying? Aside from anecdotes of the type just quoted, what evidence is there that gentrification is indeed occurring in Harlem? A review of recent socioeconomic trends in Harlem can perhaps settle this question. A definition supplied by the *Encyclopedia of Housing* defines gentrification as "The process by which central urban neighborhoods that have undergone disinvestments and economic decline experience a reversal, reinvestment, and the in-migration of a relatively well-off, middle- and upper middle-class population" (Van Vliet 1998, p. 198). This suggests we look for evidence of increased investment and an influx of those of higher socioeconomic status to discern whether gentrification is indeed occurring in Harlem.

The amount of money being invested by the private sector is a good indication of the extent to which reinvestment is happening. Unfortunately, there is no repository or database that records investment at the neighborhood level. The Home Mortgage Disclosure Act (HMDA), which requires financial institutions to record the location and characteristics of the borrowers for residential loans they underwrite, however, is a good proxy for investment. In a predominantly residential neighborhood like Harlem, one would expect residential investment to be the most important type of investment. Moreover, by focusing on conventional loans, we can get a sense of the extent to which the market views Harlem as a sound place to do business. Typically inner-city neighborhoods like Harlem and Clinton Hill were viewed as risky investments and were red lined by financial institutions. Reinvestment in the form of conventional loans would reflect increased confidence in the neighborhood and would be a sure sign that gentrification was occurring.

Figure 2.2 illustrates the amount of conventional mortgages underwritten by financial institutions in the central Harlem area during the 1991–2001 period. The increase is truly dramatic, representing a more than 1,400 percent increase! By almost any standard this would have to be counted as reinvestment. Central Harlem as defined here consists of the boundaries of Community Board 9 in Manhattan. Figure 2.2 therefore supports the anecdotal impressions that reinvestment is happening in Harlem. The renovated buildings and new construction so apparent in Harlem are indeed the manifestation of reinvestment.

That reinvestment is occurring hardly seems disputable based on the evidence presented in figure 2.2. But reinvestment is only one half of the gentrification process. As the definition implies, the arrival of the gentry is the other key indicator of the process. The socioeconomic characteristics of recent movers in Harlem is probably the best proxy for the measuring the extent to which the gentry are moving into this area.

To gauge the socioeconomic characteristics of recent in-movers to Harlem, three sources of data are utilized. The first is the New York City Housing and Vacancy Survey (NYCHVS), conducted every three years and providing socioeconomic data as well as the year the inhabitants moved into the housing unit. The NYCHVS, however, is only available going back to 1991 and because of its relatively small sample

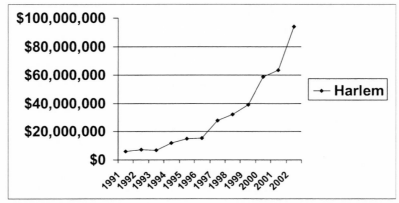

FIGURE 2.2. Conventional Mortgage Loans in Harlem 1991–2002
*Source:* Home Mortgage Disclosure Act Data

size is not well suited to providing accurate estimate for small subsets of the sample, like recent in-movers into Harlem. Thus, the NYCHVS data will be supplemented with HMDA data and data from the decennial census.

The trends revealed by the socioeconomic data are not as dramatic as the investment data, but they still tell a story consistent with gentrification. Consider the percentage of recent movers into Harlem who have college degrees, shown in figure 2.3. The general trend is clearly one of increasing educational attainment among recent in-movers. As a marker of class, educational attainment is perhaps more accurate than income because one's educational attainment is more stable over time. Education is therefore among the best proxies for capturing the class-laden connotations of gentrification, and the increase in educational attainment in the last decade depicted in figure 2.3 is strong evidence of the arrival of the gentry.

The income data also suggest a rise in socioeconomic status consistent with what one would expect with the onset of gentrification. Figure 2.4 shows trends in income from HMDA and the NYCHVS, respectively. For both trend lines, the overall pattern, though not monotonically rising, is upward. Again this is the pattern one would expect during gentrification.

It is also illuminating to look at the overall retail patterns in Harlem as an indicator of gentrification. An influx of higher-income residents will often attract retail outlets that are drawn to the increased purchasing power of the gentry. To the extent this is true, one would expect to see an increase in retail activity in Harlem where gentrification has been occurring. Data presented in figure 2.5 are based on the number of retail outlets in several ZIP codes that encompass central Harlem. There is a disjuncture in the trend line because the way retail firms were classified

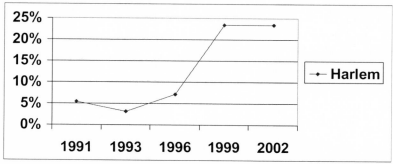

FIGURE 2.3. New Movers with College Degrees, in Percent
*Source:* New York City Housing and Vacancy Survey

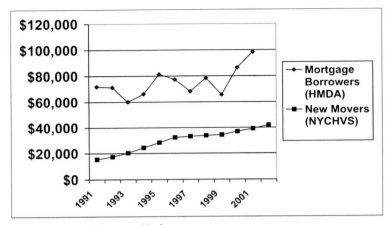

FIGURE 2.4. Annual Income, Harlem
*Source:* New York City Housing and Vacancy Survey, Home Mortgage
Disclosure Act Data

changed in 1998 with the switch from the Standard Industrial Classification (SIC) system to the North American Industrial Classification
System (NAICS). The trend is therefore best interpreted by considering
the direction of the two trend lines. The overall pattern is generally flat
with a slight uptick in the number of outlets at the end of the observation
period. As we will see in later chapters, the type of retail outlets may be of
more importance than the aggregate number from the perspective of
residents of gentrifying neighborhoods.

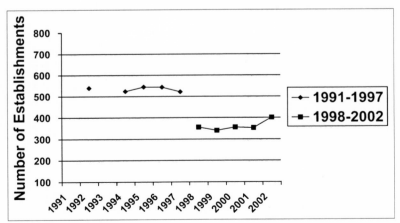

FIGURE 2.5. Retail Employment in Harlem 1991–2002
*Source:* Census Bureau County Business Patterns

## SELLING ALCOHOL IN THE 'HOOD: A TALE OF THE LIQUOR STORES

The anecdotal reports, popular media, and quantitative evidence presented here are all consistent, showing evidence that gentrification in Harlem is under way. But as noted earlier, a stroll through Harlem will still reveal all the characteristics we have come to associate with disadvantaged neighborhoods—abandoned buildings, men hanging on corners, low-rent stores. Indeed, figure 2.1 shows that despite a declining poverty rate, Harlem would still be classified as a poor neighborhood with a poverty rate of 36 percent at the turn of the last century.

The discordance between gentrification and Harlem's poverty-stricken past is easily captured by the different types of retail outlets that now sell alcohol in Harlem. In New York, liquor and wine are sold in licensed stores that specialize in the sale of alcoholic beverages. In most places in New York, a patron can browse the store, pick up a bottle, and make a selection. A few stores specialize in the sale of wine. In Harlem and many other low-income communities, however, the inventory and cashier are often shielded behind thick sheets of Plexiglas. This is presumably to protect the goods and store personnel from customers and those up to no

PHOTO 3. This is an example of the type of store selling alcoholic beverages that has long served Harlem.

PHOTO 4. This new store is emblematic of the new type of store opening in Harlem. It also sells alcohol, but for a more sophisticated clientele.

good. Recently, a store specializing in wine has opened up in Harlem, and like alcohol stores found in most places in New York, there is no Plexiglas. Both the wine and the personnel sit in the open, exposed as they do in most parts of the city. That stores specializing in wine are opening Harlem is a clear indicator that the gentry are coming. Yet the fact that liquor stores with Plexiglas still persist is an indicator that the rough edges of Harlem are not all gone.

Thus, current-day Harlem might be most aptly described as a poor neighborhood experiencing the *process* of gentrification. This is an important point to remember when considering the impacts of gentrification described in the following chapters. Whether Harlem will ever become gentrified or a solidly middle- and upper middle-class neighborhood remains an open question. But the answer to the question posed by Schaffer and Smith (1986), "The gentrification of Harlem?" would appear to be a resounding yes.

## CLINTON HILL: A VIEW FROM THE PAST

In the past, the area known as Clinton Hill was considered part of a larger neighborhood known as Fort Greene. Indeed, to this day many residents still consider the neighborhood to be part of Fort Greene and view the name Clinton Hill to be a marketing ploy by real estate professionals to attract a more upscale clientele. Clinton Hill's identity emerged in the twentieth century and was solidified with the designation of the Clinton Hill Historic District. Even during the twentieth century, Clinton Hill's boundaries have shifted depending on how far west the black ghetto of Bedford-Stuyvesant that abuts the eastern boundary of Clinton Hill had spread. Indeed, parts Clinton Hill have been considered part of Bedford-Stuyvesant at various times. Thus, in providing the historical backdrop for Clinton Hill I cite sources that refer to Fort Greene. I also use the name Fort Greene when referring to events that occurred before the name Clinton Hill became part of the popular lexicon.

The first major development to have an enduring impact on Fort Greene was the development of the Brooklyn Navy Yard in 1801. The Navy Yard influenced the ecology of the nearby area for years as numerous businesses and services sprouted to serve workers employed there. In the early 1800s, Fort Greene was primarily a squatter camp. Urbanization began in earnest in 1839 when the City of Brooklyn mapped the neighborhood into a grid pattern. The northern end was initially a built-up working-class area, and the southern end was relatively undeveloped. Reflective of this division is that Fort Greene Park was originally intended for the working class in the neighborhood. During the middle decades of the nineteenth century, Fort

PHOTO 5. Gentrified brownstone neighborhood in Harlem.

Greene grew rapidly. A case could be made that gentrification began to occur in the middle decades of the nineteenth century as more of the new housing was upscale in nature and targeted to those solidly in the middle class. Toward the end of the nineteenth century, the section of Fort Greene that has come to be known as Clinton Hill became even more upscale, attracting robber barons of the day, such as Charles Pratt, who was a partner at Standard Oil, and coffee merchant John Arbuckle. The combination of proximity to downtown Brooklyn and lower Manhattan and a relatively bucolic landscape drew industry magnates, who tore down the suburban villas that had been erected for the middle class and built mansions in their place (New York Landmarks Preservation Commission 1981). Still, the area north of Myrtle Avenue remained relatively poor, being populated mostly with tenements. In addition, pockets of poverty remained in substandard housing scattered about the community (Fein et al., 1973). Fort Greene's proximity to downtown Brooklyn and Manhattan as well as the picturesque mansions of the late nineteenth century, however, set the stage for the gentrification that came several decades later when its locational attributes were again highly prized and its distinctive architecture were in vogue.

Thus, by the end of the nineteenth century and the beginning of the twentieth, Fort Greene was an eclectic mix of stately mansions and broad streets interspersed with pockets of run-down housing, immigrants, and a sprinkling of blacks. Fort Greene's spell as a home to the elite proved fleeting as the twentieth century wore on.

With the incorporation of Brooklyn into greater New York City in 1898, Manhattan became the undisputed mecca for the New York elite, and many of the robber barons who built mansions in Fort Greene sold them and moved to Manhattan (New York Landmarks Preservation Commission 1981). Like most central city neighborhoods, Fort Greene was also impacted by the dramatic forces that hollowed out older central city neighborhoods and transformed the United States into a suburban nation. These are the forces that made once elegant housing obsolete, that brought once distant hinterlands into the easy commute by car, allowed whites to distance themselves from the burgeoning black population in the cities, and directed much-needed investment capital away from the inner city as swaths of older neighborhoods were red lined in favor of new development on the suburban periphery (Jackson 1985).

By the early decades of the twentieth century, the Fort Greene housing that was built for the middle class in the mid-nineteenth century and the housing built for the elite at the turn of the century was often subdivided into rooming houses and not well maintained (New York Landmarks Preservation Commission 1981). Tastes also changed. What was once viewed as elegant was seen as hopelessly out of date. The architecture that distinguished sections of Fort Greene during the nineteenth century was seen as unattractive during the early twentieth century. Indeed, as early as 1900 the Brooklyn Hill Improvement League considered the possibility of organizing residents to remove the detailed facades of many brownstones as a way of improving the appearance of Brooklyn neighborhoods (Fort Greene Landmarks Preservation Committee 1973), a point to keep in mind when contemplating why the middle class would be drawn to this same type of housing decades later. By 1934 there was strong evidence of Fort Greene's decline. The central and southern sections were described as previously having high purchasing power but having declined materially in recent years and as having brownstones carved up into rooming houses. In the 1934 *Real Property Inventory*, the area was referred to as rapidly decaying. The *Real Property Inventory* also classified a majority of the housing in Fort Greene as second rather than first-rate (Works Division, Emergency Relief Bureau, 1934). A decade later, in 1943, a contemporary news report described Fort Greene as a "once attractive residential area" (News Syndicate et al. 1943). A newspaper article in the 1950s aptly described Fort Greene's decline from once stately elegance:

> The worst conditions among three locations observed were at Lafayette Avenue and Cumberland Street in the Fort Greene section. There the hulks of four red-brick, three-story dwellings leaned against one another. Fifty years ago this row at 123 to 129 Lafayette Avenue had been proper, private one-family homes with the high stoops and English basements of the period. Today the mortar is crumbling from the outside walls and the plaster on the interior is in large part destroyed. Nearly every window is broken, the frames being boarded over with scrap wood or cardboard. The entry to number 125 was half-blocked yesterday with piles of garbage and whiskey bottles. The residents said refuse had not been collected for five days ... There is one bathroom on each floor. But the toilets have ceased to work, and the floors and bathtubs were covered with filth. (Freeman 1958, p. 31)

The conditions described were so bad, the tour of the area by Brooklyn officials had to be cut short out of fear that members would become ill if the tour continued (Freeman 1958). The decline of Fort Greene from its once patrician position was thus well under way by the middle of the twentieth century.

Given Fort Greene's decline over the middle decades of the twentieth century, it is perhaps not surprising that urban renewal, the paradigmatic response to urban decline during this era, left its imprint on the neighborhood. Fort Greene was the site of one of the first public housing developments in the nation with the opening of the Fort Greene Houses in 1944.

The area further west, in the part of Fort Greene that serves as the setting for this book, did not remain unscathed by the Corbusian projects that were the hallmark of housing development during this era. One of the first was the privately financed Clinton Hill Apartments. The Equitable Life Assurance Company built this development during World War II on the site of former mansions that had been subdivided as the neighborhood lost its cachet. The development was built to house workers in the Brooklyn Navy Yard during the war with the intention of returning the development to civilians afterward. In 1987 the development converted to a cooperative (Hinds 1987).

Despite the efforts at urban renewal (some critics of urban renewal might say because of) Fort Greene continued to decline through the 1960s and into the early part of the 1970s. For example, a 1973 report by the Department of Labor classified Fort Greene as a low-income area (U.S. Department of Labor, 1973). But the physical decline and failed attempts at renewal were hardly the only dramatic changes taking place in Fort Greene.

Equally dramatic was Fort Greene's transformation into a predominantly black community during the middle of the twentieth century. As blacks urbanized, they were typically relegated by housing discrimination to marginal and declining neighborhoods (the racial transition of Harlem being an exception). With the arrival of blacks, services and resources were withdrawn, furthering the downward spiral of these same neighborhoods. Fort Greene did not prove to be an exception to this rule.

Blacks were also present in Fort Greene since its initial development. Indeed in 1860 approximately half of Brooklyn's black population lived in the Fort Greene area and Colored School #1 was built in 1847 in Fort Greene (Scheiner 1965). Despite this concentration of blacks, Fort Greene was still overwhelmingly white, and Brooklyn, like most northern cities at the beginning of the last century, lacked a black ghetto (Connolly 1977).

With the great migrations of blacks from the South to Northern cities, however, the complexion of Brooklyn changed dramatically. Although the first wave of blacks from the South and the Caribbean targeted Harlem, the second wave during the middle decades of the twentieth century increasingly made Brooklyn their choice. They settled mostly along the axis of Fulton Street and Atlantic Avenue stretching from the downtown and Fort Greene areas through Bedford and Stuyvesant and into Brownsville and East New York. Blacks rarely penetrated beyond these major thoroughfares and the immediately adjoining streets (Connolly 1977, p. 54).

PHOTO 6. Myrtle (aka "Murder") Avenue in Clinton Hill.

Like dozens of urban neighborhoods across the country the growth of the central Brooklyn ghetto followed a familiar pattern of white resistance and white flight. But as long as blacks continued to pour into Brooklyn, the ghetto grew and grew (Connolly 1977). As the black population spread, the nomenclature of various Brooklyn neighborhoods changed as well. Bedford and Stuyvesant came to be known as Bedford-Stuyvesant, and as the black population spread, so did its boundaries. By the late 1960s Etzkowitz and Schaflander (1969) drew the boundaries of Bedford-Stuyvesant as far west as Washington Avenue, which was to become the heart of the Clinton Hill Historic District. Thus, with a long-standing nucleus of blacks, the massive Fort Greene public housing projects that had become overwhelmingly minority, and one of the largest concentrations of blacks in the world abutting its eastern borders, the Fort Greene/Clinton Hill area came to take on a black identity. And with white flight and black in-migration came the other symptoms of neighborhood decline, including red lining, housing deterioration, and rising crime that plagued many other black inner-city neighborhoods. As the seventh decade of the twentieth century began, Fort Greene seemed posed to become just another ghetto neighborhood.

## The Gentrification of Clinton Hill

By the 1970s to most knowledgeable observers the Clinton Hill area seemed posed to become an extension of the burgeoning central Brooklyn ghetto that would extend from downtown Brooklyn to East New York. A contemporary news report described sections as having a "rowdy climate with bars, prostitutes, and narcotics addicts" (Johnson 1971). Yet other forces were also at work, forces that would attract middle-class residents, financial capital, and commerce that would lead to Clinton Hill being the gentrifying enclave that it is today. Indeed this area was the site of some of the earliest gentrifying activity. As early as 1971 before the term *gentrification* caught on, the *New York Times* referred to "Brownstoneurbia" to describe the rehabilitation of the brownstones in the area by young professionals (Johnson 1971).

Proximity to Manhattan, distinctive architecture, repeated booms in the New York real estate market, and starting in the 1980s proximity to a resurgent downtown all combined to make the this part of Brooklyn a likely candidate for gentrification. The presence of Pratt and St. Joseph's College in the neighborhood also provided a steady supply of would-be gentrifiers. Pratt in particular, with its well-known programs in architecture, art, and design, attracted the type of individuals who might appreciate Clinton Hill's distinctive architecture as well as its gritty nature. These were of individuals with eclectic aesthetic tastes who might find renovating a deteriorated brownstone an exhilarating challenge. By 1973 Clinton Hill was described as a "revival neighborhood," a place where "brownstoners" and renovators sought out homes to be rehabilitated (Rejnis 1973).

The first wave of gentrification played out almost exactly according to script. Young professionals and students purchased and rehabilitated brownstones. Contrary to Smith's (1979) characterization of capital playing the primary or even coequal role, contemporary accounts clearly portray the gentrifiers as acting first without the assistance of capital. In 1970, Brooklyn gentrifiers are "described as having to finance the entire cost of renovation through short term personal credit" (Amster 1970). Indeed, city representatives and would-be gentrifiers hosted informal gatherings to persuade bankers to lend in gentrifying sections of Brooklyn, including Clinton Hill (Weisman 1971).

The distinctive architecture present in Clinton Hill received formal recognition with the designation of the Clinton Hill as a Historic District in 1981 (New York City Landmarks Commission 1981). This designation sent at least two signals that encouraged gentrification. First, because it was residents themselves who typically petition the city and submitted a rather complex application to designate an area as historic, this is indicative that the neighborhood now had a critical mass of concerned and educated residents. In addition, the designation as a Historic District made the area eligible for federal tax credits for the rehabilitation of historic buildings (DeGiovanni 1984). This in effect was a subsidy for rehabilitation—a crucial component of the gentrification process.

The gentrification of Clinton Hill, however, did not occur in a continuous and steady fashion. The same article that described Clinton Hill as a revival neighborhood also pointed out there were no "especially good streets," rather the "brownstoners were scattered throughout the neighborhood" in Clinton Hill (Rejnis 1973). Long-term residents, whose narratives form the basis of this book, also paint a picture of Clinton Hill in the 1970s and 1980s that despite the incipient gentrification still had the hallmarks of inner-city decline. Susan is a woman in her fifties who grew up in the Fort Greene public housing developments. Susan spent all of her formative years in Fort Greene and is thus intimately familiar with neighborhood's dynamics during the 1960s and 1970s, when she came of age. She moved to Coney Island as an adult but moved back to Clinton Hill in the late 1980s. Here is her recollection of DeKalb Avenue (a major thoroughfare in Clinton Hill) during the 1970s: "And DeKalb...I remember when DeKalb Avenue was run down tenements with rats and roaches all over the place. There was a liquor store where you could get liquor on credit. A numbers hole, places where you could go and play cards, get a drink all night for a little money. Most of the housing was rooming houses."

Tina is a black woman in her thirties who was born and raised in Clinton Hill. The 1980s were a time when crack ravaged many inner-city neighborhoods in New York, and Clinton Hill, despite the gentrification that had begun at least a decade earlier, did not emerge unscathed. Tina offers her recollection of this time:

TINA: And then when we was growing up, it was a lot of drugs sold over in this area. They used to sell drugs across the street in the building. In Citibank [an ATM outlet] they used to sell drugs. In Citibank. The boys, that, like I was growing up with, you know, they have like, they, they have like a little group going on inside the courtyard, inside the building. So they was just selling drugs all through, all through the place, so that was in the 80s.
LANCE: Was that during the crack, when crack was really heavy?
TINA: When it first came out, when crack first started...out these boys had it so down. It was, I mean they was at Citibank sellin' it. Now Waverly was really hot. The corner of Waverly and Myrtle. They block was really hot. They used to sell them drugs....It was so bad, we had a Arab store on the corner. And, um, that store right there,

the Arabs used to have, the drug dealers, they used to be scared of that drug dealer so they used to be in the store hiding their stuff in the store. Inside, the man's store! It was one of the, twenty-four hours store, but it was owned by Arabs. They would be holed up in the people's store taking sodas. It used to be funny. It, it wasn't funny but I felt sorry for them because they just started, just took over the people's store. Just putting their stuff, drugs, behind the man countertop, I was like oh, God.

Despite the prevalence of crack dealing, Tina does make a distinction between the section of Clinton Hill and the other, more violent areas of the city, in particular the nearby Fort Greene public housing development.

LANCE: Uh, so during that time when all this was going on, what was the general climate like in the neighborhood?

TINA: Just like fighting. It wasn't, it was not like now, a whole bunch of shooting and stuff. They shoot, people would shoot over here once in a blue moon, but it was mostly fighting. There was a whole lotta drugs but not nobody getting shot for any silly thing and stuff like that. None of that you know, didn't walk up and see somebody laid down in front of your building like you do down in the projects, you know, what I'm saying? You be sitting by a chair, sitting outside on the bench down here, there [in the projects] food be thrown out the window and stuff like that.

Beginning in the late 1970s and early 1980s, downtown Brooklyn re-emerged as New York's third central business district (behind midtown and downtown Manhattan). In response to the exodus of back-office functions from Manhattan to New York City's suburbs, local policy makers and civic leaders developed a strategy to keep these functions within the boundaries of New York. Developing an alternative suitable location to high-priced Manhattan was a key component of this strategy. Downtown Brooklyn, with its proximity to Manhattan and excellent subway and commuter rail accessibility, emerged as such a viable alternative. The government provided incentives and boosterism, and civic leaders provided boosterism and studies illustrating the attractiveness of downtown Brooklyn for redevelopment (Davis 1986). What this meant for Clinton Hill is that it was proximate not only to Manhattan but to a rapidly developing central business district that was literally within walking distance. This served to enhance Clinton Hill's locational assets.

The gentrification process thus has proceeded in fits and starts over the past thirty-five years in the Fort Greene/Clinton Hill area. Although there was evidence of gentrifiers as early as the beginning of the 1970s, there were sections of the neighborhood, particularly the eastern edges adjacent to Bedford-Stuyvesant and the northern reaches where multi-family developments predominate, along Myrtle Avenue that were not gentrified as of the beginning of the last decade of the twentieth century. The northern part of Clinton Hill is dominated by several apartment complexes that abut the Myrtle Avenue commercial strip. Myrtle Avenue is where signs of gentrification are most surprising. Housing north of Myrtle Avenue is dominated by mixed industrial uses and small row-houses with little architectural distinction. The strip acquired an un-savory reputation in the 1970s and 1980s and came to be known as "Murder" Avenue. Although Clinton Hill has been experiencing gentri-fication for years, it continues to be a predominantly black community. Along Myrtle Avenue, the mix of characteristics one would associate with poorer communities and those associated with gentrification are clear. For example, there are many low-rent stores, whose owners operate be-hind bulletproof Plexiglas. In addition, knots of young men still con-gregate on corners, belying the picture of a gentrified neighborhood. Conversely, coffee shops and ethnic restaurants have also staked a claim on Myrtle Avenue.

Census data also help flesh out a picture of the extent to which Clinton Hill has changed in the post–World War II era. Figure 2.6 shows trends in the value of Clinton Hill owner-occupied housing relative to New York City's for the 1950–2000 period. Despite being the home of industry magnates at the end of the nineteenth century, Clinton Hill's housing was valued lower than the city average by the 1950s. This was a pattern that persisted and indeed widened as the value of Clinton Hill's housing began to decline in the 1970s whereas for the city as a whole home prices

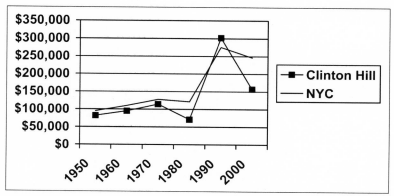

FIGURE 2.6. Clinton Hill Median House Value 1950–2000
Source: U.S. Census of Population and Housing

stabilized during the 1970s. After declining in the 1970s, the impacts of gentrification first evinced themselves in the 1980s when by the end of the decade housing prices on average were higher than in the rest of the city. This was despite some sections of Clinton Hill being plagued by drug-related crime as described. Clinton Hill was caught in the 1980s real estate boom in New York that drove prices skyward. The chart shows that real housing prices actually declined between 1990 and 2000 and does not pick up the increase in housing prices toward the end of the decade.

If we examine the socioeconomic composition of the Clinton Hill area as well, we also get a sense of how the neighborhood has evolved over time. Figure 2.7 shows median household income relative to New York City. It suggests that Clinton Hill's socioeconomic position decline relatively in the 1960s and absolutely during the 1970s. Starting in the 1980s, Clinton Hill began to close ground with the rest of the city, but as of 2000 still lagged behind the city average.

The poverty rate, an absolute measure of economic status, tells a similar story for the period after 1970 (see figure 2.8). Like many other indicators of social distress poverty peaked in 1980 in Clinton Hill at just over 25 percent. Once again, it is clear that the gentrification that began in the early 1970s was not robust enough to arrest the spread of poverty in the neighborhood. The 1980s saw ·a significant decline, which leveled off during the 1990s. The story told by the census data then is that of a neighborhood that reached its nadir in 1980 despite a decade of stirrings of gentrification in the neighborhood. The 1980s were a period of both relative and absolute growth, followed by a relatively stable 1990s period. Thus, after a generation of gentrification, Clinton Hill still lagged behind the city as a whole on at least a few key indicators of socioeconomic status.

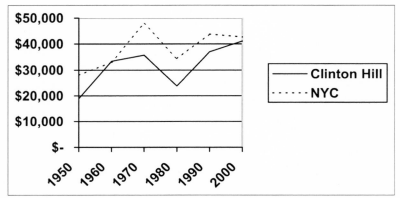

FIGURE 2.7.  Clinton Hill Median Household Income 1950–2000
*Source:* U.S. Census of Population and Housing

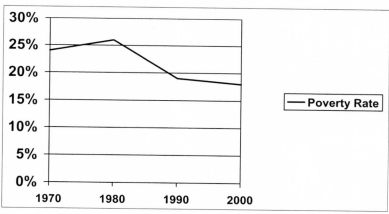

Figure 2.8. Poverty Rate in Clinton Hill 1970–2005, in Percent
*Source:* U.S. Census of Population and Housing

What the census data miss, however, is the pickup in gentrification activity during the 1990s. What the decennial census tells us about in broad epochal trends, it misses in year-to-year fluctuations associated with gentrification. Although the census indicators show that there was a socioeconomic decline between 1990 and 2000, the decadal data masks the reversal that occurred during the decade.

To get a clearer picture of gentrification trends in Clinton Hill in recent years, let us return to the HMDA data. Recall that HMDA provides neighborhood-level data on home lending activity and as such is an excellent source for discerning investment and a way of inferring gentrification activity. To the extent gentrification was taking place we should observe an increase in conventional home lending. This would be indicative of increasing private market confidence in a neighborhood that experienced significant disinvestment during the middle decades of the twentieth century.

The trends in conventional home lending depicted in figure 2.9 leave little doubt that investment in Clinton Hill increased dramatically during the last decade of the twentieth century. Indeed, even after adjusting for inflation the amount of conventional mortgages increased by a factor of eight between 1991 and 2002.

If we consider the median household income of those acquiring mortgages in Clinton Hill, however, the picture is somewhat murkier. The overall trend shown in figure 2.10 cannot be classified as moving in any particular direction. What must be remembered was that 1991 was the depths of a recession and real estate bust that halted gentrification activity

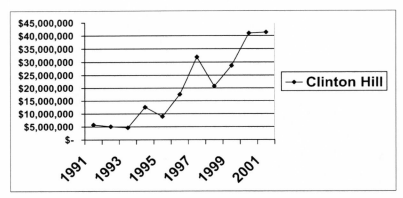

FIGURE 2.9. Conventional Mortgage Loans in Clinton Hill 1991–2002
*Source:* Home Mortgage Disclosure Act Data

in many places and lead some scholars to suspect that gentrification was a transient phase (Bourne 1993). The HMDA data suggest that during the 1990s there was a resurgence of gentrification as evidenced by the increasing flow of mortgage capital into the neighborhood depicted in figure 2.10. By the early 1990s, however, the middle class had been returning to Clinton Hill for at least two decades. Consequently, the profile (at least in terms of income) of those purchasing homes did not change much over the course of the decade. What did change was the nature of the real estate market—from a depressed one at the beginning of the decade to a

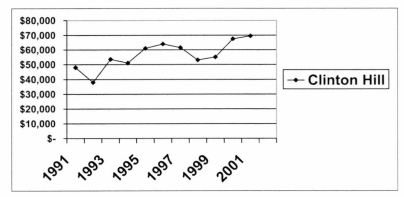

FIGURE 2.10. Median Household Income of Mortgage Purchasers in Clinton Hill 1991–2002
*Source:* Home Mortgage Disclosure Act Data

more vibrant one lubricated by the increasing availability of mortgage capital.

Finally let us consider the change in the retail scene in Clinton Hill over the past decade. Along with increasing investment and a rise in the socioeconomic status qualitative and quantitative changes in retail are also telltale signs of gentrification. Qualitatively, more upscale retail outlets often accompany gentrification, whereas from a quantitative perspective an increase in retail activity is expected. This is particularly true in gentrifying neighborhoods like Clinton Hill that had a dearth of commercial services and amenities. Though we will have to await the narratives in subsequent chapters to get a sense of the qualitative change in the retail scene, the data from the Census Bureau ZIP Code Business Patterns gives one a sense of the quantitative change in Clinton Hill's retail scene. Here ZIP code 11205, which encompasses much of Clinton Hill, is used. As noted above the change in industry classification schemes from the SIC to the NAICS in 1997 demands cautions when interpreting patterns before and after 1997. Nevertheless figure 2.11 shows a clear upward trend is apparent. This is a pattern consistent with ongoing gentrification in Clinton Hill as more stores opened up in expectation that the neighborhood could support more commercial outlets.

## The Role of Race in Gentrification

The picture painted of Clinton Hill thus far might be of the classic gentrifying neighborhoods. It was one of the first New York neighborhoods to experience the process—even before the term *gentrification* had gained

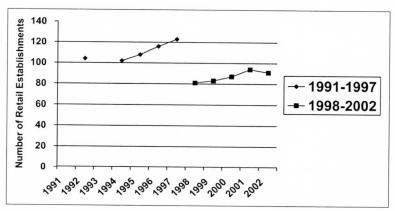

FIGURE 2.11. Retail Establishments in Clinton Hill 1991–2002
*Source:* Census Bureau County Business Patterns

currency. The area had a distinctive architecture that attracted would-be gentrifiers. The neighborhood had declined, but not as far as many other inner-city neighborhoods. Along with that decline, the neighborhood had come to take on an increasingly minority, more specifically black, character. Some of the first renovators/gentrifiers were whites from other parts of the city.

Yet in one significant way the gentrification taking place in Fort Greene/ Clinton Hill was different. Whereas the term *gentrification* conjures up images of an influx of whites rapidly displacing poorer minority residents (even among residents of Clinton Hill, as I will show later), this is not an accurate depiction of what occurred in Clinton Hill or nearby Fort Greene.

## EXPLAINING GENTRIFICATION

The history of both Clinton Hill and Harlem, then, is one of once elegant neighborhoods declining for much of the twentieth century, only to experience the beginnings of a rebirth toward the century's end. At first glance, the gentrification of these neighborhoods might appear to be just another chapter in the story of the return of the middle class to central city neighborhoods. In the case of Harlem, however, the context was different in that this was a neighborhood that had experienced extreme disinvestment and poverty concentration. Although gentrification is associated with neighborhoods that had experienced disinvestment, it was typically not areas that had declined to the extent that Harlem had. A second factor that makes the gentrification of both of these neighborhoods somewhat unique is the significant role blacks played in the gentrification process. In this section I consider both of these points in turn.

### Even the Ghetto

That the process of gentrification could even be under way in Harlem is truly stunning. As late as 1994 Nicholas Lemann could quote then Assistant Secretary at HUD, Andrew M. Cuomo, on the prospects of a community revitalization initiative: "If you expect to see Harlem as gentrified and mixed-income, it's not going to happen" (Lemann 1994, p. 255). In this controversial publication, Lemann went on to describe how ghettos were places people wanted to leave, and successful community development strategies did little more than build low-income housing or enable people to escape the ghetto more quickly. How did things turn around to the extent that brownstones could fetch prices approaching $1 million?

Gentrification in Harlem and indeed a number of other similar places seems to be the result of a confluence of factors in the last decade of the twentieth century. Like other gentrifying neighborhoods Harlem was subject to the same factors described by scholars in chapter 1 as the precursors of gentrification. New York City's economy has steadily been shifting toward white-collar jobs in industries like advertising, business consulting, finance, and fashion. These are industries that place a premium on face-to-face contact and for whom the central business district of Manhattan is their preferred locale. For the legions of professionals working in these industries, especially those without children, proximity to these jobs can be a major draw. The more affluent will choose upscale central city neighborhoods like the Upper East and West Sides. Those at the lower end of the pay scale have to look at grittier neighborhoods, like the Lower East Side and increasingly parts of Harlem. The societal wide decline in the nuclear family translates into fewer families with children and more unattached adults who are attracted to the city lifestyle and unconcerned about low-performing schools. As described earlier in this chapter, Harlem's originally being built for the upper classes meant that some of the most picturesque landscapes in Manhattan are within its boundaries. For those seeking an alternative to the cookie cutter subdivisions of modern suburbia, architecturally distinctive neighborhoods offer an attractive alternative.

In these ways Harlem was like the scores of other neighborhoods of the past few decades that succumbed to the forces that bring gentrification. Yet in many ways gentrification of the type now occurring there is somewhat anomalous. Although gentrification is typically associated with formerly poor or working-class neighborhoods, it was typically not associated with ones devastated by arson and abandonment, wracked by violent crime, nor suffering extremely high concentrations of poverty like Harlem of the late twentieth century was. Neighborhoods like this were the forlorn homes of the underclass, with hopeless futures, and immune to revitalization. So immune that the most optimistic outcomes for the Empowerment Zones, a multimillion-dollar revitalization strategy, were that it would "not harm anybody" (Lemann 1994). Thus, in addition to the conventional explanations of gentrification, one must also consider the forces that benefited inner-city revitalization in general.

In the 1990s, however, there were a confluence of factors that enticed the private market and the middle class back to the inner city. Some have referred to this confluence as a neoliberal policy regime (Crump 2002; Newman and Ashton 2004). Whatever the label, its effects were real, as I detail in the following paragraphs.

Among the most important shifts was the change in the practices of financial institutions regarding their dealing with the inner city (Wyly and Hammel 1999). Prodded by the actions of community activists who used the Community Reinvestment Act to ensure banks were meeting their statutory obligations to lend in low-income neighborhoods, and drawn by the realization that they could make money there, lending in the inner-city became fashionable (Temkin, Quercia, and Galster 2000). The dramatic rise in mortgage financing depicted earlier is no doubt partially a reflection of this.

The community development field also came into its own with best practices, lobbyists, seasoned professionals, and all the other accouterments of a mature industry (Von Hoffman 2003). This maturity meant that community developers could draw on tried-and-true methods for revitalizing neighborhoods without groping blindly in dark. Harlem, like many other low-income neighborhoods, was home to several community development corporations (CDCs) that were key in stabilizing and re-building the area. Organizations like Abyssinian CDC and the Harlem Congregations Community Initiative built housing, trained workers, and provided social services in the community. These efforts were crucial because they were among the earliest investors in the neighborhood at a time when private for-profit investors would not foray into Harlem. But once the CDCs showed that housing development could be done successfully in neighborhoods like Harlem, other investors were willing to risk their capital. In this way CDCs and other community-based organizations served as market correctives, signaling that fears of investing in the inner city were perhaps unwarranted.

These organizations also advocated for policies that could help revitalize neighborhoods like Harlem. In particular, CDCs and other community-based groups were instrumental in getting the City of New York to turn over properties acquired through tax foreclosure to community-based organizations (Von Hoffman 2003). These properties included vacant lots and abandoned buildings left behind by the wave of abandonment and arson that swept poor New York neighborhoods like Harlem and the south Bronx. To its credit, the City of New York adopted what has to be considered a relatively progressive housing policy in dealing with the thousands of properties acquired through tax foreclosure. Not only did the city transfer properties to community-based organizations for nominal amounts, but the city also devoted its own capital funds to the rehabilitation of these properties. This is virtually unheard of in local housing policy. Moreover, the city spent more of its funds on housing than the next twenty largest cities combined (Basolo 1999). The city's policy and money were no doubt instrumental in helping revitalize many distressed neighborhoods in New York.

Other locally based institutions also contributed to revitalizing neighborhoods like Harlem and Clinton Hill. For example, in Harlem, Columbia University operating through its Urban Technical Assistance Project provided technical assistance to community-based efforts to physically redevelop the area. Likewise, Pratt Institute in Clinton Hill was instrumental in revitalizing the area by making investments in the local housing stock.

The increasing importance of the Low Income Housing Tax Credit (LIHTC) as an engine of affordable housing development may have also helped revitalize poor inner-city neighborhoods like Harlem. Public housing and other federally sponsored development programs virtually ceased building housing by the 1990s. The LIHTC filled the vacuum left by the receding public housing program by providing community-based organizations with a source of capital to develop housing. As a relatively decentralized program, community-based organizations were able to apply for credits and sell them to investors in return for equity to build housing. There is also evidence that suggests that neighborhoods where LIHTC developments were built fared better than other central city neighborhoods during the 1990s and perhaps contributed to the revitalization of these areas (Freeman 2004). Thus, the community development after years of false starts may have unwittingly set the stage for gentrification to come knocking.

## Race and Gentrification

In the narratives that have dominated the gentrification discourse over the years, blacks have played a clearly defined role—that of displacees. Like other marginalized groups blacks were assumed to be priced out of gentrifying neighborhoods. Moreover, the history of "Negro Removal" under the Urban Renewal program of the 1950s and 1960s invoked images of gentrification being the postmodern version of urban renewal. Finally, the expanding black middle class was thought to be finding their place in suburban enclaves like Prince George's County outside Washington, DC, and Dekalb County outside of Atlanta. Indeed, the flight of the black middle class from inner-city neighborhoods during the post–civil rights era has emerged as one of the leading explanations for the deterioration of black inner-city neighborhoods (Anderson 1991; Wilson 1987).

A script where whites are the driving force behind gentrification whereas blacks are bystanders who are displaced, however, does not aptly describe the gentrification processes under way in either Clinton Hill or Harlem.

Consider Clinton Hill, where newspapers were reporting the beginnings of gentrification as early as 1970 (Amster 1970), but the black population actually continued to grow until 1980, at least as shown in figure 2.12. Figure 2.12 shows that the black population peaked in 1980 and has been relatively stable since then. When coupled with the evidence shown in figure 2.8, it makes clear the notion that gentrification, once

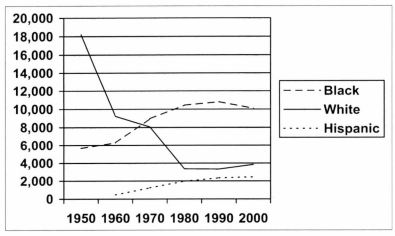

FIGURE 2.12. Clinton Hill Racial Composition 1950–2000
*Source:* Decennial Census of Population and Housing

begun, erases poor minorities from a neighborhood overnight and deserves rethinking, and that the transition period can be a long one worthy of study.

Beyond the gradual pace of gentrification, the persistent black presence in Clinton Hill despite thirty years of gentrification also points to perhaps the major difference between this area and many other such neighborhoods—the major role that blacks played in gentrification. Indeed, some of the earliest reports of gentrification in Clinton Hill noted that many of the renovators, who could be classified as gentrifiers, were black. Johnson (1971) chronicles the story of black family who moved from Queens to the area to have a shorter commute to Manhattan. A story about a brownstone tour of Clinton Hill for would-be purchasers noted that a third of the tour members were black (Rejnis 1973). By the mid-1980s, Clinton Hill was described as follows:

> There is always human and political turmoil when a city neighborhood is being retrieved from abandonment and decay and, in this regard, the Clinton Hill section of downtown Brooklyn is no exception. But unlike other minority neighborhoods that have been overrun by middle-income whites in search of affordable housing, Clinton Hill has been propelled into gentrification by an integrated mix of middle-income New Yorkers. (Hinds 1987, p. R1)

Rosenberg (1998) points to the work of local community groups like the Fort Greene Housing Office that organized and implemented programs to ensure that mortgages were made available to blacks as well as the limited alternatives for middle-class blacks seeking housing as forces that kept the area predominantly black despite gentrification. Next consider the following quote about Harlem:

> But there is evidence of impending change in Harlem. Reversing a decades-old pattern of escape to greener pastures, black middle class people are coming back. And, nearly 80 years after they first began to abandon Harlem's fashionable neighborhoods, so are middle class whites. Many Harlem observers believe that within ten years, America's most famous ghetto will be transformed into its most recognizable example of gentrification. For good reasons and bad, the Harlem we've come to know won't be the same. (Lee 1981, p. 192)

Although the quote accurately describes the sentiments of many today, it was actually written a quarter of a century ago in *Black Enterprise*. Thus, although gentrification began later in Harlem than in Clinton Hill, there has still been a considerable history of speculation about gentrification in the neighborhood. Most of this concern was less than sanguine. Schaffer and Smith (1986) specifically argued that the pool of would-be black gentrifiers was too small to foster black-led gentrification and hence Harlem was likely to be overrun by whites. Also reflective of these concerns the article titled "Will We Lose Harlem? The symbolic capital of is threatened by gentrification," from which the quote was taken.

Consistent with these fears, the white population in Harlem more than doubled between 1980 and 2000 as shown in figure 2.13. Yet in absolute terms this means the white population grew from less than 1 percent to about 2 percent of the population in 2000—hardly a threat to Harlem's black identity. Much more significant has been the increase in the Latino population, but for various reasons that will be discussed in later chapters, this increase had not registered in people's consciousness the way the increase in whites has.

Despite the fact that the white influx has been small in absolute terms, there is no doubt that gentrification has continued as described. Schaffer and Smith may have been skeptical of the possibility of black-led gentrification, but the continued growth of the black middle class in the 1990s meant that a critical mass of potential black gentrifiers was beginning to form during this time. For example, the number of blacks with at least a college degree grew from 1.9 million in 1990 to 3.4 million in 2002, according to data from the U.S. Census Bureau. In New York City, the number of blacks with at least a college degree grew from 155,000 to 202,000 during this same period, also according to the census. Figure 2.14 illustrates the proportion of the black population with at least a college degree in Clinton Hill, Harlem, and New York City, respectively. The presence of the black gentry is clear in Clinton Hill, where education

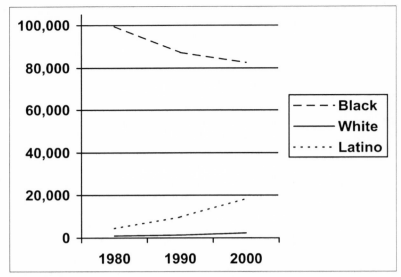

Figure 2.13.  Racial Composition of Harlem 1980–2000
*Source:* Decennial Census of Housing and Population

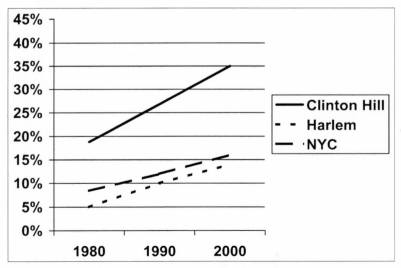

Figure 2.14.  Percentage of Blacks with a College Degree
*Source:* Decennial Census off Housing and Population

levels among blacks far exceed those in the rest of the city. Black educational attainment in Harlem lags behind the rest of the city, as would be
expected for a depressed ghetto community, but in the 1980s and 1990s
this gap slowly began to narrow. This, too, can be interpreted as a sign of
the black middle-class presence increasing in Harlem.

Along with the trends described that opened up poor inner-city neighborhoods like Harlem to gentrification and the increasing size of the black
middle class, Harlem's history as a manifestation of the new Negro also
likely played a role in its gentrification. Even at its nadir, Harlem was never
just another ghetto neighborhood. Rather, its history as the home of the
Harlem Renaissance and as a mecca for the black elite meant that it held
important historical significance to most blacks. As described earlier in this
chapter, Harlem is a neighborhood that came about and achieved its fame
through the agency of blacks and thus has inspired pride among many
blacks, including those in the middle class. Taylor (2002) describes how
Harlem's legacy was a lure to the black gentry. She describes how many of
the black gentry cherished the notion of walking the same streets as
Langston Hughes and W.E.B. DuBois and how this history contributed to
a contributed to a "black energy" that creative types wanted to tap into.
Moreover, many of the black gentry were aware of the tarnished reputation and social problems that afflicted Harlem. But they related to Taylor
(2002) their desire and near obligation as more advantaged blacks to help
Harlem achieve its former glory.

The desire by middle-class blacks to return to and stay in historically
black neighborhoods like Clinton Hill and Harlem also reflects the maturation and increasing diversification of this group. In his polemical description of the Negro middle class, Frazier writes, "they have attempted
to conform to the behavior and values of the white community in the
most minute details. Therefore they have become exaggerated Americans" (Frazier 1957, p. 193). When owning a single-family home in the
suburbs became a marker of middle-class status, upwardly mobile blacks
strove to purchase single-family homes in black suburban neighborhoods
like Jamaica, Queens, or Mount Vernon, New York.

The continuing expansion the black middle class and the rise of black
power ideology, however, changed the calculus of those coming of age
after the civil rights movement. Aping whites was no longer in vogue (Van
Deburg 1992). Instead, all things distinctively black were valued. Moreover, the increasing size of the black middle class allowed for a diversity
of means for expressing one's social status.

In pointing to the origins of the "new black aesthetic," Ellis (1989,
p. 237) describes a second-generation black middle class that is comfortable enough to reject the sometimes crass materialism of their fore-
bears and to attend "art school instead of medical school." This new

black middle-class sensibility (which I refer to as neosoul aesthetic) prefers locks to perms, the Roots to P-Diddy, and cowrie shells to gold jewelry. This neosoul aesthetic might also subscribe to values that elevate authenticity and diversity and abhor the mass-produced cookie-cutter suburbs prevalent across much of America. Where conventional black middle-class norms required striving for the single-family home on a cul-de-sac, the neosoul aesthetic might prefer older neighborhoods with charm like Harlem, Fort Greene, U Street, and Bronzeville. These neighborhoods have old but elegant architecture, street life, cafés where folks can meet and greet other bohos, and perhaps most important, a cultural legacy. As the black middle class grows, matures, and diversifies, one might continue to expect not only the expansion of suburban enclaves like Prince George's County but inner-city enclaves through gentrification as well.

Some of the same forces described that attracted middle-class blacks to Harlem were also at play in drawing them to Fort Greene/Clinton Hill. Many blacks preferred the diversity of urban living and wanted to expose their children to all aspects of the black experience, including the inner city (Newkirk 1998). Although Fort Greene/Clinton Hill lacks the historical cachet of Bronzeville or Harlem, by the last decades of the twentieth century it did have a clear black identity. Thus, a middle-class black person coming of age in New York City in the post–civil rights era for whom the suburban lifestyle did not beckon would cast their eyes about for a suitable alternative. If they were white, Greenwich Village, the East Village, or perhaps Williamsburg would be hip, funky neighborhoods to migrate to. The continuing significance of race in social life, however, has resulted in the urbane black middle class looking for their own neighborhoods with "flava." Fort Greene/Clinton Hill has come to be such a neighborhood.

By the 1990s, Fort Greene/Clinton Hill was a mecca for black creative types and entrepreneurs. Some were longtime residents like vocalists Betty Carter and Noel Painter, pianist Geri Allen, and photographer Roy De-Carava. Newer arrivals included actors Laurence Fishburne and Wesley Snipes, saxophonist Branford Marsalis, neosoul songstress Erykah Badu, rapper Common, and movie producer Spike Lee. The concentration was so great that many spoke of a second Harlem Renaissance that was taking place in Brooklyn (Brown 1992; Shipp 1990; Washington 1991). Unlike the Harlem Renaissance of the early twentieth century that was purposely put in motion to improve blacks' standing in America, however, this clustering of artists appears to be the result of creative types simply being drawn to this particular neighborhood. Unlike the suburban amenity package that offers good schools, low densities, and a predictable if sterile environment, neighborhoods like Clinton Hill offer an opportunity to be around creative types who do not necessarily conform to the American dream: "There is an incredible psychic energy that comes from living in a place full of so many people who are artistic, progressive and culturally aware and young" (Lisa Davis, as quoted in Brown 1992, p. 48).

Although the concentration of artistic types in Fort Greene was coincidental in contrast to the purposive gathering of artists in Harlem during its Renaissance, the impact of these communities on the conscious of America was in some ways similar. Like the artists of the Harlem Renaissance, many of Fort Greene's artists see shaping the image of blacks to be part of their larger calling. Whereas the artists of the Harlem Renaissance aimed to humanize blacks by showing that blacks could also create art, today's artists are speaking to the notion of black identity, seeking to refine, shape, and stretch what it means to be black at the cusp of the twenty-first century (Shipp 1990).

Along with being a magnet for creative types, Clinton Hill appears to have attracted a black entrepreneurial class as well. Along Fulton Street and throughout the neighborhood are black-owned restaurants, clothing stores, and other retail outlets. At least some of these entrepreneurs seem to be motivated by black nationalism, that is, a desire to keep capital in the community, and create the option to buy black (Lamb 1991). Thus, for many black entrepreneurs, their ventures were more than mere money-making propositions. This was a way to help build a stronger black community, one that was prosperous and economically self-sufficient.

Thus for middle-class blacks seeking a neighborhood that was the manifestation of their neosoul sensibilities, Clinton Hill or Harlem would fit the bill. It was a place where other progressive blacks resided, where one could patronize black-owned stores, yet with a gritty enough edge to allow one to "keep it real." People like Spike Lee, Laurence Fishburne, and certainly many anonymous others could certainly choose to live elsewhere. Yet they chose to reside in a predominantly black inner-city neighborhood.

That some middle-class blacks would shun suburbia can be viewed as a variant of Ley's (1996) "new middle class" thesis refracted through the prism of race. Ley argued that demographic, economic, and political changes created a new middle class that was drawn to the city. For blacks, there were also significant changes that differentiated the middle class—a point I elaborate on in the concluding chapter. Suffice it to say here that the expansion and maturation of the black middle class allowed it to diversify, and at least one strand of this diversity manifested itself in gentrifying inner-city neighborhoods like Clinton Hill and Harlem.

## CONTEXT RECONSIDERED

Both Clinton Hill and Harlem were witnesses to some of the major trends in urban history that defined the twentieth century. The neighborhoods had auspicious beginnings and the homes of the elite and middle class. Yet the forces of suburbanization sapped both of their vitality. The apartheid that characterized urban America surely characterized Harlem as well and appeared to be the fate of Clinton Hill, too. Both neighborhoods came to take on black identities and with that all of the history of struggle and maltreatment that has been the fate of black neighborhoods in modern America. Attempts at urban renewal while improving the housing conditions of some failed to stem the decline of these neighborhoods after World War II. Yet in their grand beginnings the seeds of revival lay dormant, bursting through when conditions were ripe. Clinton Hill began its renaissance before declining as far as Harlem did. But Harlem followed, so that by the turn of the century gentrification was in full sway in both neighborhoods. And for both of these neighborhoods, gentrification did not mean the end of their black identity, rather, it was their black identity that in some ways contributed to their revival.

This is the historical context of Clinton Hill and Harlem that served to color residents' reactions to the gentrification swirling about them.

# 3  There Goes the 'Hood

THE ABHORRENCE WITH WHICH gentrification is viewed in many circles is illustrated clearly by the results of an online search of the term *gentrification*, which turned up the following:

> The term is often used negatively, suggesting the displacement of poor communities by rich outsiders. (Grant 2003)

> "They're pushing poor people out of the city and in the process breaking up the power bases of their struggle," he says. "It's gentrification, but you could also almost call it apartheid by both race and class." (Lydersen 1999)

> As such, gentrification is almost always a displacement of poor residents to remote and less economically favored areas with similar substandard housing, and a theft of public and private resources from other poorer neighborhoods which deserve to be improved for the people who already live there, and should be understood and resisted as such. (Dixon 1998)

These snippets are illustrative of the popular wisdom of gentrification as anathema. It is a process that benefits the haves to the detriment of the have-nots. It is a continuation of the history of marginalized groups being oppressed by the more powerful. And always, gentrification leads to the displacement of poor marginalized groups.

Outside of the ivory tower, *gentrification* has become a dirty word, at least outside of real estate interests and city boosters. Although initial reports of gentrification in the 1970s tended to be favorable, this view was quickly erased by ongoing concerns about displacement and class conflict thought to be inherent in the gentrification process. Community-based organizations often sprung up to combat gentrification (McGee 1991). For example, in my neighborhood a community-based organization sponsors an annual antigentrification block party. As early as 1985, the Real Estate Board of New York felt it necessary to take out a full-page ad in a paper defending the positive benefits of gentrification. A nonprofit research, communications, capacity building, and advocacy organization at one time had an antigentrification Web site.

The political economy approach portrays gentrification much the same way. This school of thought typically portrays moneyed real estate interests, yuppies, and government elites as the beneficiaries of gentrification. Through gentrification, the political economy critique has it, yuppies gain access to space that is conveniently located to downtown employment and cultural amenities. Real estate interests profit by speculating on previously marginal properties. Government elites see a rise in their tax base and perhaps a decline in social services needs associated with the poor. Smith and LeFaivre (1984, p. 17) write:

> Thus the benefits of gentrification appear to accrue to the capitalist class, defined as those who own and control capital for the purpose of investing it for profit or interest, as well as to the middle class in general, who are the beneficiaries not only of new living space but also of profitable, if comparatively small investments.

My conversations with residents of Clinton Hill and Harlem, however, reveal a more nuanced reaction toward gentrification. If gentrification were a movie character, he would be both villain and knight in shining armor, welcome by some and feared and loathed by others, and even dreaded and welcomed at the same time by the same people.

A positive reaction to gentrification was a clear theme that emerged during my conversations with residents of Clinton Hill and Harlem. Some of the positive reactions were based on narrow economic self-interests. Especially in Clinton Hill, where many of the respondents were homeowners or cooperative owners, the escalating housing prices increased the return on their housing investment substantially. Renee grew up in a nearby public housing project moved into a Clinton Hill coop in the mid-1990s. (The names and some identifying characteristics of the people quoted in this book have been changed to protect their anonymity.) Since then she has been considering purchasing her apartment, lamenting the opportunities lost:

> 1999, 2000 things turned around, the co-op stabilized a lot, and we began to attract, uh, what we call a different market. In 1999 apartments here sold, one-bedroom apartments, sold for maybe $35, $40, $45,000. That's when I should have made my move. Today that same apartment will sell for $160,000. Little steep for an apartment.

Or, consider the experience of James, a man in his forties who grew up in nearby Bedford-Stuyvesant and attended college for a few years before settling in East New York as an adult. He moved into Clinton Hill at the age of twenty-eight: "I paid $18,000 in cash for my apartment in 1988. Now this unit would go for a couple of hundred thousand dollars. That's because people are coming from areas that are even more expensive." For these homeowners, gentrification has been a boon. Whatever their discomfort about whites moving in, increased police protection, or other facets of neighborhood change, it would be impossible for them to ignore the economic benefits associated with gentrification.

That homeowners would stand to benefit from gentrification is an obvious if sometimes overlooked result of gentrification. Moreover, because of disinvestment in these neighborhoods, housing prices in the past were extremely depressed. Those who purchased in earlier years were not necessarily affluent but now stand to reap a considerable windfall should they decide to sell their property. To some degree this is happening for people who were fortunate to become homeowners in Clinton Hill and Harlem. Naturally some people are enthusiastic about this facet of gentrification. Barbara is a graduate student who moved to Harlem seven years ago. She was initially a renter, but her building turned into a cooperative several years ago. She summed up how the recent changes in Harlem were affecting her personally: "To sum it up I am experiencing the changes, I'm rolling with the punches. I'm excited about the possibility of making money. And I look at this as an investment—I'll be making money from my apartment."

The increase in housing values for homeowners of Clinton Hill and Harlem is clearly a good thing for these homeowners. Given the paltry homeownership rate in Harlem as shown in table 1.1, however, the economic benefits of gentrification are unlikely to accrue to many Harlem residents. In contrast, in Clinton Hill, where there is a substantial presence of black homeowners, these economic benefits are meaningful. Indeed, in recent years much has been made of the vast inequalities in wealth between blacks and whites. It has been pointed out that the disparity in wealth is much larger than the income disparity, and much of this difference has been laid at foot of unequal housing values (Oliver and Shapiro 1995). Oliver and Shapiro (1995, p. 147) write:

> In general, homes of similar design, size, and appearance cost more in white communities than in black or integrated communities. Their value also rises more quickly and steeply in white communities.... Whether or not discrimination is intended, the racial housing-appreciation gap represents part of the price of being black in America.

Conley (1999) has also pointed out the costs of differences in wealth accumulation due in part to lower housing appreciation among blacks. These increases in home equity, particularly in Clinton Hill where much of the property is owned by blacks, are perhaps a long time coming.

That homeowners who moved into gentrifying neighborhoods would benefit from gentrification is perhaps not surprising even if this fact is relatively overlooked among commentators. But the economic benefits stemming from increased property values for homeowners was hardly the most prevalent source of goodwill expressed toward gentrification. More prevalent and perhaps more surprising was the reaction of some long-term residents to other aspects of gentrification. Many residents appreciated the improvements in amenities and services. Gentrification often brings to mind yuppies and the upscale specialty shops that serve them, leaving the impression that these services would do little for long-term residents. To some extent this characterization is accurate, but it is not always complete. The changes taking place in Clinton Hill and Harlem in some ways might be perceived as the normalization of commercial activity in these neighborhoods after decades of disinvestment. A supermarket with decent produce, a drugstore, and a moderately priced restaurant are amenities taken for granted in many neighborhoods but were in short supply in inner-city areas like Clinton Hill and Harlem.

Associating increased retail activity with gentrification does beg a chicken-or-egg type of question. Is the arrival of a Duane Reade drugstore really a sign of gentrification? In recent years there has been a revival of many depressed inner-city neighborhoods (Von Hoffman 2003). When this revival occurs either in a hot market, a neighborhood with an attractive housing stock, or a neighborhood with a good location, gentrification will often accompany the revival. Certainly higher-income residents make the opening of a store like Duane Reade more attractive. Likewise, the presence of basic stores and amenities like a Duane Reade certainly make inner-city neighborhoods more attractive to those we might classify as the gentry. Although a Duane Reade certainly could

PHOTO 7. A sign of the old and new. A check cashing place, common sight in low-income neighborhoods, abutting a Starbucks, a ubiquitous symbol of gentrification.

open without gentrification, the arrival of higher-income residents and other kinds of investment make the arrival of these types of investment more likely to occur. Certainly residents of these neighborhoods considered all of the improvements as part of the package of gentrification—as will be discussed in the next chapter.

The lack of retail amenities is not only an inconvenience but may have significant affects on quality of life. Indeed, scholars in the United Kingdom have coined the phrase *food deserts* to describe neighborhoods where affordable and nutritious food is not readily available (Wrigley 2002). Instead of markets where fresh fruits and vegetables and other nutritious options are available, residents of many poor neighborhoods have to make do with corner stores with higher prices and fewer nutritious options. Some have linked residence in these food deserts to unhealthy lifestyles that contribute to morbidity and illness (Acheson 1998). Although evidence of food deserts in the United States is anecdotal, if their existence is an empirical reality, gentrification might make more nutritious food readily available and affect the health of poor residents in these neighborhoods. As will be shown shortly, several residents pointed to the improved availability of fresh produce and other grocery items as one of the more salient changes they associated with the changes in their neighborhood.

Aside from possible health implications, residents relished the options that gentrification afforded them. Juan is a mid-forties resident of west Harlem, where he has lived all of his life. He witnessed the waxing and waning of the neighborhood. The urban renewal programs, the heroin plagues, the crack epidemic, and the disinvestment that beset the neighborhood from the 1960s on. This disinvestment left the neighborhood with few satisfactory retail options. He is very cognizant of the changes in this area: "But, uh, as I was mentioning the things, there's a Fairway [a new supermarket]. You know. Uh, and that's terrific. Because the, you know they have a nice price range on things. If you want to buy something that is upscale it's there. If you wanted something reasonable it's good. But the quality is good." Tina is a single mother in her thirties native to Clinton Hill. As such she was born when the first stirrings of gentrification were beginning in parts of Clinton Hill, and when Myrtle Avenue, the main thoroughfare up the street, was called Murder Avenue. Her overall reaction to the changes was as follows:

> I just like the change…and all the people. I really like the changes. You know, you get to see, different people, different stores being opened, even though those people's kind of snotty. Some of them are, some of them is kind of friendly, so…me and my kids go up on DeKalb Avenue to the different restaurants. Then, we went to the sushi restaurant. My son was like, what is this? I was like, let's just try it, 'cause I've never had it before.

PHOTO 8. New coffee/bakery shop on the once notorious "Murder" Avenue.

What is particularly surprising about Tina's response was her positive reaction to amenities like a sushi restaurant. This is the type of neighborhood change that many would assume would benefit only the newly arrived gentry. Tina's response suggests that this is not always the case. Her response should not be interpreted as indicating that all long-term residents are appreciative of the more boutique type of amenities that often accompany gentrification. Most residents did not mention such amenities, instead focusing on those that impacted their daily lives, such as supermarkets. A few were even openly hostile to restaurants that they viewed as being targeted for them. Terry, native of Harlem in his fifties, said, "We don't eat there. I went in there for a piece of cake and it was like four bucks! I can get a whole cake for four bucks. Obviously they don't want too many of us in there. We don't get down like that spending four dollars for a piece of cake, know what I'm saying?" Terry lives in the same public housing project where he was born and raised and provided the comments in response to a query about some of the new restaurants that had opened in the neighborhood. The prices, though standard for restaurants in New York, seemed outlandish to him and his peer group—"we don't get down like that." But for the most part, residents were appreciative of at least some of the changes taking place in their neighborhood. Ms. James migrated to New York City from the South as a child and has been living in Clinton Hill for some forty years, since she was a teenager. She witnessed the decline of the neighborhood and is now witness to the change and seems amenable to these changes.

> Now we have um, see, a lot of things changed in that community after the, the Watts rebellion. And then you had several of the many rebellions, okay, and each time that something like that would happen, things would change. It used to be all Italian merchants on Myrtle. But after the rebellions things was real tense. Then Italian merchants left um, when it became, when Clinton Hill became all black. You know the dairy, the drugstore, and the other things changed when it became um, a black community. One of the drug stores on Myrtle put in a Plexiglas all over, so, you could no longer go behind, um, you could no longer walk through and just pick up whatever you want. Stores was leaving or hiding behind Plexiglas. But it was bad. It was bad, but, when the man is being robbed every day. And they, they had a pharmacy underneath. It was this, this was robbed twice in one day. So could you blame them? So, now I like the stores. I think um, most of us the tenants who have been here for a long time are really delighted to see all of these things come back, because at one time when, we only had like the um, an Italian restaurant that was a, you know, and then they, when it got black they left, so, we didn't even have anything.

Carmen is a single mother of three who is native to Harlem. She expressed her appreciation of the improvements in shopping options this way: "More stores are coming, like downtown stores are in our neighborhood. Before I used to go downtown, 34th Street, 14th Street. I take the bus to 125th Street, you can find every store that you find downtown there. It's wonderful."

The convenience afforded by improved amenities and services was a constant theme in my conversations with residents of Clinton Hill and Harlem. To some degree, this speaks to the dearth of commercial activity that plagues many black communities like these. The exodus of people from many inner-city neighborhoods in the 1960s and 1970s was also accompanied by receding commercial activity. The civil unrest of the 1960s, red lining by financial institutions and insurers, and seeing their customer base steadily shrink caused commercial enterprises to flee neighborhoods like Clinton Hill and Harlem in the 1960s and 1970s. It was not uncommon for a supermarket or a video store to simply not exist in some neighborhoods. Being able to go to grocery shopping or eating out in one's neighborhood are things that are available in many middle-class and mostly white neighborhoods and are often taken for granted. This was not always the case in recent years in many black inner-city communities. Juanita is mid-thirties native of Harlem who moved out to one of the outer boroughs after attending one of the CUNY schools. She has since returned to Harlem, where she now lives in her mother's rented apartment. Juanita's narrative illustrates how living in a commercial desert might predispose one to be somewhat receptive of gentrification.

> Like the new stores, the shops and things of that nature, I appreciate that. Like I know there's a Pathmark that's opening up on 145th and 8th Avenue. That's like unheard of. I was really surprised at that, and then up the block, it's, uh, Duane Reed opening up. 'Cause we used to have the travel so far just to get prescriptions filled. 'Cause you're leaving from 8th Avenue and going, not, only ten blocks, but then you have to travel avenues further west to get to a pharmacy. So that'll be a lot more convenient.

Given this backdrop, it should come as no surprise that the respondents I spoke with often appreciated the improvements in amenities, even when they were suspicious of why additional amenities were being provided. Ms. Johnson is a native of South Carolina who migrated to Harlem in the 1940s. After living in several sections of Harlem, she now lives in an apartment building in central Harlem. Her perspective on the improving services and amenities was as follows:

MS. JOHNSON: But to me I think it's, it's helpful, because you see more policemen. They respond faster. So here to me, I enjoy the change in the neighborhood. Okay. As I, as I said, the supermarkets are different, and I don't see where it could hurt. I don't have no reaction, except that I think the improvement is for all the best. Well it's actually much better and since they've built it up it's much cleaner. Because with the empty lots, the people used to bring their garbage from all over, and there was all these rats would be around. Now they've built it up with new homes, so that I think the neighborhood looks better, and it's much cleaner. I don't see how it affects you know because as I've said we now have supermarkets, we always have transportation so that was one of the good thing about living in Harlem and now that we have better supermarkets and have much more umm—drugstores because I remember we went down to about one drugstore you had to walk about ten blocks to get to that one. And now we have drugstore all around the corners. So, I think it is more convenient, expensive but it is convenient.

LANCE: Okay. All right, is there anything else you think we should know about this neighborhood or how it is changing and how these changes might effect neighborhood residents?

MS. JOHNSON: Well I—I imagine everyone don't like it because we have other people living here. But to me it helps so because you have a better source of living. For example if they weren't here we would have still had those old supermarkets with their dried out vegetable and spoiled meat—Where in now we don't have that. And they didn't do it because of us, because if they did it would have happened years ago. So to me they staying here it makes, doesn't make any difference. For us and it is better to me but then I can't speak for nobody but myself. Because I have some neighbors that despise it [laughs] but when I said to them—I said look at the supermarkets, look how nice and fresh the food, I think you go there and you can buy fresh vegetable like you can downtown. Well, we would go— and load them on the buses downtown in a better neighborhood to get fresh meat, fresh food, fresh vegetables, you don't have to do that now. But you know you can't please everybody. And so I only go and say what's best for me.

Ms. Johnson is an African American who clearly subscribes to the notion that the improvements taking place in Harlem were not for "us," meaning blacks, but for "them," meaning whites. As an African American myself, I feel confident that she was using our shared race to designate "us" in contrast to whites or "them." Certainly other racial/ethnic groups have also been moving into Harlem, notably Latinos. But given the shared history of discrimination and disinvestment, especially in New York, it is probably safe to assume that she is referring to whites. Her view is ultimately pragmatic. Although the improvement in services in her mind reflects the discriminatory treatment black neighborhoods receives, she is more than happy to take advantage of these improvements. That residents would appreciate improved amenities, in hindsight, seems like common sense. Who wouldn't appreciate better stores in which to shop?

Increased commercial activity, however, has been derisively coined "Disneyification." Powell and Spencer write:

> Gentrification transforms public spaces into privatized consumption spaces. Urban leaders, developers and economic elites provide a package of shopping, dining, and entertainment within a themed and controlled environment which some scholars call "Disneyification" ... This commodification of culture is perhaps most jarring in Harlem, where recent redevelopers have packaged race as culture and art, using frontier motifs to "tame" the neighborhood while keeping it exotic enough to attract consumers. (2003, pp. 443–44)

These critiques make valid points. Certainly the capitalist class continues to benefit from gentrification. A Disney Store has indeed opened on 125th Street (although it has since closed), the main thoroughfare in Harlem. Nonetheless, this does not mean that long-term residents will not witness any benefits. To be sure, some of the positive feelings toward gentrification were often ambivalent. This ambivalence often stemmed from the disrespect residents felt their communities had experienced in the past, as discussed. But the fear that the neighborhood would lose some of its character because of rising prices also figured into the ambivalence that many people felt. Nate is a mid-forties native of Bedford-Stuyvesant who moved to Clinton Hill fifteen years ago. As such, he moved in when his section of the neighborhood was somewhat dicey. He was nevertheless attracted to the neighborhood because of its black identity and the fact that compared to other predominantly black areas in Brooklyn it was a "good" neighborhood. As a civil service worker he is solidly middle class but squeezed out of some New York's pricier neighborhoods. He is thus ambivalent about the improvements to what he sees as an up and coming black neighborhood: "I am concerned about people leaving the area because it is too expensive. But I'm also happy. They will bring a stabilizing element in reference to police protection and many access to many resources. To me it's like half and half. I see good and I see bad."

Other Harlem residents, though appreciative of the new stores, recognize some of the benefits of the older mom and pop stores.

CAROL: One of the not so good things is that I see a lot of mom and pop shops being moved out, forced out, you know, because of all the new, um, construction and high, high cost, you know, places, I guess all the real estate around, around those places are going out so people can't afford their leases. You know, the laundry mat I used to go to on the corner that was there for so long, they put a super kind of laundry mat that stays open twenty-four hours right across the street and drove him out of business, and that's one of the things that I think is kind of negative.

LANCE: So most of these stores are leaving because of the increases in the, in the costs?

CAROL: I think they can't afford to pay. When you, when it's time to renew the leases they can't afford, and another thing is that they, you know, he's in business in the case of the laundry mat, he's losing business, it was a smaller place. So everybody's going over to the larger place with the bigger machines and, you know, things of that nature. And to a certain degree I thought that although you can always use a lot of laundry mats in the neighborhood, to have them right across the street from the other, it seemed like the target was to force the little man out of business.

LANCE: All right. Could you talk a little bit more about why you think that's a, a negative, um, because the, yeah—

CAROL: Well, because that's a laundry mat that has been in the neighborhood for years owed by someone who lives in the neighborhood, and has always been supported by the neighborhood, and then you have people that do not live in the neighborhood, the money's not going back into the neighborhood, that'll weaken benefits off the people in the neighborhood, so that's why it's kind of negative. And not being refunneled in the community because the, the gentleman was very involved in different kind of things, uh, positive things, um, and you know, it wasn't just about the money, I mean, it was about the neighborhood opposed to being just about the money.

As a native of Harlem in her late thirties, Carol is all too familiar with the lack of retail options in the neighborhood. She is well aware of the fact that the stores that did persist in Harlem through disinvestment were often small, lacked variety, and charged higher prices. Yet she is also aware that as mom and pop stores they often provided other services for the community. Terry, who was introduced before, elaborated on another potential drawback to the decline of the local mom and pop store:

> If you look at the stores they used to be little mom and pop shops. You know? And these stores whenever we had a party or an event they would pitch in, soft drinks, a little money whatever. But now you're seeing all these little boutiques and chains open, but they don't give anything to the community. You know? If you go in there and ask them to contribute, it's a problem. And the other thing is, we don't see these new stores opening up hiring anyone from the community. Either they hire college students or someone from outside the community. You know?

This type of sentiment was most often expressed in Harlem, which has seen an influx of national chain stores that clearly are not indigenous to the community. Clinton Hill, in contrast, has not experienced such as influx, although nearby downtown Brooklyn has. This is a complaint hardly confined to gentrifying neighborhoods, as communities across the country have bemoaned the loss of the mom and pop stores while voting with their feet and patronizing the nearest Wal-Mart.

Despite these fears about the changing character of the neighborhood, my interviews clearly revealed a positive sentiment toward the gentrification taking place in their areas. Below are three examples from individuals that typify these positive feelings.

LANCE: Well, just to conclude how would you say the changes that are taking place are affecting your life there?

CAROL: The one thing that it has, it, the way I, you see, I've never really thought about, you know, like the idea of just paying rent. And having ownership or part whatever, you know, the co-op thing, 'cause that's another confusing thing for me, I'm but, part

PHOTO 9. Multifamily housing development in Clinton Hill that was converted to cooperatives in the 1980s.

shareholdership in something. And, that's a good thing, wanting to strive, it's making you want to strive to, to do those things. I'm feeling the changes and it's also made me appreciate my community a little more, and understand the strong history...within the community and the importance of maintaining that history and rebuilding. You understand?

MS. JONES: It makes me feel good. It makes me feel good. I feel, I feel safe, you know, I, you know, I kind of feel a little bit like back when we, when I first moved in now it's getting better.

MS. JOHNSON: But then you should, you can question yourself, you've been living someplace that nobody wanna live. So if other people wanna live there then there is something good about Harlem. And we have some nice places in Harlem

The narratives point to an appreciation for the improvement in the quality of life that was taking place. After years of seeing their community decline, improvements were welcome. Not surprisingly, this inspired pride in some. This, after all, is their home. Why shouldn't residents of gentrifying neighborhoods want their home to be viewed as desirable and a place that others want to live?

The discourse on gentrification, however, has tended to overlook the possibility that some of the neighborhood changes associated with gentrification might be appreciated by the prior residents. Even apologists or boosters for gentrification often ignored the potential for the process to benefit existing residents. Early proponents of gentrification focused on the need to bring the middle class back to the city, the improved appearance of rehabilitated neighborhoods, and the strengthening of the tax base associated with gentrification. Detractors focused on displacement almost to the exclusion of any other impact that gentrification might have. Clearly the narratives expressed here are inconsistent with this depiction of gentrification as villain and suggest benefits extend beyond improving the tax base and attracting the middle class back to the city.

The context of inner-city decline in the latter part of the twentieth century is instructive in making sense of positive sentiments toward gentrification. This is especially true in Harlem, but to some extent in Clinton Hill as well. Many inner-city neighborhoods truly reached their nadir in the last decades of the twentieth century. Poor neighborhoods are nothing new. Since the advent of industrialization, slums, ghettos, or whatever we choose to call them have always been with us. But the ghettos of the late twentieth century were truly unique in some ways. They were unique in the extent to which so many people, institutions, and capital totally abandoned these neighborhoods. The Lower East Side of the late nineteenth century and even Harlem of the early twentieth century were famous for their density. They were places that no matter how deplorable their physical condition, which was worse in absolute terms than anything in recent decades, were still places of opportunity to the thousands of migrants who continued to pour into them. Although conditions were bad and there was a criminal underworld that flourished, poor neighborhoods were historically viewed as stepping stones to a better life. Moreover, these teeming masses, no matter how poor, were able to support bustling commercial districts.

In contrast, the slums of the late twentieth century are notorious for their depopulation. In the decade of the 1970s alone, Harlem lost nearly a third of its population. Like other depressed communities, commercial enterprises followed this out migration. Wilson (1987) has characterized the outmigration of residents from neighborhoods like Harlem as one that depleted these neighborhoods of middle-class residents who would form a social buffer in the event of economic decline. Although there is some debate about the characteristics of this type of decline, it undoubtedly included some of the most able members of the community.

This further weakened an already vulnerable community. When the crack epidemic hit in the 1980s, communities like Harlem were ill-prepared to cope. Thus, Harlem was a neighborhood that had experienced the flight of many of its residents, disinvestment, and widespread abandonment. Against this backdrop, positive reactions toward the improvements associated with gentrification in Harlem are perhaps not so surprising.

Clinton Hill, although suffering from some of the same maladies affecting neighborhoods like Harlem, never declined to the extent that Harlem did. Nevertheless, its proximity to poorer neighborhoods like Bedford-Stuyvesant and Bushwick may have tainted expectations about the neighborhood's ultimate trajectory before gentrification began. As a result, Clinton Hill also experienced decline and disinvestment during the 1970s.

The positive reactions toward gentrification described here suggest a rethinking of the impacts of gentrification may be in order. Clearly there are benefits that may accrue to residents of gentrifying neighborhoods who themselves would not normally be classified as gentrifiers. The lack of even basic services in many inner-city neighborhoods means that many will welcome at least some aspects of gentrification. This does not mean, however, that gentrification did not have its downsides or detractors. As one respondent aptly stated: "What good is a nice neighborhood if you can't live there?"

## FEARS OF DISPLACEMENT

More than any other aspect displacement is pointed to when the villainous nature of gentrification is discussed. For example, in her summary of the literature on gentrification, Wittberg (1992) focuses on displacement when describing the potential negative impacts of the process. Moreover, some observers go so far as to define gentrification as the displacement of low-income households. A report by the Brookings Institution states that "gentrification requires the displacement of lower income residents from their neighborhoods" (Kennedy and Leonard 2001, p. 5). Defined as a household having to move for reasons beyond its control, displacement can indeed be traumatic. Moreover, in cities like New York where housing is scarce, displacement can threaten households with homelessness. Given the potential havoc that displacement can wreak and the emphasis placed on it in the popular and scholarly literature, one would expect fears of displacement to be paramount among residents' reactions.

Carol, like many other residents I spoke with, expressed such a sentiment:

LANCE: Well given your, uh, experience living in the community, maybe, could you tell me, um, what significant changes you've seen in the neighborhood?

CAROL: Well, first I'm gonna start with my building. Tenants in my building as, like myself and whatever, they're really trying to push him, the management and, um, they want certain people out.

JUAN: Well yeah, I do worry about the rent going up.

These narratives correspond to the well-known criticisms of gentrification as a force of displacement. The threat of increasing housing costs could lead to some having to move. The theme of fear of displacement, however, was not always personal. Much to my surprise, most respondents did not report personal experiences with a fear of displacement. Despite the lack of a personal fear, there was a general concern about displacement that permeated the air. This concern meant that people were worried about being "pushed out." The neighborhoods were indeed changing, and what the end result would be no one was sure, much like a thunderstorm that inspires fear of lightning. Someone may have never witnessed a lightning strike, and the odds of being struck personally might be low, yet a thunderstorm still has the power to inspire fear and concern.

This general concern about displacement, although not always personal, did manifest itself in the stories people told me about others in their community. Below are snippets of some of the stories that were related to me.

JUANITA: A lot of people feel like they, they're being pushed out. There's people that, you know, trying to carry more than one job and, and, and actually, you know, this, this whole thought of, or this feeling of, really, because there's a lot of single-parent households, right? But this, this real feeling of the need for more than one person to make, to make it, you know?

JAMES: Well, if you go to personal comfort, probably for me doesn't make a difference. Uh, my experience has been that gentrification has, because of the increased prices, forced some people to have to move African Americans for the most part. Many residents that have been in Clinton Hill for a long time if they happen to not have the benefit of rent-stabilized apartment having rents almost double in the space of four years has caused some residents to have to move out. That's very unfortunate.
LANCE: How widespread do you think that is, where or—
JAMES: Uh, in terms of those long-term residents that did not have the benefit of rent stabilization, I think it's been pretty widespread.

Anthony is in his early thirties and has been residing in Clinton Hill for four years. Although he is African American, his college degree and suburban Maryland upbringing might classify him as a gentrifier. Moreover, as someone who recently purchased a co-op in Clinton recently he might be viewed part of the reason housing prices were rising. He was nevertheless attuned to the fears of long-time residents, as he states here.

> People think there is a shift, especially to kick people out, you know. But I mean, people have serious concerns, and these are people, these are people who usually have been in the neighborhood a long time. It was not a nice neighborhood. I heard of a lot of people wouldn't walk on Myrtle Avenue. I think it was nicknamed "Murder Avenue" [laughter]. And there is DeKalb Avenue, which they now call "Restaurant Row" which up to about eight years, it was kinda scary as well. So now it's finally good and they are afraid they are losing their neighborhood. It's, I finally get something And and, now the rent is so high that they have to leave. Like "they are taking over, we are getting pushed out," I think that's their only fear. A lot of people I talked to have rent control, it's a weird for them, because they have rent-controlled, excuse me, rent-stabilized apartments, so they rent, I mean, they get the best in the world, by all the new services coming in, the neighborhood looks nice, the crime goes down, the rent only goes up 2 percent.... So, I don't really think they have a legitimate beef. But I think, think that maybe it's maybe a historical thing, or like, you know, for something their parents thought taught them, or something from back, who are really angry about just seeing....

These examples show that concern about displacement permeated conversations about gentrification. Some people spoke of people who they knew who were displaced. Mason, a late thirties native of Harlem who is living in the same public project he grew up in, related to me an example of someone he knew that had been displaced:

> What I'm hearing is that people who have been living in a building for years are being given thirty days notice to leave. I don't begrudge a developer for making money, but thirty days notice, that's not right. I know this ninety-two-year-old guy been living on 123rd and for years. They were renovated and he had to move. Now he has to scramble around and figure out what resources are out there. At ninety-two he's paid his dues. That's not right.

More common was the refrain that people felt they were being "pushed out." The struggles that residents of the community were undertaking, such as working two jobs, to avoid being pushed out also feature in these narratives of displacement. Anthony, however, proves to be an armchair sociologist with an especially insightful view of the displacement narrative that permeated discussions about gentrification. He alludes to the fact that many of those expressing fears of displacement indeed had rent-regulated apartments and so in his mind did not have "a legitimate beef." But history or something lends credence to fearing the displacement powers of gentrification. This comment hints at the way people interpret gentrification, and this is elaborated on in depth in the next chapter. For now it suffices to say that this is further evidence of the extent to which fear of displacement was part of the perception of gentrification.

Given the widespread concern about displacement expressed by respondents and in literature on gentrification, it is somewhat surprising that more experiences with displacement were not more personal. This appears to be due mostly to the housing situation of the persons I spoke with and just plain luck. A few individuals were lucky to have landlords who did not charge as much as they could for a unit. Despite the depiction of landlords as greedy or rational profit maximizers, there a few instances in which landlords defied both these stereotypes. Jake, who grew up in the nearby Fort Greene housing projects, went to the Pratt Institute and now resides in Clinton Hill, related this dynamic to me in the following conversation:

LANCE: Do you know many people who have had to move because of rising prices?

JAKE: I really don't have the pulse on that. But not really. Because you have these pockets of affordability.

LANCE: How are they able to maintain affordability?

JAKE: Some landlords aren't greedy. They may have bought their property way back when before prices went sky high. So they can afford to charge a reasonable rate. Others that just bought have to pay their mortgage. So they charge what the market will bear.

Sometimes the landlords' own self-interest might make them hesitant to raise rents drastically, particularly if they are small owners of a few units. For small landlords, the transaction costs of finding new tenants who pay the rent on time, don't abuse the property, or make a lot of noise might make some hesitant to raise rents to a degree that would force one of their good and reliable tenants to leave. Alicia, a college student with limited means, lives in Clinton Hill and thought that her being a reliable tenant discouraged her landlord from raising her rent excessively: "This year he hasn't, he didn't increase the rent. I figured because he may have overheard a conversation that I was having with Susan downstairs. I was like he better not like raise our rent, because doesn't he realize that we're good tenants. So, it's like, okay."

Aside from the few who were lucky enough to have landlords who did not simply charge what the market would bear, other types of housing situations served to protect people from displacement due to gentrification and thus also limited any personal experience with the threat of displacement. As was pointed out earlier, some were homeowners in the form of shareholders in cooperatives. Others were fortunate to live in a rent-regulated apartment or a government subsidized unit. As table 1.1 indicated, a substantial portion of the sample were either homeowners or residing in rent-regulated or subsidized units. Homeowners face little threat of displacement because the bulk of their housing costs are tied to maintenance and servicing the debt used to purchase their home, neither of which will be affected by gentrification. Property taxes for home-owners, however, may increase as the assessed value of their home in-creases. But in New York City, where property taxes are skewed to favor homeowners against commercial and large multifamily unit owners, this is unlikely. Not surprisingly, none of the homeowners I spoke with ex-pressed a fear of being displaced due to rising property taxes. Those in subsidized units are for the most part not at risk of displacement due to gentrification. Likewise, those fortunate enough to have secured rent-regulated apartments also had a modicum of protection from rapid in-creases in their housing costs.

What rent regulation also did, however, was provide an incentive to landlords to encourage current tenants to move. Under New York City's rent regulations, when a tenant moves the unit is deregulated and the landlord can charge the market rent. Given the wide disparity between the market rent and regulated rent in many instances, it is not surprising that landlords might actively seek to empty their occupied rent-regulated units. Sometimes landlords offered cash as incentive for the tenant to leave. Other times, they resorted to more nefarious methods to encourage occupants of these apartments to leave. Tales of landlords withholding services, harassing tenants, and hiring detectives to make sure tenants adhered to rent regulation guidelines (i.e., their regulated unit is their primary residence) abound. These stories are perhaps more common in changing neighborhoods because gentrification increases market rents and therefore widens the gap between regulated rents and market rents.

In response to this landlord harassment, a number of tenants' rights organizations have sprung up to protect tenants from landlord harass-ment. Harlem Operation Take Back and the West Harlem Tenants Or-ganization are examples of such groups. These groups apprise tenants of their rights, provide free legal clinics, and generally serve as advocates for the interests of tenants and low-income households.

Viewed from the lens of these organizations or those making use of their services, gentrification poses a threat in two ways. One, by in-creasing market rents it gives a landlord more of an incentive to en-courage them to leave as the following narrative by Juan suggests:

JUAN: They are always trying find ways to get people out.
LANCE: How, like what is some of the types of things they do trying to get people out?

JUAN: Well they'll contest the lease. I had to fight for my lease. I was
living a few years with great-grandmother, so I had succession
rights or whatever you wanna call it. And so with some other people
they've done that also. For whatever the reason is, whether it's,
it's a son that was there for a few years or whatever. And they thought
they had a legal angle in not giving that apartment. They, they
would do it. Um, someone went on a vacation and I think this is a, a
certain guideline on when how long you can be away from your
apartment. And because she made a mistake on something they were
able to bring that in. She lost her apartment. Although she fought it
for a long time. And, um, they'll, they'll play dumb on something and
make, uh, you prove that you're right about whatever the issue or
point might be in, in terms to uh, uh, um, lawfully um, being the
tenant. And they'll take you to court. Because a, how many people
can afford to miss, uh, work? How many people can afford the lawyer
sometimes? Sometimes it's not a person who's uh, uh, articulate in
English or whatever. Sometimes it's elderly so there's the intimidation
factor. So you know, whenever they can. Um, hey, but in our building
it's been a handful of little tricks that they try and they haven't suc-
ceeded. Except for that one person that was evicted and, uh, you
know it's a shame because, uh, she, she didn't protect herself better.

Under New York rent regulations, there are various guidelines governing not only how much the landlord can raise the rent but whether the
unit can be deregulated when the original tenant moves out. If a family
member remains living in the unit, the unit maintains its regulatory status
even after the original tenant moves or dies. These are known as succession rights. The rent regulations also stipulate that a regulated unit
must be the tenant's primary residence. Consequently, landlords will
challenge tenants on the grounds that the unit is not the tenant's primary
address or that they are not related to the original tenant in a way to have
succession rights.

During one legal clinic that I attended, a tenant described his predicament. He had shared an apartment with the mother of his child. The
apartment was in her name, and she paid all the bills out of her account,
although he gave her money. She eventually moved to Georgia, leaving
him with the apartment. The landlord had apparently hired a detective
who uncovered the fact that the original tenant was now in Georgia.
Because they were not married and did not have joint accounts, he had no
legal claim to succession, at least in the opinion of the legal clinic attorney. The landlord's efforts to evict him were thus likely to succeed.

These narratives are perhaps as suggestive of the way that rent regulation can distort landlord–tenant relations as they are in speaking to the

way gentrification is viewed by residents. Moreover, it is not clear that harassment of this type was increasing concomitantly with gentrification in Clinton Hill and Harlem as the following dialogue with Juan suggests:

LANCE: Is the harassment something that you notice that's happening more frequently now? Or is that something that's always been going on?
JUAN: You know it's always being going on. That's when one of the reasons why the tenant's association for our area came up, because they were trying to get people out.

One might expect, however, that increasing prices associated with gentrification would give landlords an incentive to harass occupants of regulated units and through their actions contribute to a fear of displacement permeating the air.

A second way gentrification contributed to the aura of concern about displacement was that by increasing housing prices in the neighborhood the option of staying in the neighborhood was all but eliminated for those who did want to move. Tammi is in her mid-twenties and native to Harlem. For college she left New York and went away to school. Despite the upward mobility that is associated with obtaining a college degree, rising housing prices prevented her from moving out of her mother's apartment and setting up her own household:

> I went away to school, for five years, with the intention of not coming back home and getting my own place and you know, establishing my independence and coming back home. During that five-year period, the rents have increased, the neighborhoods have changed drastically and that's like kind of disheartening that, you know, I come back and want to return back home to stay in my community and I, I really can't.

Thus, the fear or concern of displacement or being pushed out was a common refrain during my conversations with residents of Clinton Hill and Harlem. As already noted, this concern was not always personal. Rather, people pointed to displacement they had witnessed or fears that others had expressed. The narrative of displacement has become part of the community lore regarding gentrification—a point I will return to in the next chapter. The housing status of many individuals, in the form of regulated or subsidized units, undoubtedly contributed to some not having personal experiences with displacement. That many residents have some form of rental protection—be it in the form of a subsidy or regulated unit— is not surprising in New York. Data from the 2002 New York City and Housing Vacancy Survey show that citywide, 68 percent of all rental units have some form of subsidy or regulation; in Clinton Hill the figure is 62 percent and Harlem this figure reaches 89 percent (author's calculations)! With relatively few units unregulated or not subsidized, widespread displacement is perhaps unlikely. It may also be that those most vulnerable to displacement have already been displaced and hence unlikely to be reached through my sampling methods. Nevertheless, as the narratives make clear, concern about displacement continues to be a common theme.

It should also be kept in mind that due to speculation, housing inflation in gentrifying neighborhoods is likely to be worse in the ownership sector than in the rental sector. Whereas rising prices are often an inducement for owners to purchase in anticipation of the capital gains they will realize, rising rents seldom encourage people to rent. Consider figure 3.1, which illustrates trends in housing prices and fair market rents (Fair Market rents are set at the 45th percentile of all rents), in the New York metropolitan area. The trends show a much steeper appreciation in the ownership sector than in the rental sector. Although rents have been steadily increasing, the increase in the past few years has been nowhere as sharp as in the ownership sector. Were rents increasing as rapidly as prices, displacement pressures would be more severe.

The feelings toward gentrification discussed so far have focused on the process or end results of the process, better services, increasing housing prices, displacement, and so on. But gentrification also implies a gentry and a change in the type of people residing in these neighborhoods. In the next sections I explore the reactions to the coming of the gentry.

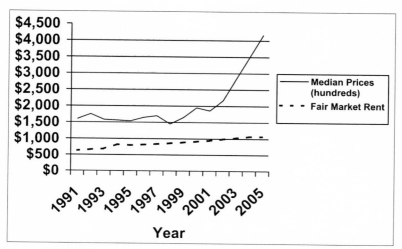

FIGURE 3.1. NYC Metro Area Housing Prices and Fair Market Rents
*Source:* National Association of Home Builders and U.S. Department of Housing and Urban Development

## DIVERSITY IN THE 'HOOD

The gentrification of both Clinton Hill and Harlem, predominantly black neighborhoods, had significant racial overtones. Here I will touch briefly on some of residents' reaction to the influx of nonblacks into these neighborhoods. It is important to remember the context of the study neighborhoods when interpreting these responses. Harlem and to a lesser extent Clinton Hill are overwhelmingly black neighborhoods, despite noticeable gentrification in recent years. As noted in the preceding chapter, a stroll through either of these areas will be reveal more brown faces than not. Thus, both neighborhoods still have a black character, complete with services such as barbershops, churches, hair salons, and so on that target a black clientele.

In both neighborhoods an increasingly visible presence of whites was perhaps the most noticeable change associated with gentrification. To some, the increased presence of whites was the very definition of gentrification. Nate expresses this sentiment: "Once you see white people hanging out in a neighborhood where they generally wouldn't come through, it's gentrification."

When asked about the neighborhood changing, many residents pointed to the time when they first noticed whites walking around as evidence that gentrification was occurring. When whites came that meant the neighborhood would improve and that significant changes were under way. Moreover, whites were assumed to be gentrifiers—either artists, students, or some other demographic—that fit neatly into preconceived notions of who gentrifiers are.

Although social scientists have shone a spotlight on the process of white-to-black succession, the integration of whites into black neighborhoods is relatively unexamined. This may be because until recently the change from predominantly black to white has been a relatively rare occurrence (Lee 1985). This rarity is reflected in the shock that many residents expressed at seeing whites moving into these predominantly black neighborhoods. Black neighborhoods perhaps differ from other types of minority areas in that not only do they have a black majority but they have historically been relatively homogenous with few whites. Although ethnic enclaves of various nationalities are a common occurrence, they are seldom dominated by one group to the extent that some neighborhoods have been dominated by blacks (Massey and Denton 1993).

Consequently, in the racialized landscape of urban America, black neighborhoods not only have black identities but have been devoid of a white presence as well. Thus, a black identity for a neighborhood came to mean not only a substantial black presence but an absence of whites as well. This identity means the neighborhood "belongs" to blacks. Those not of this background are viewed as outsiders and perhaps interlopers. Outsiders, whites in this case, are not expected to be seen walking down the streets of these neighborhoods. If they are passing through, they are not expected to linger. Consider the following reactions of Kenneth and Takeesha, both of whom are in their late twenties and moved into Harlem after attending predominantly white colleges. Although they spent considerable time in the white world, Harlem was seen as a black world, a place where whites did not venture. Thus they were still taken aback at the presence of whites in Harlem:

LANCE: When did you notice significant changes taking place in your neighborhood?

KENNETH: And then I would walk along 125th Street and notice [white] people just strolling, and there used to be a time where it was a threat! You would be scared to be in Harlem and be white it was like known! But now I see them strolling like at midnight you know passing me by.

LANCE: Since you moved into the neighborhood [Harlem], have you, um, noticed any changes?

TAKEESHA: Well, obviously, um, in addition to, I guess the, um, rehabilitation to a lot of the buildings I've noticed that, uh, different types of people moving in, um, obviously a lot of white people,... so you, and I've seen the, the thing that, that, uh, I guess shocked me the most was the day that I, um, got up, I was out about six o'clock in the morning, this was during the wintertime when it was cold, and I saw a young white girl jogging down the street, which to me was shocking.

LANCE: Why did that, why did that shock you?

TAKEESHA: Because, I mean, first of all a lot of people think of Harlem as being very dangerous, um, and I wouldn't, although I don't feel threatened, I wouldn't be jogging like at that time of day, you know, um—

LANCE: It was still dark or—

TAKEESHA: Yeah, it was just, the sun was just coming up and, you know, so to see, you know, a young white girl jogging through Harlem is just to me just crazy, you know.

Surprise at the visibility of whites was even evident in Clinton Hill even though the white population has always been at least 20 percent. Nevertheless, in the past whites ceded certain spaces in the neighborhood to blacks, particularly at night. This is no longer the case. James, a resident of Clinton Hill for over fifteen, years described the increasing visibility of whites in Clinton Hill this way:

I moved here in '88. I can tell you that I would not have been comfortable walking around the neighborhood at night. Today it's a very different story. The streets are vibrant. You see people at all hours of the day. And oddly enough when you walk Myrtle Avenue at night, which still has a reputation although not to the extent it did years ago, now I see many Caucasians and Asians walking around Myrtle Avenue at, to the extent that, almost to the exclusion of African Americans.

According to this view, whites are expected to fear and avoid black spaces. The black neighborhood as a place of crime, danger, and unpredictability has been etched into the national psyche. Writers have described them as "deadly neighborhoods" (Jencks 1988), and activists as "third world countries" (Chinelyu 1999). Social scientists have posited that the equating of black neighborhoods with crime, poverty and general undesirability is the reason whites are reluctant to share residential space with blacks (Gould Ellen 2000; Harris 2001). Whites with the privilege and wherewithal to do so are expected to avoid black neighborhoods. When whites move into predominantly black neighborhoods, they upset the prevailing notions of who belongs in particular areas. This surprise at seeing white people was certainly more apparent in Harlem than in Clinton Hill. Although Clinton Hill is also predominantly black, it has a shorter history as a black neighborhood, dating back to the late 1960s and 1970s, and has always had a substantial white population due to the presence of Pratt Institute.

A visitor from overseas who walked down a major thoroughfare in Harlem or Clinton Hill for that matter might wonder what all the fuss and concern about whites in the neighborhood is about. The faces are still overwhelmingly black and brown. Moreover, as illustrated in the previous chapter, in absolute numbers the increase in the white population has not been that dramatic. Indeed, in Harlem the biggest change in terms of racial/ethnic groups has been the increase in the Hispanic population. But the long history of blacks sharing residential space and socioeconomic status with Hispanics in New York renders the Hispanic influx a nonevent (Massey and Bitterman 1985)—at least thus far. In contrast, the modest increase of whites signifies a sharp break from past patterns and hence engenders much surprise. What this surprise signifies is just how racially isolated many of America's inner-city communities had become. A white face was truly a rare occurrence.

What the surprise may also indicate are changes in whites' use of public space in these two predominantly black neighborhoods. As one respondent astutely noted, whites appeared to be more comfortable using public spaces in these neighborhoods. Given the dramatic and well-publicized drop in crime in New York City, a plausible speculation might be that despite all the negative stereotypes still associated with black neighborhoods, whites feel safer in these areas now (Beveridge 2004). Harlem in particular has received much publicity about the second renaissance, with magazine articles and TV shows highlighting the attractions of the neighborhood. This publicity, combined with the drop in crime may have made whites more willing to invade black space, even at times when it would have previously been unthinkable—like six in the morning.

Much of the literature on gentrification points to the influx of whites as something loathed by long-term residents. Powell and Spencer (2003, p. 437) write: "Then at some point in the future, and in part because the neighborhood values are depressed, whites move back in and force residents to leave, often to strange neighborhoods that are in distress. Even if minority residents remain, they fear their way of life will not be the same." Figure 3.2 is also illustrative of the hostility directed at the influx of whites. The flyer depicts gentrification, in part, as whites taking over black neighborhoods. More revealingly, the flyer issues a call to stop the takeover. Whites moving into the neighborhood is not viewed here as an innocuous trend toward more integration. Likewise, the black popular media has also reflected the anxiety surrounding white movement into black neighborhoods as the following headlines attest: "Invasion of the Hood Snatchers: How Black Neighborhoods are Being Gentrified" (Montgomery 2002) and "The Whitening of Black Neighborhoods" (Watson 2003). Thus, the scholarly literature, popular media, and the actions of community activists paint a picture of black resistance to white infiltration.

My conversations with residents of Clinton Hill and Harlem did reveal an undercurrent of hostility toward whites moving into these neighborhoods among at least some of the interviewees. The hostility was seldom directed to whites per se, or even what the coming of whites foretold for the future of the neighborhood. Rather, the hostility emanated from how people made sense of the causes of gentrification, or more specifically the neighborhood improvements associated with gentrification. This is a point I discuss in considerable detail in the next chapter.

To be sure, there were some who expressed antagonistic feelings toward whites moving into these neighborhoods just on general principle. Henry is a mid-sixties native of North Carolina who moved to New York as a teenager. He has spent almost all of his life living in the black ghettos of New York—Bedford-Stuyvesant, Brownsville—and has been living in Harlem for the past twenty years or so. As such he is not used to living around whites: "Well it make me feel less comfortable. Because for one I'm not used to being next to whites, and I prefer not to. Prefer to stick with my own." Takeesha also expressed a degree of antipathy toward whites moving into Harlem, despite interacting with them on a regular basis:

# Saturday February 28th 2004

## THE STATE OF BLACK NEW YORK

# CITY WIDE CONFERENCE ON GENTRIFICATION

### 2nd Gentrification Summit

# Major Community Town Hall Meeting 3:00pm

**Subject: What Is Gentrification? : How And Why Whites Are Taking Over The Black Community and What We Can We Do To Stop It"**
Conference Begins At 10:00 AM

Workshop #1 **Tenants Rights-** *"How To Avoid Being Victimized By Your Landlord"*
-11:00 am
Workshop #2 **Buy Black!** *"How To Keep Black Businesses Alive In New York"*
-11:00 am
Workshop #3 **Money, Land And Property** *"How To Move From Renter To Owner and Independence"* (Credit issues, Finance, Programs That Can Help)

-1:00 pm
Workshop#4 **The Politics Of Gentrification:** *"From City Hall To The Streets. How To Hold Politicians Accountable"*

-1:00 pm
Workshop #5 **Commercial Real Estate** *"Buying Apartments, Landlord, Renovations "*-6:00 pm
Workshop #6 **Self Improvement**: *"How We Stop Deterioration In Our Neighborhoods"*
- 6:00 pm

Featuring: Harlem Fight Back...Nellie Bailey...Harlem Tenants Council.... Real Estate Agents & Brokers...Mayoral Candidate/ Councilman Charles Barron...Other Elected Officials...Dr James McIntosh (CEMOTAP).... Morris Powell (Harlem Activist)...Nation Of Islam...Lawyers...Committee To Honor Black Heroes and Others...Kevin Williams from Kev's Copy Center....Delois Blakely (Mayor Of Harlem)...National Action Network.... Other Activists and Leaders.... Business persons, Pastor Dennis Dillon...Written Information on Laws, Rights, Research and Programs and Money that Can Aid You
Consistent Questions And Answers........... Participation From The People
The Forming Of The Anti Gentrification Movement ....... The 1st Conference Was Great!

**Sponsored By: The Black Power Movement; New Black Panther Party;**
**Black Lawyers For Justice; African Nationalist Pioneer Movement**
**Hosted By: Attorney Malik Z. Shabazz (NBPP Chairman/ Black Lawyers For Justice)**

FIGURE 3.2. Flyer Announcing Anti-Gentrification Meeting

Yeah, you want better services, you want a safe neighborhood, you want a clean neighborhood, but, at the expense of, you know, of whom, uh, and so, and that, that's why I feel conflicted because, you know, you want the neighborhood to, to improve but not in terms of, its resources, not in terms of, improve doesn't always mean, you know, white people ... in general I just felt like it seems like whenever, you know, black people have something, it's really hard for them to, to retain it, white people have always operated, as, you know, sort of, you know, conquistadors, just, you know, basically taking over ... and it affects me because I've never known such hatred inside of me until this started happening, and I can't explain it, because it's not that I haven't worked with white people, I haven't been around white people, but for some reason this just, it just means something more to me and so when I see them in the stores and, you know, I just, I'm just filled with such anger I got on even, uh, I mean I've been dealing with it, I'm like, okay, to me obviously there's really nothing I can do.

Such antiwhite sentiments, however, were relatively rare during my conversations with residents. Most residents did not express negative reactions toward whites or other groups typically not found in black neighborhoods moving into Clinton Hill or Harlem. Sandy, a native of Harlem in her mid-thirties, remembers when nonblack faces in Harlem were relatively rare. He nevertheless appears to be somewhat open to the notion of others moving into Harlem. "You see not only whites, you see all nationalities such as Asians, up in Harlem now. Which I don't think is a bad thing." Nate, the civil service worker, was also amenable toward whites moving into the predominantly black Clinton Hill:

Well I'm a realist. I think gentrification is good in certain respects in that it brings things to a neighborhood what it really never had. Like an all black neighborhood never had as much police protection as their white counterpart. So it brings that. Plus it brings investment. Plus I have no problem being in a neighborhood that's um, you know, mixed.

Ms. Johnson was reflective about the importance of integration and questioned why Harlem should be all black:

I think it is good. And why should we want a neighborhood that nobody lives but African American. Just like some neighborhood are only Asian, Jewish and you think people it shouldn't be that way. How can we learn each other if we gonna to be living separate. So—I think, in every neighborhood it should be you know different people. I don't think it should just be one nationality living there. I don't think so. So then the improvement I would welcome it. Because I don't want to say well, okay I live in Harlem but nobody live here but African American. So what's wrong with Harlem so that nobody else wanna live there in Harlem? But then you should, you can question yourself, you've been living someplace that nobody wanna live. So if other people wanna live there then there is something good about Harlem.

Gary was twenty-nine at the time of our discussion, grew up in East Orange, New Jersey, and moved to Clinton Hill six years before. He values the juxtaposition of the 'hood with gentrification, which creates a neighborhood dynamic found in few neighborhoods.

GARY: I like the variety we have in the neighborhood. I like the French restaurants. I like Modeba which is South African. I like that we have Sol, a little spot owned by an African American doing his own thing. I like that it's accepting to gays and lesbians. I like the fact that you have the old black grandmas who go to church every Sunday and will give you a lecture on what's good and what's bad you know. I like that it's a cross between, what my girlfriend calls, what does she call it, the 'etto. Because it's on the verge of being ghetto on Myrtle.

LANCE: What does she call it?

GARY: The 'etto without the *gh*. Cuz it's not exactly ghetto cuz you have this nice side going this way from Myrtle Avenue and then on Myrtle Ave you have sort of ghettoish things. You have people selling drugs and that sort of thing. And its that mix. That's what I like about it.

The implications of the unique mix created by gentrification and the 'hood, or the 'etto as Gary and his girlfriend call it, is a dynamic I alluded to in chapter 2 and will discuss in more detail in the concluding chapter. Here, it serves to support the notion that there was a general acceptance to a more integrated neighborhood. Residents certainly noticed the increase in diversity. But few spoke in overall negative or positive tones.

This pattern of responses is consistent with the notion that blacks are amenable to residential integration as some writers have posited (Massey and Denton 1993). But remembering the context is again important. Both Clinton Hill and Harlem remain predominantly black communities. Residents may not be adverse toward some diversity in the form of a few whites moving into their neighborhood. Were these neighborhoods to become predominantly white, overall reactions might be more be negative. Indeed, several respondents indicated that although they did not have a problem with whites moving into the neighborhood, they would be disappointed if the neighborhood became predominantly white. This is also consistent with what has been written about blacks' preferences for residential integration. Although blacks have been found to be amenable to and actually prefer integrated neighborhoods, integration does not mean an overwhelmingly white neighborhood (Farley et al. 1994). Tina expresses this sentiment. Although she claims to be comfortable with integration, her view of the area is still a predominantly black neighborhood:

LANCE: Well, does the fact that the neighborhood was, uh, predomi-
nately black and is becoming more white over time, do you, do you
have any feelings about that one way or the other?

TINA: No.

LANCE: No?

TINA: It's all right for me.

LANCE: So if the neighborhood became, say 90 percent white, that
wouldn't bother you or it would?

TINA: Maybe not 90 percent. [laughs.] Maybe 30, you know, I wouldn't
be bothered, but 90, come on. Where they coming from?

In sum, the increase of whites in Clinton Hill and Harlem was probably
the most notable aspect of gentrification. Although this proved troubling
to a few, the themes that more commonly emerged from my conversations
were a guarded indifference and to a lesser extent, appreciation. Outright
hostility was relatively rare. In this way, interviewees' reactions to residential integration with whites appear to mirror those found by other
social scientists who generally find blacks to be amenable to residential
integration with whites. Though my conversations with residents of
Clinton Hill and Harlem revealed a somewhat blasé attitude toward the
notion of sharing residential space with whites, these same conversations
indicated that a great deal of significance was attached to the coming of
whites. This is a point I discuss in detail in the following chapter.

## WHAT OF THE BLACK GENTRY?

Although the residents I spoke with most quickly associated gentrification
with racial change, the scholarly literature elevates class over race as the
defining feature of gentrification. Although definitions of gentrification
explicitly mention class, race is often ignored. With the correlations between class and race being what they are in urban America, however, it is
difficult to discuss class without alluding to race. In this case, the reactions described suggest a notable awareness to what is a modest increase
in the white population. Nevertheless, to the extent gentrification is occurring, it also suggests there is a class change as well. Moreover, if one
subscribes to the scholarly definitions of gentrification it becomes clear
that a substantial component of the gentry are black. Figure 2.13 suggests
that in both Clinton Hill and Harlem, the "black gentry" or college-
educated blacks have been increasingly represented.

In contrast to the agitation that surrounded the arrival of whites, reactions toward the black gentry were much more muted. When asked
how they perceived their neighborhood to be changing, an increase in
the black gentry or middle class was seldom volunteered by any of the

interviewees I spoke with. Barbara is a black graduate student who attended an Ivy League university, pledged an elite black sorority, grew up in a New York City suburb, and moved to Harlem within the past five years. She perhaps fits the profile of a black gentrifier. Maybe because of her own class background, she was also cognizant of class differences among black Harlemites:

LANCE: Maybe you could tell me how you think the neighborhood has changed, or if maybe it hasn't changed since you've been there.

BARBARA: I see more businesses developing. I see St. Nicholas Avenue has gotten just cleaner, renovated brownstones. Of course, I see the construction coops, condos going up every other week. I also think it's become diverse, Now I see a little of everything. I see Asian, I see white and different blacks too.

LANCE: What do you mean by that?

BARBARA: You see people coming off the train dressed in work attire, so you assume that they're professionals.

But this was an atypical response. More typically interviewees volunteered noticing new stores opening, buildings being renovated, and as noted an increased presence of whites. An increased presence of blacks of higher socioeconomic status was rarely volunteered. This is not to say that interviewees never noticed the changing class composition in their neighborhoods. As will be discussed, this was also an important theme. But it was one that typically had to be drawn out of respondents through direct questioning or additional prompting. This is instructive. It speaks volumes about the extent to which race can trump class as a marker of social status in America.

In the context of gentrification in these predominantly black neighborhoods the relatively muted reaction toward the influx of the black gentry is due to the lack of obvious class distinctions among blacks in these communities and the long-term presence of the black middle class in these same communities.

Unlike white skin, which automatically signifies membership in the gentry class in the context of a predominantly black gentrifying neighborhood, there is no such obvious mark of the black gentry or middle class. Income is a criterion one might use to identify the black gentry, but one's income is not always obvious from outward appearances. To be sure, there are outward trappings of class in urban America—one's address, one's clothes, the car one drives, one's diction, and occupation, to name a few. But for a number of reasons none of these make the same type of mental imprint as a white face in a predominantly black community.

Address is no clear marker of class in gentrifying neighborhoods, because by definition gentrification takes place in formerly less than prestigious neighborhoods. In addition, various housing subsidy programs, such as public housing, rent regulation, Mitchell-Lama, and particularly in Harlem various housing developments sponsored by HPD, allow those with limited means to reside and continue moving into these neighborhoods. Thus, although Clinton Hill and Harlem are gentrifying, one cannot easily assume that someone living or recently relocating to these neighborhoods must be of a particular class.

One might assume that the black gentry would stand out based on their style of dress or comportment. The American ethos, however, is to downplay class distinctions. Class is undoubtedly an important determinant of life outcomes in the United States. But this does not necessarily translate into the advertisement of one's class in all situations. In everyday anonymous interactions, it is often difficult to determine one's class unless he or she is at one of the extremes of the socioeconomic spectrum. This is reflective of the overwhelming ethos that posits ordinary middle-class status as normative. Thus, many of the elite, like the son of a blue-blood family who is now president, claims to be "just folks," while the poor strive to be accepted into the middle class. Putting on airs is frowned on in America. Likewise in the black community, "keeping it real" is a popular phrase meant to convey one's desire to relate in an everyday manner with the common folk. Characteristic of this everyday, plain folks ethos is the ubiquity of casual dress as well as casual language.

Another important factor contributing to the relative inconspicuousness of the black gentry is the fact that income differences between the black gentry (and the white gentry for that matter) and other residents of Clinton Hill and Harlem are not always that great. Indeed, during the early stages of gentrification, many of the gentry seek out these neighborhoods because it is some place they can afford. Many of those that might be classified as the gentry may be starting their careers or be in relatively low-paying occupations, like the arts. Therefore, not only are differences in income likely to be inconspicuous, but the differences may be small or nonexistent to begin with.

The inconspicuousness of class contributed to the muted reaction toward the arrival of the black middle class that was associated with gentrification. A further contribution, however, is that both Clinton Hill and Harlem have always had some socioeconomic diversity, and hence an increase in the black middle class is not perceived the same way as if theirs were a sudden appearance. To some extent they have always been there. Wilson (1987) talks about the flight of the black middle class from black neighborhoods like Harlem in the wake of the civil rights legislation that outlawed discrimination and putatively opened up previously all white neighborhoods to the black middle class. Though the veracity of Wilson's thesis has been debated extensively, it is clear that even if true, it does not mean that all of the black middle class has left these neighborhoods.

Clinton Hill, for example, even when it was experiencing white flight and the major thoroughfare was known as Murder Avenue, seems to have had a stable middle-class presence. Indeed, many of my respondents had solid middle-class credentials. Consider the following examples. Yolanda is a black resident of Clinton Hill in her mid-fifties who grew up in a public housing project in Fort Greene. She now has a master's degree and has been a resident of Clinton Hill for seventeen years, before the gentrification. Louis is a black resident of Clinton Hill in his late sixties who went to college after being in the military and has been residing in Clinton Hill for thirty-five years. Jake is an African American resident of Clinton Hill in his early forties who grew up in public housing just blocks away from where he now lives (and has always lived). Jake attended Pratt Institute and now works as a teacher. None of these individuals have backgrounds that one would normally associate with the gentry, and they were living in Clinton Hill long before it began to gentrify. Yet all have college degrees and have worked in white-collar or professional occupations. Given the long-term presence of individuals like these, it is not surprising that blacks who might fit the profile of gentry might not attract much notice.

Likewise Harlem has always had a black middle-class presence. Harlem's heyday as a mecca for the black elite is well known and touched on in chapter 2 of this book. Sections of Harlem like Strivers' Row and Hamilton Terrace have long been and continue to be enclaves of the middle and upper middle class in Harlem. In addition, Harlem is home to several middle-income housing developments like the Lenox Terrace Mitchell-Lama development that houses middle-class households. Thus, even when Harlem reached its nadir in the 1970s and 1980s, there was still a significant middle-class presence. Carol is a black woman in her mid-thirties who has spent her entire life in Harlem. She now has a master's degree. Tammy is a black woman in her mid-twenties who also has spent her entire life in Harlem. She went away to a state college in upstate New York and returned to Harlem after graduation. Both Carol and Tammy are examples of long-term Harlem residents who because of their educational backgrounds might be classified as part of the gentry. But they have been there all their lives and would hardly be seen as gentrifiers.

Barbara reinforces two of the points I have been making about the inconspicuousness of the black gentry in the narrative below:

LANCE: Well, maybe you could tell me a little bit about why you chose to move into Harlem.

BARBARA: I was attending grad school, and the commute was too difficult, so I was looking for a place in New York City. Plus my family was moving, their house was being sold, so I had to become a little more independent. And a soror of mine from college said she had lots of room. Her mother moved out of state, and she was the only one living in this brownstone on 148th. So she rented a floor out to me. And it was very affordable. And I thought, great, I'll stay there. [laughs]

LANCE: So you chose it primarily because you knew someone that was there, and the affordability.

BARBARA: Right. And my friend, soror, Tonya, she grew up in the area, since her mother was always there, she knew a lot of the history. And she reassured me that there were decent people living in the neighborhood despite the reputation that Harlem had.

LANCE: In your mind what kind of reputation did Harlem have?

BARBARA: You know, a has-been reputation. It's almost like the negative is always highlighted. Actually, while I was living up in Westchester, we would drive through Harlem, and people would say—comments like, "This was once a beautiful place to live. What has happened?" So just a situation that has gone progressively worse, it has gotten worse. That was pretty much what people would say, almost like it's a shame, almost that feeling some sort of regret when they speak of Harlem, what has happened to Harlem. So that's the only reputation that I knew of.

LANCE: So then you had these perceptions of what the neighborhood was like. And then you moved in. Your friend reassured you that, as you said, there were some good people in your neighborhood. Is that—that was—what do you mean when you say that?

BARBARA: Well, "good," meaning upwardly mobile folks, and "good" meaning educated people. It's sad that—I shouldn't even use the label "good," but what she meant was that growing up on the block she knew that there were people who had similar values as her family. They believed in just, you know, family and education and similar type things. And since her mother was of that background, I guess that was her way of reassuring me that you're not going to be surrounded by people who don't care about the area, or who just don't care about life, you know. I know that Tanya's mother would come back and forth from Florida, and she would say things like, "I wish Tonya wouldn't look as if she was a part of this community," which sounded like a snobbish statement to me. But she said, "Because our daughter was an attorney"—but Tanya's so cool and down-to-earth that—you know, baseball cap wearing, jeans, sneakers all the time. So she felt like unlike her presence, which was the sophisticated lady, well-dressed, that stands out, who would often be noticed, Tanya didn't have that same presence and was never going to have it. So she kept saying, "You guys look like you belong." [laughter] So Tanya would say, "Well, if we was, you know, uppity like you, we probably wouldn't have gotten along so well."

The narrative illustrates how Harlem always had a middle-class presence despite its unsavory reputation. Families sent their children to Ivy League schools and on to become attorneys. Barbara's friend fits the profile of a black gentrifier as an attorney, sorority member, and graduate of prestigious school. Yet she always lived in Harlem and was familiar with an area that had middle-class folks and values. In this way there is little to distinguish Barbara as a black gentrifier from her friend who has always lived in the community.

Barbara and her friend are nevertheless aware of the differences in class between them and many others in the community. By dressing down and keeping it real however, they are easily able to blend in, get along, not draw much attention to themselves, and are probably not perceived as outsiders.

Although the black middle class or gentry was perhaps a more potent force than whites behind gentrification in demographic, economic, and political terms, their presence did not attract the attention that the statistically smaller white populace did. Nonetheless it was whites who figured prominently in narratives about gentrification. The prominence of race will emerge again in the following chapter when I discuss how residents of Clinton Hill and Harlem make sense of the gentrification occurring in their neighborhoods. This prominence, though, signifies the central role race played in reactions to gentrification.

## THE DILEMMA OF GENTRIFICATION

The narratives reported herein attempt to portray the general attitudes I found toward gentrification. They tell a conflicting story, as well they should. Conflicting feelings most aptly describe the residents feelings toward gentrification. Juan said, "Yeah, that I was thinking about what, how I would be coming out in case you have asked, um, that you think gentrification is good or bad. That's a hard one. You know." Betsy commented,

> We've been getting, we are getting sort of a face-lift, so and that's a good thing, um, that's the major thing in the neighborhood. One of the not so good things is that I see a lot of mom and pop shops being moved out, forced out, you know, because of all the new, um, construction and high, high cost, you know, places, I guess all the real estate around, around those places are going out so people can't afford their leases.

Yolanda said, "And the neighborhood is probably gonna change for the better, maybe, meaning that it's gonna become more upscale. But is upscale always good?"

These examples further illustrate the dilemma gentrification poses for these neighborhoods. Residents were surely appreciative of the improvements associated with the process. But at the same time, the threat of displacement hangs in the air, making many wonder if the improvements are even worth it. Thus the narratives suggest that an ambivalent view is perhaps the only way to capture complex and conflicting feelings that gentrification can inspire. Rather than cheering for gentrification or accusing it of "knocking out" the disadvantaged, a more even-handed perspective would recognize that gentrification brings both cheer and grief.

The context of this inquiry are also worth remembering when considering how the narratives presented here were interpreted. It could be argued that given the disinvestment these neighborhoods had experienced, especially Harlem, some gentrification was sorely needed. These neighborhoods had experienced particularly stark days in the 1970s and 1980s, and few would be nostalgic about returning to those times. In some ways these areas did not provide their residents with an acceptable quality of life when the landscape was dotted with abandoned buildings, the crack epidemic was in full force, and basic amenities like a supermarket were scarce.

This context is important because not all "gentrifying" neighborhoods reached the depths of disinvestment that Harlem or even Clinton Hill did in the 1970s and 1980s. *Gentrifying* is put in quotes to signify how the process can take on different forms and mean different things in differing times and places. Gentrification in a working-class ethnic neighborhood is different than it would be in a neighborhood devastated by arson and abandonment like Harlem. There are similarities, but key differences as well. A working-class neighborhood might not have a gourmet supermarket but would still have a well-stocked grocery store. Likewise, gentrification in Harlem at the turn of the century is likely different than the gentrification that took place in Boerum Hill, Brooklyn, in the 1970s. Even at its nadir, Boerum Hill would never have been confused with an underclass neighborhood or a place where mortality rates rivaled those found in some developing countries.

The importance of context could even be seen between Clinton Hill and Harlem. Clinton Hill, for example, had a much higher home-ownership rate, and therefore its residents had a much greater economic stake in gentrification. Consequently, although residents of both Clinton Hill and Harlem were appreciative of the improvements in amenities and services, Clinton Hill was where people were more likely to see an improvement in their financial well-being. The range of feelings toward gentrification expressed here may different from those found in other neighborhoods, depending on their context.

Context may also help explain some of the discrepancy between some descriptions of gentrification and the sentiment of some respondents presented here. Gentrification's reputation as a "yuppie boutique" phenomenon may have been cemented by the experience of the first wave of gentrification during the 1970s. At that time, gentrification seldom occurred in the poorest inner-city neighborhoods like Harlem or predominantly black neighborhoods like Clinton Hill, Clinton Hill perhaps being the exception.

Consequently, the dearth of amenities and services that have afflicted inner-city black communities in recent decades was perhaps not a problem in the first gentrifying neighborhoods, and hence the notion that gentrification could introduce amenities and services appreciated by long-term residents has perhaps not taken hold in our imagination.

The context of Clinton Hill, Harlem, and perhaps other neighborhoods suggest a more ambivalent view of gentrification. In this way the findings of this research echo the thinking of Kennedy and Leonard (2001) who concluded that gentrification was neither "good or bad" but posed a set of challenges and opportunities for communities.

In Clinton Hill and Harlem, gentrification thus poses a dilemma. It was acknowledged to bring good, but it also created a foreboding of things to come. A fear of displacement hung in the air. This fear of displacement played a significant role in the negative sentiment that was sometimes expressed toward gentrification. This fear, however, was hardly the only source of malcontent. As one of the interviewees expressed it, there was a "historical thing, or like, you know, for something their parents taught them" that inspired the negative reactions toward gentrification. In the next chapter I argue that indeed history does play a role in how people interpret and make sense of gentrification.

# 4 Making Sense of Gentrification

THE DRAMATIC CHANGES associated with gentrification inspired Clinton Hill and Harlem residents to think about why their neighborhoods were changing as such. Many had witnessed firsthand the decline of the black inner city in urban America. Beyond their personal experience, the image of decaying black neighborhoods is one that has been etched in the popular imagination and reinforced by the popular media. Movies like *Boyz N the Hood*, *New Jack City*, and *Straight Out of Brooklyn* all attest to the dismal reality that the urban ghetto had become. A reversal of fortunes in such neighborhoods necessarily calls out for explanation.

Although there are well-developed theories on the causes of gentrification in the scholarly literature, a common wisdom has also evolved on the streets of urban America. Henry, a Harlem resident who was introduced in chapter 3, has only a high school education. As such he might not be expected to have been exposed to scholarly debates on the causes of gentrification. Nonetheless, he articulated some of the common demand-side explanations for gentrification:

LANCE: What do you think made the whites want to move in?
HENRY: Well, the economy. Most of them are staying out on the island [Long Island, a suburb of New York City]. And now since the jobs are a little tighter, money is a little tighter. So they're getting in places that they can easily get to work. They're tired of that long commute.

Zanetta, a native of Spanish Harlem who moved to central Harlem as an adult, related a common refrain when describing the onset of gentrification in Harlem—the relatively cheap housing cost.

LANCE: Do you have any ideas about what's attracting people to the neighborhood?
ZANETTA: The, the price of living is cheaper. Um, I moved into my apartment, well, I moved in, I had a studio apartment, and my rent initially was $525 a month, a nice spacious studio, you know, and then I moved to a one bedroom, it was $660. I would say that probably just in general Manhattan is just getting expensive and people need to find a place to live, so this just makes sense.

In addition to the commonly held perceptions that proximity to downtown and cheap housing costs were driving the gentrification, residents of Clinton Hill also pointed to a singular event—the terrorist attacks of September 11, 2001. Anthony (introduced in chapter 3), who had recently purchased a cooperative apartment in Clinton Hill, told a common version of this explanation.

LANCE: What do you think attracted people to this neighborhood?

ANTHONY: There's some sort of shift after 9/11. I think to Brooklyn, a lot of those people who lived downtown, left New York and came to Brooklyn. And, something happened where, I think the suburbs of New York City are, really, really high priced now, in West Chester the taxes are like ridiculous and this is very close to Manhattan, it is fifteen, twenty minutes, right? Clinton Hill is not that far, so you got Brooklyn Heights, right over the bridge, way too expensive now for most people. Then after that, you know, there's like, Cobble Hill, in all it is too expensive, then like the next kind of neighborhood on the verge of change is Clinton Hill and Fort Greene, and the housing stocks are amazing, I mean, I'm sure you've seen it. Here on Clinton Avenue and these historic brownstones. And, so, I think it was the, it's the housing stock, I think drove people to it, and like the infrastructure is nice, and soon it started to get better, I think people were scared to go there for certain reasons and it started to get better, you know, and the more it gentrifies, and a memo goes out and [laughter], out to everybody's friends, I don't know how they hear about it but it's like a flood now, like, it can't be stopped now.

Excepting the idiosyncratic case of September 11, these explanations sound similar to those described in the scholarly literature. For example, explanations of gentrification generally fall into two camps: ecological/economic and political economy. The demand-side school generally emphasizes the following: demographic changes, particularly the decline of the two-parent nuclear household that made urban living more attractive and dampened concerns about inner-city schools; changes in cultural tastes, such as an appreciation for older architecture found in many gentrifying neighborhoods that results in increased demand for inner-city living; and economic considerations like the increasing costs of commuting from the suburbs. The political economy perspective points to the supply side of the equation, arguing that the cyclical nature of capital and its constant search for the highest rate of return in laying out an explanation for gentrification. The cyclical nature of capital portends to the waxing and waning of the profitability of urban land (Smith 1996).

Elements of the economic/ecological theories can be seen in the explanations offered by residents on the causes of gentrification. The importance of economic considerations is perhaps the most obvious. To residents of affected neighborhoods, the increasing attractiveness of their environs could be explained vis-à-vis what it offered compared to other areas. Given the skyrocketing costs of housing in other parts of New York City, even predominantly black neighborhoods like Clinton Hill and Harlem were beginning to draw more interest because of their relatively low prices. These sentiments echo London and Palen (1984, p. 17) who wrote "the decreasing availability of suburban land, rampant inflation in suburban housing costs, rising transportation costs, and the relatively low cost of slum shells interact to encourage [gentrification]."

This is not to suggest that residents of gentrifying neighborhoods keep up with the scholarly literature. But it does illustrate the extent to which a common wisdom has emerged that explains this type of neighborhood change. Ms. Henry, a Mississippian in her sixties with a tenth-grade education who migrated to New York as a teenager, was able to relate the common wisdom on gentrification, a wisdom that for the most part dovetails with the scholarly wisdom: "Harlem is almost like at the center to where you wanna go. If you wanna go uptown, you go uptown, downtown, and you get to the airport real quick. Going to where you want to go is no problem from Harlem. And see now Harlem has some of the greatest brownstones, old buildings, good buildings and, these people want it."

Both Harlem and Clinton Hill have some of the classic ingredients that made them ripe for gentrification, as described in chapter 2. The combination of a growing and diversifying black middle class, the changing economy of the city, shifts in urban policy described in chapter 2 that directed private investment toward black neighborhoods, along with dramatic events like September 11, which may have caused the gentry to look in ever more unconventional neighborhoods for housing, precipitated both areas as being neighborhoods whose time may have come.

## THERE GOES THE 'HOOD: THE ARRIVAL OF WHITES

The changing economy, an appreciation for the housing stock in Clinton Hill and Harlem, and the convenience of these neighborhoods were offered as rationales for why whites had begun to move there en masse. That their neighborhoods were now attracting whites was nevertheless a surprise. Beyond surprise, however, the respondents associated the arrival of whites with neighborhood improvement. Nate's (the civil service worker introduced in chapter 3) quote about integration captures this sentiment precisely:

LANCE: How do you feel about the changes taking place in your neighborhood?

NATE: Well I'm a realist. I think gentrification is good in certain respects in that it brings things to a neighborhood what it really never had. Like an all-black neighborhood never had as much police protection as their white counterpart. So it brings that. Plus it brings investment. Plus I have no problem being in a neighborhood that's um, you know, mixed.

That white people equaled better services was considered a given. Without even asking, respondents freely volunteered their perceptions about how the neighborhood was changing and the role whites were playing in these changes. Samantha grew up in one of the public housing projects in Fort Greene. She moved to Coney Island when she was an adult, but moved back to Clinton Hill almost twenty years ago when the section where she now lives had a less than savory reputation.

SAMANTHA: I remember when I noticed things were definitely changing. There used to be a time when you did not see whites on Myrtle Avenue after the sun went down. That was unheard of. But I remember after about five years after I moved back [this would make it around 1992] saw a white guy using an ATM on Myrtle Avenue after dark. And this was an ATM that wasn't even enclosed. And it was like he was comfortable, "I'm home." That's when I realized things had changed. So now they're making Myrtle Avenue look real nice. It looks like Park Slope. I'll give you another example. For the longest time there's an A&P right around the corner. But I usually went shopping outside of the neighborhood so that I could get fresh meat, fresh produce. Just in the past couple of years they have been totally modernizing the store. To the point you would hardly recognize the store. So my son and his friend went in there and asked the manager "why are you fixing up the store now all of a sudden?" And they said "Because more whites are moving into the area."

LANCE: Really? Are the store owners white?

SAMANTHA: The manager was Hispanic.

This narrative describes the process of neighborhoods improving because of the coming of the gentry. As the complexion of the neighborhood lightens, amenities and services will improve, and this was viewed as an accepted law of urban living. This was a feeling that cut across age, gender, class, and length of time in the neighborhood and was prevalent in both Clinton Hill and Harlem.

When explaining why this was so, three types of responses were generally given. One explanation was that whites were more affluent, politically savvy, and more demanding of better goods and services. This explanation puts the onus for better neighborhood conditions on the actions of whites themselves. Henry, a mid-sixties resident with a high school education, Ms. James, a woman in her late fifties with two years of college education, and Celia, a woman in her late twenties who went to a prestigious undergraduate college and was a graduate student at the time of our interview, all articulated versions of the whites as agents of change thesis:

CELIA: It's because a certain type of people are moving into the community, and they demand, basically better resources, and so when I go to certain stores and they're like out of this and, you know, the service is incredibly slow, you're just like this, you know. I'll just say the word *white*. But like, as more whites would move into a community, certain things that have just been commonplace will no longer be accepted, you know, like to go into a grocery store and have every apple rotten. That's just not going to fly, you know, and to only have that Kraft packaged cheese and not have like feta, whatever, I mean, but that's just, but it's not like the people in the community didn't want it, it's just, it doesn't. . . . it wasn't available, you know, so that's problematic.

HENRY: Neighborhood's—uh just getting a little better, I guess. You're getting more police protection and everything, as expected. I guess the whites demanded more of the Police Department and they're just doing their job—what they say are their job.

MS. JAMES: But, I've seen the improvement, and services that um, to having more things available, and um, the park you can go to Fort Greene Park and there are activities. During the summer. Whereas before you were afraid to go to the park. But, there is double security, because white people, make sure that they get good security!

Here whites are viewed as a group that will not tolerate inferior services. Cognizant of this, stores and providers of public services step up their performance to accommodate the new clientele. Anderson in *Streetwise* alluded to this dynamic in his ethnographic account of a gentrifying neighborhood in Philadelphia:

> The new residents pressure government official for municipal services, including better police protection. These demands are often met, and the whole neighborhood benefits. The once segregated schools gain some middle class-white students, whose parents become involved and require the schools to respond to their needs. Thus the schools improve. (Anderson 1991, p. 139)

Some were also cognizant of the correlations between class and race that are common in America. Typical of this perspective are the comments of Jerome, a community activist in his early forties in Harlem, and Tammi, the young Harlem native who returned to Harlem after college and was introduced in chapter 3:

LANCE: Do you have a sense of why the neighborhood is improving in terms of services?

JEROME: I think it is more about class than race. More about money. People with money can contribute to the politicians. But, it's the case that the people with more money tend to be white and the people with less money tend to be black. Some people say, "oh it's the white people." But I think it is more of a class thing.

TAMMI: I think there's more of class issue than a race issue, because like I see like wealthy politicians coming back into Harlem, like we had, politician who owns a brownstone in Sugar Hill [a neighborhood in Harlem].

LANCE: Well, how do you think that translates in to, like you said the streets are being paved more or, uh, all the sidewalks are being fixed up?

TAMMI: Because if they're paying a certain amount of money they wanna live in "luxury," you know. They don't wanna pay like, $350 to $500,000 for a brownstone and down the block there's trash or abandoned buildings. So that politician for example made like she had this big issue about her trash, you know, like, a couple of months ago, you know, but I'm sure, she doesn't have broken sidewalks, or homeless people sitting down in front of her building. That is the type of thing they're doing.

LANCE: They, being the—

TAMMI: Middle class.

This class-based view accepts that some people are able to command a better neighborhood. But the ability to wield such power is one that transcends race and is more determined by one's class. People with personal experience in community activism seemed more likely to subscribe to this view. Ms. James, who was introduced earlier in this chapter, is a resident of Clinton Hill with a long history of activism with various local groups. Through her activism she has been able to witness the varying ways that people try to affect change in the neighborhood:

> You know everybody keeps talking about when it is theirs and this is my community. I am just so tired of hearing that. It is whoever get into that community and lived, to make it a livable, and a decent place that's all.

When people really want a safe and decent community, you'll always find at the meetings, they will always work, they will be the people who go to Connecticut Muffin, who go to the Thai restaurant, who really appreciate that. The rest of the people they will complain, but they will never ever do anything. And there are some white homeowners on Vanderbilt, not many, who were very active when they wanted to turn the Brooklyn Navy Yard into um, a prison. But they [the whites] were against that. But, you know, the white people in just that one block, said "Now you know our children live here we don't want that." And they were able to stop it.

This resident is juxtaposing the perceived lack of community involvement among her black neighbors to the activism of the white gentrifiers in Clinton Hill. This example illustrates how things are accomplished and neighborhoods improved—by voicing one's complaints and working to achieve what's best for the community. This is something that some whites and to a lesser extent the middle class in general was perceived to be more adept at.

Like Ms. James, other persons I interviewed that worked with neighborhood groups or were on the board of their cooperative appeared to have intimate knowledge of how levers of power could be pushed. Often they spoke of their own efforts at neighborhood improvement. They described their meetings with the local police precincts, their discussions with local merchants and others, all with the aim of improving the neighborhood. For example, Shawn, a worker at a community-based organization, described her mother's personal battles with drug dealers on her block:

My mom would tell the drug dealers, "look y'all have to go somewhere else with this. We have kids on this block and you can't stand here with this." I really think it was folks like my mom and others who helped turn this neighborhood around. When there was crack houses on our block they harassed the drug dealers and fixed up these bombed-out shells. All of that made the neighborhood acceptable to people who would have never thought about moving up here.

In Shawn's view, the work of residents of Harlem made Harlem safe for outside investors and the gentry. Several residents of Clinton Hill who were active on their cooperative board thought the same way. Both James and Louis (introduced in chapter 3 as residents of Clinton Hill) are members of their coop board and argued as such:

JAMES: We also have a local development corporation it's the Myrtle Avenue Revitalization Project. They've been extremely instrumental in bringing new types of businesses to Myrtle Avenue. And, uh, along with those businesses you have people going out to patronize them. That's helped a lot to change the feel of the block.

We're actively working to establish a Business Improvement District on Myrtle Avenue so that we can take it to the next level.

LOUIS: They're starting to come back now after we fixed it up. When I first moved in it was all white. They all left. We weathered some hard times. But we got the place back on our feet. Now they're wanting to come back.

Some of the people involved in community activism were proud to take credit for what they viewed to be their accomplishments. They interpreted the improved services and amenities in the neighborhood as the fruits of their labors. Much more so than other respondents, those who were actively engaged in community-based organizations attributed at least some of the local improvements to the actions of indigenous residents themselves. The common theme here is that this view sees the actions of residents themselves, whether the gentry or indigenous residents like themselves who are active in the community, as integral to the neighborhood improvements that are under way.

A second way some people described the improvements occurring was almost as a side effect of an increase of whites. Yolanda, a resident of Clinton Hill introduced in the last chapter, attributed the increasing presence of restaurants was to the eating habits of whites:

LANCE: Do you have any ideas why there's a major influx of restaurants into the neighborhood, uh, people eating more or, uh—
YOLANDA: Eating more? No, I guess. Again I, I'll just point out to, uh, maybe the last four years or so with a greater influx of, um, you know, white people into the neighborhood, I think a lot of them probably have a tendency to eat out a lot more.

Rather than whites demanding better services, the businesses are simply responding to the market created by whites. Barbara, the graduate student who moved to Harlem after attending college, also described the improvement of police protection to coincidental forces. She described the police as naturally more protective of their own kind:

LANCE: Have you noticed any changes in public services?
BARBARA: The police. Their response to any crime, any problems. I don't know what's causing it, but I can speculate. I think that I would say that maybe there's concern now. Someone who looks like you calls for help you can now relate to their need and maybe I'm thinking. Let's say I walk into the police precinct and make a complaint it may be business as usual. But if it is someone they can identify with they may be heard. When I first moved there I would call the police about noise and my roommate would laugh.

It was a joke because she knew they wouldn't come. But if someone called them today they probably would.

LANCE: When you say the police identify, what is it, I don't want to make assumptions, what is it they identify with?

BARBARA: Race. It's not necessarily class because that same police officer may not be able to afford a $700,000 brownstone. But it's history, it's race.

LANCE: The police are mostly white. And the people who are mostly calling are white?

BARBARA: Yes.

LANCE: So there's not that many black cops.

BARBARA: Nope.

Viewed this way, the improvements in amenities or services are coincidental. Because the police are mostly white, naturally they are more responsive now that whites are moving into the neighborhood. It is not that whites are more demanding or savvy, but things have just worked out that way.

A third explanation views the forces determining the level of amenities and services in a perhaps more nefarious light. The powers that be take notice of the changing complexion of the neighborhood and through whatever mechanism decide to dole out services more favorably. The exact mechanism through which this occurs is not always clearly understood as the following exchange with Miriam, an artist in her mid-forties who grew up in a Midwestern suburb, illustrates.

MIRIAM: When I first moved in you always saw the undercovers having someone up against the wall. From what I am told it used to be really bad. I mean my area was known for drugs. In fact the building I am living in used to be a crack house.

LANCE: Do you have a sense of why they're trying to clean up the neighborhood now as opposed to in the past?

MIRIAM: It's for the white people. Obviously, I mean it's not for us.

LANCE: Because the white people are moving in the neighborhood they are cracking down?

MIRIAM: Yes, yes, that's always the case anywhere. Because the real estate is valuable and they are jumping on it.

LANCE: How does that work? You have a neighborhood with a lot of crime and the whites move in and . . . The question may sound stupid, I'm just trying to get your thinking about this process. The whites move in, how does that translate into increased police presence?

MIRIAM: I don't know where it trickles down from or who puts the word out that you have to be more proactive on this or whatever, all

I know is it happens, I don't know how, or who, or what. It does happen and it is very obvious.

Given Miriam's background—raised in the suburbs, migrated to Harlem as an adult, and a struggling artist—one might classify her as a gentrifier. Yet she clearly makes a distinction between herself and the whites who have moved into Harlem. It is for them that the neighborhood benefits are being made.

Dave, a native of Harlem in his mid-thirties, concurs:

LANCE: Are the parks and public spaces safer now?

DAVE: They're becoming cleaner, they're becoming safer. There are a lot of Caucasians living here now so they have to make them cleaner and safer, so they have to make it safer for them as well. They got to live here, right? Of course these changes are happening for the Caucasians coming in. Not too many African American households can afford $1500 a month for rent, so it is designed to replace them.

The feeling that a conscientious decision was being made to devote more attention to whites and other newcomers also inspired some resentment and bitterness toward the whole gentrification process. For people who had been living in a neighborhood for years with inferior services, the sudden improvement, even if beneficial, was also insulting. Dave went on to describe his feelings of resentment.

> Its funny just when they are moving up, that's when they feel like doing something with the neighborhood. Because they're moving uptown, and we've been here for forever. Basically they didn't think of making this before everybody moved uptown. I mean, it's good that it's happening, but it is happening for the wrong reasons. It should have been happening a long time ago.

Kevin, a mid-thirties man who has lived in Harlem all of his life except the time he spent away at college, and Takeesha, introduced in chapter 3, were also indignant about this.

KEVIN: I mean, you see maybe a more police presence, but that's for them. That's not really for the older residents. And, and you could really feel that. So, um, it's just . . .

LANCE: When you say that, when you say the police presence is for them and not for the older residence, could you elaborate on this point?

KEVIN: If it's, if it's for the older residents, they would have been there prior to the new people coming into the neighborhood. So when you see like an improvement of services because of your new neighbors, or I guess, uh, the income of your neighbors, it sorta is a slap in a face, because you should have been getting that prior to people coming in. Just cause, you know, somebody comes in doesn't mean all of a sudden you step up your services. Services shoulda already been plentiful prior to.

TAKEESHA: Yeah, that's, I mean, like that to me, that's sort of like the problem is, just why is that a certain, you know . . . type of people, you know, have to move in, uh, in order for that to happen, I mean, you know, you can talk about on one hand, they're bringing in, you know, wealth or whatever, but, I mean, that should have nothing to do with whether or not the police is . . . you know, or whether or not, um, the sanitation department is picking up the trash and things like that.

These remarks suggest resentment directed not so much at whites per se but at perceived white privilege. The improvements taking place are perceived as being targeted to others and not themselves. Gentrification is then a process designed to benefit whites and certainly not long-term residents. To be sure, sometimes changes in services are specifically targeted at some people. Take for example the practice of hanging on the corner or loitering that is common in many inner-city communities. If this practice is suppressed, it is hard to argue that this is for the benefit of would-be corner hangers. Mason, introduced in the previous chapter, described a change in the permissibility of loitering that he views as for the benefit of others:

MASON: There used to be a corner where the Puerto Ricans and Dominicans hung out and played the bongos and drank beer. Now they can't do that. But you can do that in Washington Heights. So there's this double standard. That's wrong. How can neighborhoods under the same mayor be treated so differently? Now you can't even stand in front of your own building without being harassed. Or if you sit on the benches the police will come along and point to the no loitering sign and say you can't stay here.

LANCE: Why do you think this double standard exists?

MASON: Because of new people moving in and putting pressure on the police to make things orderly.

What used to be acceptable no longer is. What is acceptable in some neighborhoods is not acceptable in others. How else to make sense of this other than to assume that certain people are able to command a change in the rules? Henry, the older native of North Carolina who frequents the corners, also viewed a change in police activity that aims to curb such activity as being for the benefit of someone else, as the dialogue below illustrates:

HENRY: Well—I haven't seen any change in the last ten years, but
the last three years, there have been great change with the
whites moving in. Neighborhood's—uh just getting a little better,
I guess.

LANCE: So that's—that's happened since the whites moved in you said?

HENRY: Such as sanitation, noise level, people standing around on
the street, which at one time it was permitted but now, it's—
they're a little strict on it.

LANCE: They—you mean, they don't allow people to stand around on
the street?

HENRY: They—not much.

LANCE: Hmm. So, what rule is that, that—that they used to—

HENRY: Well, they say it's a rule that had been on the book—it's an
ancient rule. But now, getting—it's being enforced now. Well we,
we go along with the flow, if the police come, we stops and hide
whatever we doing. Even when they pass, we go back to it sort of
thing, we go back to, ha, ha, normal.

LANCE: Okay. Hmm. It almost sounds like harassment, you know?

HENRY: Hmm. You know it—it depends on what side of the street
you're standing on.

LANCE: How do people feel about that? I mean the people that already
had been living here, the fact that the law has rules and—

HENRY: Ha, ha, I think most people are pissed off.

Those being harassed by the police would be expected to view the influx
of whites in relatively harsh terms. Obviously selective enforcement of
laws is not being done for the benefit of those being harassed. Terry, who
was introduced in the previous chapter, was able to point to specific
events that illustrate how certain behaviors were now proscribed with the
onset of gentrification.

But if you move into a new place you shouldn't try to take over, and be like
"we're here now so you got to do things our way." For example, we have a
celebration every Father's Day across from the school on the corner. Been
doing it for twenty years. So there's a building they renovated and last year
someone calls the cops. Police come and say you know you can't be out here
drinking that beer. We're like "we're grown men." Some of us in our
seventies, we're not gonna be causing trouble. If it wasn't for one black lady
who was living there for years that came out and said "leave them alone
they been doin' this for years" we would have had to move. Then we used to
stand around on 123rd we would relax in front of the school, drink a beer.
Can't do that no more. They put a fence around the school. If we on the
corner or stoop with a beer the police is coming. Meanwhile Danelo's [a
local restaurant] put a patio out and people is sitting out there drinking
wine. But I can't have a beer?

In Terry's story, old (presumably harmless) rituals are being disrupted by the gentry who are trying to "take over." By using the police to enforce what they deem to be the new regime, the gentry inspire resentment. What is even more galling is that certain activities, such as drinking in public, are proscribed unless they conform to the gentry's idea of what is acceptable. Drinking outside is drinking outside. As long as someone is not disorderly, what difference should it make whether someone is standing on a corner or sitting behind a restaurant cordon? This type of differential treatment is not surprisingly laid at the doorstep of gentrification and is resented.

But other changes in amenities and services would presumably benefit everyone. The resentment thus also stems from something else. The sentiment seems to be "Why should a neighborhood have to have white residents to receive better services?" Gary, introduced in chapter 3, summed up his feelings this way:

GARY: I don't like having whites making the difference or creating the impression that because now it's safe or now its ok to live there.... Our neighborhood is definitely gentrifying, I'm like is it so much a bad thing? Well depends on how you look at it. I liked the vibe of our community before. I don't like that our property values have to go up when white people fucking move in. Excuse my French. Ha, ha. But that's what happens. Once you see white people hanging out in a neighborhood where they generally wouldn't come through, it's gentrification. I hate that you know. I hate that has to be the legitimating factor for property values to go up or for your neighborhood to be a nice neighborhood that sort of thing.

LANCE: So you're not so much against property values rising, it's just the fact that it seems like there has to be whites that cause it?

GARY: Yeah, yeah. That's what makes it legitimate. And then like when blacks move into a neighborhood that's predominantly white then property values go down. Absolutely ridiculous! I don't like that, like I told you before, white people moving into the neighborhood legitimizes our property values going up. I don't even know if that's the case, it may just be my impression. Maybe you have people with higher incomes moving into the neighborhood driving prices up. I don't know what the statistics are, that sort of thing. But it just *seems that way*.

Gary was a coop owner and thus stands to benefit from an increase in property values. So naturally he would prefer that the value of his property value rise. But the fact that property values increase seem linked to race, a point he makes clear by presenting a counterexample of when property values decline due to an influx of blacks, is irksome.

That neighborhoods differ in terms of access to amenities and services is well known. As the popular real estate mantra says "location, location, location" are the three most important determinants of property values. To many residents, gentrification has meant an improvement in both private and public amenities. That these improvements have occurred simultaneously with an influx of whites has not escaped their attention.

A common explanation for differences in neighborhood services like police protection is the political boundaries that separate affluent communities from less prosperous ones. According to this view, the higher tax bases and fewer social problems in suburban communities affords them the ability to provide high-quality public services. Indeed, a substantial body of literature exists describing the motivation of households to sort themselves into relatively homogenous clusters with similar preferences and demands for services and amenities provided at the local level (Tiebout 1956).

Interjurisdictional differences in resources and demand for public goods and services certainly explain some of the disparities in services and amenities across localities. In the minds of some residents of predominantly minority communities, however, these differences are beside the point. They see neighborhoods *within the same city*—"How can neighborhoods under the same mayor be treated so differently?"—with better schools, better police protection, cleaner streets, and the like, and they attribute these differences to the relative power of certain groups. Whites are clearly viewed as the more powerful group. Some respondents attributed improvements in amenities and services to a mixture of benign and perhaps conspiratorial forces. Barbara expressed this view to me in the following dialogue:

BARBARA: I just heard they did a sweep on 125th Street. A friend of mine said they just saw a bunch of young African American males get picked up. They said "what's the reason?" They were questioning the cops as they were saying to them you have to get off of these corners.

LANCE: Wow! This is recently?

BARBARA: Yeah. She said "I'm telling you they are cleaning up the area." That was the term she was using, *cleaning up*. Meaning you can't even just be seen. She said what she perceived was that someone or the white people made complaints and they want it to look like say west 70th Street looks like. *You* are out of place if you are standing on the corner. I don't care if it's your right to stand on the corner. We don't owe you an explanation. So you just have to move unless you would like to be arrested.

The remarks of the respondents suggest one of the great ironies of gentrification and point to a perhaps overlooked source of antagonism.

Certainly increased police protection and better stores are items from which everyone can benefit. After all, when stores carry better produce, anyone, including longtime black residents, can purchase it. A decline in crime will also benefit black residents making them less likely to be robbed or killed. But some are suspicious of the motives behind this neighborhood improvement. Ms. Henry, the native of Mississippi, expressed her cynicism in the following conversation:

LANCE: Well, uh, let me ask you something. Do you have any thoughts about why more stores have been opening up in Harlem?

MS. HENRY: Yeah, I have given, given some thought. They're trying to, to draw, um, people from all over. I mean that's my thought. Um, they want people that, from all over the world.

LANCE: What about the people in the community?

MS. HENRY: In the community? It's not for the people who are in the community. It's not for us at all. This is what I'm telling you. It's not meant for us. Anything that they're doing in Harlem, it's not meant for the poor blacks.

Likewise, a decrease in crime benefits all residents, except perhaps the few criminals in the neighborhood. But the notion that these benefits were intended for members of the community often did not occur to most respondents. Michael is a native of Harlem who attended Columbia University and moved back into Harlem after graduation and is in his late twenties. As such, some might view him as part of the gentry, although with his native roots he could claim to be an indigenous resident. His Ivy League education notwithstanding, he nevertheless interprets neighborhood improvements as something for outsiders, of whom he does not consider himself.

> I remember right before HSBC [a local bank] and Subway opened up there was this huge influx of police presence. It was ridiculous. They set up one of those mobile police stations right by the subway. I just noticed there being so many police officers flooding the streets. My neighborhood is notorious from the drug dealing going on there. Not violent, we don't have a lot of violent crime, I've never heard of a purse snatching or mugging or rape, but everyone is pretty much aware that there are millions of dollars in drugs being moved. All of a sudden you saw fewer people hanging on the corner, less drug dealers, so we all assumed they were clearing the way for something big. So we realized there was going to be a larger commercial presence in the area, we just weren't sure who or what it would be.

According to Michael, an increased police presence certainly must herald someone or something coming from outside the neighborhood. Otherwise why would the police attempt to crack down on crime? Certainly, not because current residents should not have to live in a drug-infested environment. Moreover, an increased police presence may now mean you are more likely to be harassed. In the following story, Michael illustrates the way the increased police presence is thought to service particular groups, even in the same neighborhood.

MICHAEL: For instance, no one sat and ate at the Chinese restaurants. But now people sit down and you know eat. It's like the table next to you is reserved for the drug dealers. But the white people just don't know or don't care.

LANCE: So people wouldn't sit there because they knew it was used by drug dealers?

MICHAEL: Right. Everyone knew. But if you don't know, you just sit down. You don't see the drug dealers saying anything. But if it was me who sat down, the drug dealers would be like "What are you doing?" and I would promptly get up.

LANCE: So that's interesting. The drug dealers would say something to you, but not the other people. Why do you think that is?

MICHAEL: Because you have the police outside. A white person sitting there if you say something to them, they go outside and say "The drug dealer told me I couldn't sit there," and the cops are going to cause problems.

LANCE: Whereas the perception is that you wouldn't say anything to the police.

MICHAEL: Nah, I'm not saying anything to them. The cops aren't there for us, that's for sure.

The characters in this narrative are black (Michael) and Dominican (the drug dealers). According to Michael, both the drug dealers and he perceive the police presence to be there to serve whites. Hence, they would harass him and other nonwhites who unwittingly interfered with their drug-dealing operations. But whites who interfere are left alone.

In addition, some neighborhood improvements, such as an increased police presence may make some people feel *less* comfortable. Because of the way young black and Latino men have been targeted by police, many in this demographic will not welcome an increased police presence—even if they are law-abiding and well educated. Michael went on to describe how he felt about the increased police presence in his neighborhood:

Well there's been an increased police presence. That's something that makes me feel less comfortable. . . . I've gotten stopped on a number of occasions. One time I'm coming out of my building with a bag of laundry, Tide and bleach and the police said where are you going? I'm like pointing to my stuff and walking away. They say to me "you can't just walk away." I'm like why not? They were undercovers I guess looking for dealers.

In most communities, the default assumption would be that improvements in services are designed to benefit residents of these communities. The narrative above, however, suggests that this assumption is challenged in many poorer minority communities, even those experiencing gentrification.

That neighborhoods receive better treatment as a result of whites moving in perhaps also reminds some blacks of their subordinate status in American society. The perceived inability of blacks to achieve the type of community they desire, whether because the powers that be refused to provide services or blacks lacked the political savvy to demand the services they desired, all serve to reinforce notions of blacks as a subordinate caste. To the extent that black neighborhoods, for all their problems, have served as havens from white racism, being reminded of one's subordinate status in one's own comfort zone is probably unsettling. Both Takeesha and Nate expressed this ambivalence toward whites moving into Harlem and Clinton Hill:

TAKEESHA: Yeah, you want better services, you want a safe neighborhood, you want a clean neighborhood, uh, but, at the expense of, you know, of whom, uh, and so, and that, that's why I feel conflicted because, um, you know, you want the neighborhood to, to improve but not in terms of, uh, its resources, not in terms of, improve doesn't always mean, you know, uh, white people. It doesn't mean, you know, to change the racial composition or class composition.

NATE: Well, I mean, I like the diversity, that's great, and I like more services coming to the neighborhood and I like the neighborhood being paid more attention to. But the only problem I have, and, and I wish I could see some statistics on this, I don't like that it takes white people moving into our neighborhood to legitimize our concerns, to legitimize the realization of our property values, and to uh, make it a safe neighborhood, you know, that sort of thing.

These interviews suggest that among some of the residents of gentrifying Clinton Hill and Harlem, an influx of whites means improved amenities and services. For some, however, this improvement inspires feelings of anger and racially based disrespect.

The narratives just illustrated allude to conspiratorial decisions made for the benefits of whites. Some respondents viewed the conspiracy as part of a wider plan to take these neighborhoods from blacks, speaking in explicitly conspiratorial terms. Ms. Henry spoke in these terms:

Every day you got people sitting up there. Why aren't they [blacks] dead yet? How do they, how do, how do they do this, this and what are they thinking? Believe it or not, these people, uh, they, their minds are on black people a great deal. How do we get them to work for us, but we, we, we need that whole place. We need, we need Harlem but we want them. So in other words, they're using great strategy. Every day there's a strategy going on here. I may not be able to say it like a professor or whatever, but there's a strategy and, uh, don't let, don't let anybody fool you that they don't watch us. And they say, well, hum, these people, they, they ain't got no education and, uh, they ain't trying to do nothing. I mean, hey, you know, it's just laying up there.

Jake, introduced in chapter 3, described the conspiratorial view of how neighborhoods evolve under gentrification:

JAKE: It seems like a certain area will be designated by planners or whoever for gentrification. Then the police presence will increase markedly. Crime will go down. More stores open up. Then property values go up. Pretty soon only certain people can afford it. Very few African American. Mostly white.
LANCE: How does this happen? Who does the designating?
JAKE: I don't know. Probably businesses working with government. Businesses work to influence in a capitalist society.

Ms. Tate is a mid-fifties native of Harlem residing in the home her parents bought several decades ago. One might expect her, as a homeowner, to have a more benevolent view of the gentrification process. But she, too, expressed a conspiratorial view of the changes under way in her neighborhood: "I don't wanna be pushed out. You know what I'm saying, because I truly believe that there's a conspiracy in trying to push people, black people, out that own homes in Harlem."

In some instances "they" became specific actors who were moving to take these neighborhoods from blacks. For example, Ms. Henry described her feeling that the residents of her public housing development would soon be displaced:

MS. HENRY: Now they're doing that, they, there, they change the outside of the building. The building looks great outside, but they don't care about the tenants inside. So, you know, what are you getting ready to do here, okay?
LANCE: Why, why do you think they want to fix up the outside but don't care about the tenants?
MS. HENRY: Well, it's been discussed among tenants quite frequently that, um, it's because we understand that this [Columbia] university would like to own our property, as, you know, dormitories for the

students, incoming students because there seems to be a shortage of housing for all the students. These projects have a fifty-year lease. That lease will soon be up and it's, and it's really up for grabs. So, Columbia, uh, they got a good shot at it, once, once that lease is up. They've been trying to get it for a while.

Ms. Syndemon, a native of South Carolina in her mid-fifties who moved to Harlem as a teenager and now lives in an apartment complex, related to me an apocryphal story about changes pending in her neighborhood. Although she recognized the conspiratorial nature of the rumor, she nevertheless entertained the veracity of it, or at least thought it was worthwhile to mention:

MS. SYNDEMON: Eventually, like this little project right here, 155th Street. It was rumored that they were selling, city was selling that to, um, what's his name? Trump. Yeah. People was saying that, so we are saying, "What is Trump gonna put up here?" You know, I'm saying, Trump? But I don't believe that. I don't believe that any more. You hear things. Then they said it was the polo grounds.

LANCE: Oh, that Trump was gonna buy that building?

MS. SYNDEMON: Uh huh, yes. But anything he buy, you know minorities are excluded. It's only for the rich. So eventually, I think, I think eventually a lot of blacks [laughter] are gonna have to leave Harlem, because so many homes are only one, one income.

The naming of specific actors in these cases, rather than dispelling the conspiratorial nature of the narratives, actually reinforces them. In both cases, the actors can be viewed as powerful agents almost above reproach. Columbia University is the largest private landlord in New York City, is part of the Ivy League, and has a history of influencing development in upper Manhattan. Donald Trump is a larger-than-life real estate developer whose name is synonymous with the rich and powerful. These two actors stand in as metaphors for powerful forces that act in ways to the detriment of residents of gentrifying neighborhoods.

These narratives clearly indicate a view among residents of neighborhoods that changes associated with gentrification, such as an influx of whites, improved police protection, and new and improved stores, are interconnected. This interconnection is one with which most observers would agree. Many scholars have written about the inequality of place. What differs is some residents' views of this interconnection. Whereas social science tends to view this inequality as an unintentional consequence of larger macrostructural forces, the residents' views puts agency squarely back into the picture. They specifically cite actors or describe a conspiracy or plan, talk about word going out or calls made by whites to get better services.

Contrast that with some of the dominant explanations for neighborhood conditions proffered by social scientists. Wilson (1987) for example, argues that job losses due to deindustrialization along with the flight of the black middle class lead to concentrated pockets of poverty and social pathos. Massey (2001) points to the cumulative effects of actions by individual whites who discriminate and avoid living with blacks, which results in high levels of black segregation and consequently concentrated poverty and social problems in these neighborhoods. In both of these explanations there is no conscious, coordinated effort to create ghetto neighborhoods; rather, these neighborhoods are the unintended consequence of a multitude of actors.

Likewise, most explanations of gentrification point to impersonal society-wide forces as culprit. Changes in commuting costs, demographic change, and consumer tastes and the restructuring of the economy are typically offered as explanations as to why gentrification is occurring. The improvement in amenities is typically attributed to the market responding to the increased purchasing power of the gentrifiers. Even political economy explanations of gentrification, which seek to point out the beneficiaries and losers of the process, places impersonal concepts like the inexorable cycles of capital accumulation at the foci of its arguments. In this view, capital is like a force of nature, inevitably seeking the highest rate of return, like water seeking its own level.

The narratives on gentrification described, however, move beyond impersonal forces like the market in explaining changes taking place. For example, take the comment that new stores were being opened for "them" and not long-term residents. The market serves whoever has the capability to pay. The reference to the stores, many of which are not exclusive by any stretch, being for whites moving into the neighborhood points to human agency rather than the market as the driving force behind gentrification.

The narrative of gentrification that emerges from neighborhood residents is one where rising housing costs, dissatisfaction with suburban living, and an increasing appreciation for the proximity of neighborhoods like Clinton Hill and Harlem coalesce to make whites, the middle class— otherwise known as the gentry—take notice of these neighborhoods. Thus far, the narrative is consistent with conventional academic of gentrification. But for the person on the street in gentrifying neighborhoods, the explanation diverges when the mechanics of neighborhood improvements are discussed. People are consciously deciding to treat the newcomers to gentrifying neighborhoods better. Moreover, this better treatment is not a coincidence of the market or a preceding factor that led to gentrification in the first place. Rather, it represents the contempt (or at best indifference) with which the prior residents of gentrifying neighborhoods are viewed.

## FACT OR FICTION: GENTRIFICATION AS CONSPIRACY?

The conspiratorial tone of the narratives described might strike some as far-fetched and question whether the equation "white people = better services" is as simple as presented here. Skeptics would probably concede the numerous empirical studies of neighborhood conditions strongly suggest that the proportion of whites in a neighborhood is positively correlated with the level and quality of amenities and services (Helling and Sawicki 2003; Logan and Alba 1993; Logan et al. 1996; Massey, Condran, and Denton 1987). But the skeptics would also point to institutional inequalities and the cumulative effect of individual decisions rather than an active choice to deprive black neighborhoods. Moreover, empirical studies that have attempted to document disparities between neighborhoods in levels of municipal services have found mixed results. Some studies have found that low-income minority neighborhoods receive lower levels of service, but other studies have found no such pattern (Sanchez 1998).

Further skepticism is also invited by the fact that some of the conspiracy-like claims, such as Trump or Columbia University acquiring public housing, are demonstrably false. The New York City Housing Authority has no plans to sell developments to private investors, nor is there a fifty-year lease that will soon expire.

Skeptics could also point to alternative explanations for improvement in gentrifying neighborhoods besides a conspiracy or conscious decision to "step up" their services in the wake of the gentry arriving. For example, consider the issue of crime; New York City's dramatic decline in crime and changing police tactics are well known by now (Blumstein and Wallman 2000). This decline, however, was not limited to poor black neighborhoods experiencing gentrification. There were declines in crime across the board. A perhaps more plausible explanation is that changes in police activity predated the influx of whites. Declines in crime may have made once dangerous places viable living alternatives to whites and middle-income households.

Also consider the widespread increase in investment activity in many inner-city communities. Although economists traditionally have described the market as hyperrational and not prone to discriminatory behavior, the reality is that markets are often irrational and behave more like frenzied herds. This has been noted by behavioral economists

(Shiller 2005). Once a few stores opened up in neighborhoods like Harlem, other investors were willing to take a chance. Indeed there is evidence of chain stores opening in inner-city communities that are not experiencing what would typically be considered gentrification. It also seems likely that at least some of the recent reinvestment in inner-city communities like Clinton Hill and Harlem has been driven by financial institutions responding to the prodding by community activists indigenous to these very same communities.

As I described in chapter 2, local community-based organizations have also played an integral role in revitalizing these neighborhoods. Some of the best known community development corporations in New York City, such as Abyssinian Development Corporation and Harlem Congregations for Community Improvement in Harlem and Pratt Area Community Council in Clinton Hill, were actively engaged in revitalizing these neighborhoods. The efforts of these groups should not be discounted. Residents who were active in such groups were eager to take credit for the revitalization taking place in their neighborhoods. Consider Reginald's explanation of the turnaround in Harlem:

> Well, um, we saw the neighborhood crumbling right before us. So we, this is about 1985, we, um, started pressing the city to do something with all the abandoned buildings. With all of our churches we have a significant major political force. So Koch and the city wanted to get rid of these buildings and started agreeing to work with us. So that's how it started. People, uh, were seeing something done with these buildings and people started moving back into the neighborhood. After a while even whites were moving in too. Getting rid of all those abandoned buildings made it harder for the drug dealers and addicts to congregate. So the neighborhood got a little better, and more people came. And it's like a cycle. Though we've had a harder time getting businesses to come and stay, but even that's changing now. So that's how we started the whole thing.

Reginald has been a resident of Harlem for twenty-five years and through his church has been engaged in community development activities. He views the actions of community-based organizations like the one he belongs to as the progenitors of the revitalization under way in Harlem. Likewise, Ms. James has been living in Clinton Hill for forty years and has always been very active in the community. In describing the improvement of the community, she points to the efforts of the residents, but she infers that the black residents did not do all they could have to achieve these changes:

> You know I've really, I've gotten a lot out of the community, I enjoy raising my kids in the community, and I've worked hard in the community, to build an after school center to make sure that you know we get the, police, um,

police protection, you know everything so I'm, I'm glad to see that you know, at last you know, that you have some of the things that you spent all these years fighting for and you thought will never happen. But I'm very disappointed, that, that black people didn't do it on their own.

Earlier, I described how Ms. James thought whites in the neighborhood were important in organizing to effect change. She reiterates this belief here, but again points to the actions of the residents like herself to explain the changes happening in Clinton Hill.

In addition, the role of longtime middle-class residents in these communities also should not be discounted. These individuals provide some of the critical mass of those with disposable income to support more stores and the social capital to demand better services. They also served as role models and provide the base of support for neighborhood institutions as described by Wilson (1987).

I can also relate my firsthand experience attending a neighborhood meeting in Clinton Hill. The meeting was held in a new Senegalese restaurant, itself a sign of gentrification. Residents were gathered to begin the process of forming a block association. Present were a mix of black and white residents, although given the overall demographic character of the neighborhood, whites were overrepresented at about half of those present. Residents introduced themselves—most were homeowners and had moved into the neighborhood within the past five years. Given the recent nature of their arrival and their status as homeowners in an overheated housing market where only those with substantial means could afford to own homes now or in the recent past, one could classify the attendees as gentrifiers. Also present was a member of a local community development corporation, a city council representative, a representative from the Parks Department, and two officers from the local police precinct. Residents talked about how to organize a block association and how to improve the local greenery, but the bulk of the attention was directed at the police. Residents wanted to know what could be done to address neighborhood criminal activity and discourage youths from congregating on the corner. Ironically, a group of youths were congregating in front of the restaurant as the meeting took place. The police made clear that resources flowed to areas where complaints were being lodged. Although the officers made it clear that it was not a crime to stand on the corner, the residents did implore them to do something. It would not be surprising if the police did indeed do "something" to satisfy the complaints of these residents. Those who stood on the corners were absent to plead their case to their new neighbors or the police. This dynamic is consistent with explanations that services improve or change because the gentry are better organized to demand what they want.

Given these alternative explanations some, would be tempted to dismiss the conspiratorial tone of many residents as another conspiracy theory by paranoid blacks. Skeptics might point to other conspiracy theories that posit intentional harm behind social maladies afflicting the black community. Stories such as AIDS being a plan to kill blacks and other nonwhites in the world, or construing the presence of drugs and guns in black communities as evidence of a conspiracy to destroy black neighborhoods are examples of other conspiracy theories (Waters 1997). The gentrification story in many ways sounds like a conspiracy theory but has just enough truth to make it credible.

The view of gentrification and indeed the condition of black inner-city communities in general as part of a conspiracy is in evidence in the movie *Boyz N the Hood* (dir. John Singleton, Columbia Pictures, 1991). The semi-autobiographical movie (Singleton also wrote it) takes place in the black ghetto of south central Los Angeles and contains a scene where Furious Styles (Laurence Fishburne), a self-styled street intellectual and race man, explains the process of gentrification and neighborhood decline in black neighborhoods to an "old head" and a group of youths congregating on a street corner:

FURIOUS: Know what that is? [Pointing to a "Cash for Homes" sign]
YOUTH: A billboard.
FURIOUS: I'm talking about the message and what it stands for. It's called gentrification. That's what happens when the property value of a certain area is brought down. They bring the property value down. They can buy the land at a lower price. Then they move all the people out, raise the property value, and sell it at a profit...
OLD HEAD: Ain't no one from outside bringing down the property value. It's these folks [Pointing to the nearby youths]. Shootin' each other and sellin' that crack rock and shit.
FURIOUS: Well how you think the crack rock gets into the country? We don't own any planes. We don't own no ships. We are not the people who are flying and floating that shit in here. I know every time you turn on the TV that what you see, black people, sellin' the rock, pushin' the rock. But that wasn't a problem as long as it was here. It wasn't a problem until it showed up in Iowa and Wall Street where there aren't hardly any black people. Now you want to talk about guns. Why is it that there is a gun shop in almost every corner in this community?
OLD HEAD: Why?
FURIOUS: I'll tell you why. For the same reason there's liquor store on almost every corner in the black community. Why? They want us to kill ourselves. You go out to Beverly Hills, you don't see that shit.

Yeah they want us to kill ourselves. The best way you can destroy a people you take away their ability to reproduce themselves. Who is it that is dying out here every night on these streets? Y'all.

Here Furious describes gentrification as a deliberate plot to make money. Current residents are to be discarded without a thought. Moreover, the conditions that make gentrification possible in the first place—low property values—results from an intentional plan to destroy black people. Neil Smith could not have said it better.

The director, John Singleton, is here conveying some of the thoughts percolating in the black community. But Singleton is not presenting Furious as a bitter, paranoid, ill-informed angry black man. Instead Furious is presented as man whose words should be accorded great weight:

YOUTH: Damn, Furious is deep. He used to be a preacher?
YOUTH [FURIOUS'S SON]: Nah, he ain't no preacher, he just reads a lot. Pops was talking, speakin' the truth.
YOUTH: Your pops is like motherfuckin' Malcolm, Farrakhan.

Furious is a man who reads a lot and is assumed to be a learned man or preacher. The message conveyed here is that the conspiratorial view of neighborhood dynamics is one worthy of respect. Indeed, the director may have been attempting to plant the seeds in the audience as much as he was reflecting current wisdoms in the black community. Gentrification as conspiracy would appear to have deep roots within the black community. The narratives depicted earlier in this chapter clearly touch on this current of thought.

Some scholars look askance at such conspiracy theories. Attributing such thoughts to angry people with flawed judgments who withdraw from society, this school of thought sees conspiracy theories as something to be challenged and corrected.

I choose, however, a different tact taking heed of what Duneier (1999) warns as the ethnographic fallacy. As described by Duneier, such a fallacy occurs when a researcher takes respondents' stories at face value, without considering the larger context or macrolevel forces that shape the respondents' realities. In Duneier's study of homeless sidewalk vendors, he found that his respondents typically attributed their homelessness to their own actions without any reference to deindustrialization, discrimination, the lack of affordable housing, or other society-wide forces that contributed to their predicament. Duneier wanted to allow individuals to tell their stories but also wanted to inform these stories with what he saw as the larger picture. Despite ignoring the larger forces that may have predisposed the men in his study to become homeless, the men's stories still had meaning—namely, that these men still felt that they exercised control over their lives in the face of overwhelming structural obstacles. Thus, the men's claims to be solely responsible for their homelessness can be interpreted as a way of maintaining their sense of control over their fragile and vulnerable existences. Taking a similar analytic tact here suggests the meaning of the whites equals better services or gentrification as conspiracy narrative may be as important as the empirical veracity of it. This approach seems warranted in a situation where residents are asked to voice opinions about a complex phenomena like the forces that change amenities and services in gentrifying neighborhoods for which their firsthand experiences are necessarily limited.

Turner (1993) describes the currency afforded to many malicious conspiracies in the African American community. She attributes beliefs in these rumors not to inadequate education but rather to a historical legacy of oppression that makes such stories credible. Although the rumors described in Turner's work are typically untrue or unverified, the collective memory of having whites control blacks' fates makes these stories believable. For example, the notion that AIDS is a disease created by white doctors to harm blacks or other marginalized groups may seem incredible to some. But then the notion that the federal government would withhold treatment for a curable disease to observe the effects of that disease, as in the case of the infamous Tuskegee syphilis experiment, would also seem incredible if it had not actually happened once already. Turner (1993, p. 136) writes, "In seeking to fill the gaps between what is known and what remains a mystery, the folk will rely on their sense of black history to construct motifs consistent with the past experience but applicable to the issue at hand." Thus, these rumors serve as metaphors to the racial oppression that many blacks continue to perceive today. Continuing inequities, whether actually motivated by racism or not, only serve to reinforce suspicions about how public services are doled out. Michael provides an example of such suspicions:

MICHAEL: The train unfortunately the skip stop service on the $\frac{1}{9}$ train only begins at 137th Street. That's the last time you can catch the 1 or 9 and it doesn't really matter. I always felt that was a racist thing that occurred cuz the 1 train ran and then they threw in the 9 and they started doing this leapfrog thing and I never understood why.

LANCE: Why do you say it's a racist thing?

MICHAEL: Because you have all of Manhattan and 'til it gets to a section where the skin color changes there's skip stop service, leapfrogging and so you want to get to work to you plan $x$ amount of time and you're watching trains just race by you. I've never heard the MTA's argument for doing such a thing... out of all of Manhattan you begin this skipping at this one particular section. It just strikes me as odd.

Likewise, the stories of neighborhood improvement being attributed to whites, whatever their veracity, may also serve as metaphors to the inequality of place that is still evident in urban America. If we consider the history of neighborhood change and development in urban America, one can easily point to policies that sound like conspiracies but were actually implemented. Many municipalities did for a short time try to use zoning to keep races separate. Until 1948, homeowners often used restrictive covenants to forbid sales to blacks. The federal government actually codified the practice of red lining, or refusing to insure mortgages in predominantly black neighborhoods. Urban renewal did disproportionately target black neighborhoods for demolition and the resultant displacement, so much so that it came to be known as Negro removal. Public housing was intentionally segregated and targeted to black neighborhoods. When such practices were outlawed, some cities simply stopped building public housing. And so on. When this historical record is taken into account, the notion that whites can make a few calls to "clean up 125th Street" or force stores to stock better produce might seem plausible to some.

Indeed if we look to the work of social scientists on trust, such cynicism as that expressed earlier in this chapter might even be expected. Social scientists seeking to explain the existence of trust typically employ a learning model view of trust. That is, people learn to trust to the extent that past experiences have provided a basis to assume trustworthiness (Hardin 2001). This experience does not necessarily have to be personal. A group's collective memory can supplement one's personal experiences when making decisions about whom to trust. *Collective memory* here refers to experiences of the group an individual identifies with that may be related across generations provided a basis to assume trustworthiness. This experience does not necessarily have to be personal. The learning model view of trust thus suggests the cynicism described earlier stems from the historical maltreatment of black neighborhoods. Years of discrimination and institutionalized racism have seared mistrust of whites and white institutions into the collective memory of blacks. Like any other situation where actors have proven themselves untrustworthy, cynicism will abound. A number of studies have found that trust is in short supply in black and inner-city communities (Campbell 1980; Demaris and Yang 1994; Lee 2002; Ross et al. 2001; Smith 2003). The cynicism described earlier in this chapter is therefore consistent with a learning model view of trust as well as studies of trust in the black community.

The point here is not to suggest that services have not improved because of whites. I have not attempted to validate these stories by checking alternative sources. But these stories should not simply be taken at face value. Stories about public housing being taken over by Columbia

University or Donald Trump are better viewed as apocryphal. Columbia University and Donald Trump are names that help flesh out the story of a plan to treat whites better and take over the neighborhood.

Rather than taking these narratives at face value, I argue for viewing them as representative of the cynicism that decades of unequal neighborhood treatment have wrought. The cynicism toward how outside forces treat the ghetto has long been prevalent in neighborhoods like Harlem. In his autobiographical account of life in Harlem, Claude Brown in *Manchild in the Promised Land* describes the ruminations of his friends and himself. "We'd laugh about how when the big snowstorms came. They'd have the snowplows out downtown as soon as it stopped, but they'd let it pile up for weeks in Harlem. If the sun didn't come out, it might have been there when April came around. Damn sending snowplows up there just for some niggers and people like that" (Brown 1965, p. 199).

Scholars have long pointed to a history of oppression that has left blacks relatively mistrustful, especially of whites (Campbell 1980; Demaris and Yang 1994). This mistrust translates into blacks being likely to believe that whites will behave in ways detrimental to themselves and other blacks. Against this backdrop of cynicism, the stories of malfeasance will gain currency. Stories that allude to whites or the powers that be plotting to take advantage of blacks or treating whites favorably are consistent with what is expected and thus readily believed. In contrast, stories that allude to equal and fair treatment, such as the notion that better stores are opening because of increased demand, or private capital recognizing the untapped potential of black neighborhoods are inconsistent with the history of unequal treatment that blacks have experienced. Consequently, this type of narrative is probably less likely to gain traction and become part of the way people make sense of the changes happening around them.

The cynicism expressed in the narratives quoted also provide additional insight into why gentrification is not always a welcome force, even among those not personally threatened by displacement. To the extent that gentrification and accompanying neighborhood improvements are for "them," this represents a slap in the face.

Here, the narratives presented suggest the improvements in the study neighborhoods are due mostly to the presence of whites. But these stories tend to ignore some of the other forces at work in Clinton Hill, Harlem, and other inner-city communities that may have also attributed to the changes they attested to. The narrative of whites equals better services, however, is perhaps more congruent with the history of urban inequality in the United States. Moreover, because whites are so visible in these communities, it is also a more obvious explanation than one that points to the black gentry. The notion that the presence of whites is somehow responsible for neighborhood improvements serves as a sort of ethno-sociology (Waters 1997), that is, how everyday people make sense of their world. When confronted with a phenomenon that is not entirely under-stood, ethnosociologies offer a reassuring way for people to make sense of their world. In a world where exogenous forces and the larger white community have acted to disadvantage predominantly black neighbor-hoods, such ethnosociologies should not be dismissed out of hand. Rather, they point to the way many residents of gentrifying neighbor-hoods make sense of their world.

The discussion suggests three types of explanations that dominated residents' thinking about how gentrification translates into an improving neighborhood. One school sees neighborhood upgrading to be the end re-sult of residents, indigenous or gentrifiers, exercising their power to create and demand a better neighborhood. This is a school of thought that, not surprisingly, seemed to be more prevalent among those who engaged in activities to improve the neighborhood themselves. A second, less com-monly offered viewpoint perceives these neighborhood improvements as coincidental or the result of market forces. A third perspective pointed to exogenous forces that favored whites and to a lesser extent the middle class in general in deciding where and when to dole out services to the com-munity. This last perspective is much more cynical about the process of gentrification.

Somewhat surprisingly, these perspectives did not break down along class lines. One might expect that homeowners or those with more edu-cation might be less cynical about gentrification. To some extent I an-ticipated these groups to view gentrification in a less conspiratorial way. As noted, however, some of the most cynical comments were made by those with Ivy League educations. In explaining the cynicism of many blacks toward white-dominated institutions, Turner (1993) also did not find class to be an important predictor. Because this is an interpretive inquiry, I do not attempt to correlate perceptions about gentrification with class background or other factors in a quantitative way. But the patterns I observed do allow me to speculate inductively about the sources and possible antidotes of the widespread cynicism I found. In particular, to policy makers and planners wishing to foster democracy in the process of developing and revitalizing communities, the cynicism expressed here should be troubling. It suggests that nearly four decades of citing the mantra of community in redevelopment efforts has not erased a cynical view toward the powers that be in many minority communities.

Yet these findings also suggest a ray of hope. Some of my conversations revealed a dogged determination to engage the forces of neighborhood change in ways that would be beneficial to the area. Although they did not naively believe in the benevolence of local government or commercial institutions, they were not so cynical as to believe that these actors only worked to benefit outsiders or could not be influenced to the advantage of the indigenous community. These are folks who could be viewed as the children of the community development movement and represent the possibility of empowerment for disadvantaged communities.

Thus, the way that residents of gentrifying neighborhoods interpret the changes occurring around them has important implications, which I will amplify and discuss in the concluding chapter when I discuss the planning and policy implications of this book.

# 5   Neighborhood Effects
in a Changing 'Hood

THE PREVIOUS CHAPTERS have illuminated the myriad ways that
residents of gentrifying neighborhoods perceive and interpret the changes
swirling about them. The discussion thus far suggests that gentrification
affects communities and people in ways more complex and as yet uncon-
sidered than portrayed in much of the literature. This chapter considers
the personal interactions between the gentry and older residents. How do
long-term residents perceive the relationships (or lack thereof) between
themselves and the gentry? Their perceptions are particularly germane to
ongoing debates over the mixed-income housing and neighborhood effects.
These narratives thus have important implications both for our thinking
about gentrification and for policies to address it, which I will consider
in the following chapter. But they also speak to ongoing debate on the
importance of neighborhood effects. In this chapter I analyze residents'
perceptions of interactions between the gentry and long-term residents
through the lens of the neighborhood effects thesis.

The neighborhood effects debate was brought to the fore by Wilson's
(1987) seminal work that suggested that the socioeconomic composition
of one's neighbors plays an important role in determining one's life
chances. More specifically, the presence of upwardly mobile, stable, and
middle-class households helps others become upwardly mobile and helps
stabilize community life. Wilson argued that it was the flight of the black
middle class from inner-city communities in the post–civil rights era that
left many ghetto neighborhoods bereft of stabilizing forces that would
enable them to withstand economic deprivation without descending into
chaos. As a result, the economic shocks of the 1970s transformed many
black communities from relatively poor but stable communities into
isolated ghettos rife with crime, despair, and family disintegration.

Although there has been considerable debate about some of the tenets
of Wilson's hypothesis (see, for example, Massey and Denton 1993 for an
alternative perspective on the putative flight of the black middle class),
the notion that concentrated poverty leads to deleterious consequences
has achieved close to a consensus in the policy and scholarly communities. Intuitive appeal, a strong theoretical foundation, a plethora of quasi-
experimental studies, and more recently, evidence from a true experiment

have coalesced to cement in our minds the notion that neighborhoods do matter—and that a mix of classes is preferable to high concentrations of poor people.

This consensual view has led to dramatic changes in affordable housing and community development policy. Deconcentrating the poor has become the mantra, and a number of initiatives aim to do just that. There has been a major shift in federal affordable housing policy away from public housing toward vouchers,[1] in part because vouchers are less likely to concentrate the assisted households in poor neighborhoods. Mobility programs, whereby tenants are given not only a voucher but counseling to encourage them to move to low-poverty neighborhoods, have been adopted in a number of cities (Turner 1998). Through the HOPE VI program, the Department of Housing and Urban Development (HUD) has encouraged demolishing and replacing public housing developments with mixed-income housing, leading some critics to characterize it as state-sponsored gentrification (Fitzgerald 2002). In some of the most devastated communities of New York City, homeownership has been sponsored as means of bringing in families that would help stabilize these communities (Von Hoffman 2003). Mixing classes—whether through dispersing the poor to middle-class neighborhoods or bringing the middle class to poorer neighborhoods—is, with few exceptions, the accepted wisdom among policy makers in the affordable housing community.

Gentrification by bringing more middle-class residents to relatively poor neighborhoods would appear to have the potential to contribute to these efforts to create mixed communities. The scholarly community, however, has been slow to seriously examine neighborhood effects in the context of gentrification. The voluminous literature on gentrification has tended to treat the residents as either an afterthought or as pawns to advance a larger argument against gentrification. More specifically, gentrification's boosters have tended to downplay or ignore the process's potentially adverse consequences and even while singing its praises, seldom described the benefits in terms of neighborhood effects. For example, in an early review of the literature on gentrification Sumka (1979, pp. 480–81) refers to "improving the housing stock, increasing the tax base, attracting jobs and commercial activity, and improving the quality of services" as the "hope" of gentrification. Another author listed increased home values, municipal services, access to mortgage capital, and improved goods and services, with nary a thought about any benefits

---

[1]Under the Section 8 voucher program, the tenant is responsible for locating an acceptable unit. The government pays the difference between the fair market rent and 30 percent of the tenant's income. The fair market rent is a level at which approximately 45 percent of rental units in a given market would rent below.

more affluent residents themselves might bring, and when thinking about the poor specifically did not list the potential for any benefit (Cicin-Sain 1980). A more recent review of the gentrification literature does acknowledge that poverty deconcentration has been offered as a putative benefit of gentrification (Atkinson 2002). But this review cites only one article that mentioned the issue of poverty deconcentration, and in the end the review concluded "there is no current empirical evidence to support this" and the belief that "incoming affluent residents benefit local residents ... remains as much a value judgment as a position based on research evidence" (p. 15).

Gentrification's detractors, not surprisingly, have typically not addressed the issue of neighborhood effects and how these effects might manifest themselves in light of gentrification. Low-income households were the losers in gentrification, the victims of displacement, and a loss of the community they called their home. In *The New Urban Frontier* Smith (1996) likens gentrification to policies that sought to remove the homeless from the public view and as part of a broader trend of "taking back" the city from the dark hordes. Others have defined gentrification as the displacement of the poor by more affluent residents (Marcuse 1986). Logan and Molotch (1987) describe renters as "victims" of the gentrification process.

As described earlier in this book and elsewhere, however, displacement is not an axiomatic outcome of gentrification. Some households are fortunate to have housing circumstances that immunize them from displacement pressures, and others may be upwardly mobile and able to stay in a gentrifying neighborhood. Whatever the reason, the process of neighborhood change in gentrifying neighborhoods is often gradual, driven more by succession or a change in who moves into the neighborhood than rapid and widespread displacement (Freeman 2005).

Moreover, although the potential and reality of gentrification harming residents by increasing housing costs and tearing asunder existing social relationships is certainly real, the neighborhood effects thesis suggests the possibility that gentrification could also benefit the disadvantaged under certain circumstances. This notion is for the most part based on the neighborhood effects thesis that posits that more affluent neighbors are beneficial.

If the gentrification literature focused too myopically on displacement, the poverty concentration literature failed to consider how neighborhood effects might manifest in the context of gentrification. The quasi-experimental studies typically failed to distinguish gentrifying neighborhoods from other types of neighborhoods. It may be that some of the neighborhoods included in analyses of neighborhood effects were gentrifying, but the authors made no indication as such. Rather the distinguishing feature would usually be a neighborhood's poverty rate or some other measure of socioeconomic status. These measures no doubt correlate with gentrifica-tion, but whether the putative benefits of more affluent neighbors ever took place in the context of gentrification in these quasi-experimental studies is unclear. A poor neighborhood that was gentrifying was treated the same as any other neighborhood. We therefore have no way of knowing if gentrifying neighborhoods were included in the quasi-experimental studies of neighborhood effects.

The experimental studies conducted as part of the Moving to Op-portunity (MTO) program provide perhaps the most convincing evidence of the veracity of the neighborhood effects thesis. Alas, the neighbor-hood context focused on here was again the poverty rate. Some of the neighborhoods' poor households were moving into and reaping benefits under MTO may have been gentrifying, but this was not a consideration of researchers who have written about MTO thus far (Goering and Feins 2003).

Intuitively, to the extent that the neighborhood effects that Wilson (1987) hypothesized about, numerous researchers attempted to measure, and policy makers take as a given are indeed real, it seems likely these effects would manifest themselves in the context of gentrification as well. Or would they? When Wilson spoke of the benefits of middle class neigh-bors he was speaking of a time when race was more important than class and hence middle class blacks were perforce part of the same community as their poorer brethren. Whatever the class differences, the commonality of race would have forced poor and middle class blacks alike to be part of the larger black community. Under gentrification, the middle class arrives from elsewhere and may even be of a different class or racial background. As such, they may not be viewed as part of the community even if they live in the neighborhood.

Consider also the contrast in contexts between the MTO program and gentrification when considering neighborhood effects. Under MTO a self-selected group of residents volunteer to move to a low-poverty neigh-borhood. These households might be especially amenable to changing their ways and taking advantage of their new environment, they have, after all, decided to uproot their families and move to a neighborhood where they perhaps know no one. Under gentrification someone wakes up to find new and perhaps unwanted types of people moving into their neighborhood. Are they just as likely to change as someone who voluntarily moves to a new neighborhood? Do the neighborhood effects manifested under MTO manifest themselves when the migration process is reversed?

The remainder of this chapter considers the likelihood of neighbor-hood effects in the context of gentrification, drawing on the interviews I conducted, my observations in these neighborhoods, and the theoretical foundations of the neighborhood effects thesis. I begin by opening up the black box of neighborhood effects, that is, the processes through which neighborhoods are thought to affect life chances. I focus on the socio-economic characteristics of a neighborhood's residents as gentrification directly affects this neighborhood attribute and much of the neighborhood effects literature focuses on this dimension of neighborhood life as well. I then consider the findings of my research and synthesize the two. In the end, I conclude that overlooking the nexus of gentrification and neighborhood effects is flawed and those who wish to understand the city would be better served by considering this nexus.

## THE BLACK BOX OF NEIGHBORHOOD EFFECTS

Drawing on the work of Jencks and Mayer (1990) and Gould Ellen and Turner (2003), I focus on the social aspects of neighborhoods to identify the mechanisms through which they operate to affect life chances. These social aspects include the myriad ways that neighbors influence one's behavior. Most common in the popular imagination is the notion of peer effects. Peer effects suggest that like follows like and individuals will be influenced by the behavior of their peers.

In addition to the notion of peer effects, social ties have the potential to influence the life chances as well. *Social ties refers to the relationships people have with one another and, in the province of neighborhood effects, the nature of those ties in the immediate neighborhood. These connections are sources of social satisfaction providing love, friendship, and a sense of belonging. But these ties can also play a role in facilitating upward mobility by providing sources of information about jobs, accessing services, and other important resources (Kleit 2001). Once again, better-off neighbors are an advantage in that they offer ties that are more "leverageable," that is, ties that foster upward mobility or offer access to important social and economic resources.*

The perspectives just described examine how an individual's behavior is shaped by the socioeconomic composition of his or her neighbors. The collective community, however, also has a voice in shaping the neighborhood milieu through collective action. A neighborhood is more than the sum of individuals but is an entity itself and can be thought of as more or less effective in achieving its objectives. This collective action can be directed internally, to set behavioral norms, for example, or externally, such as to secure adequate resources for the community. The setting of behavioral norms also encompasses the notion of role models in the common parlance. That is, individuals base their behavior on the behaviors of those they see setting examples. When this action is directed toward the behavior of local residents it is often referred to as collective socialization or efficacy (Jencks and Mayer 1990) but when directed externally referred to as collective efficacy exclusively (Sampson, Raudenbush, and Earls 1997). In both of these scenarios the socioeconomic composition of the neighbors is thought to matter.

As a collective entity, the neighborhood may be able to set norms of behavior for inhabitants and visitors to follow, protect its turf from threatening forces, and secure resources for the neighborhood. Neighborhoods with these capabilities are likely to be cohesive with consensual norms and neighbors who trust one another. Conversely, neighborhoods rife with mistrust and instability will be less capable of enforcing norms or securing resources for the neighborhood. Sampson et al. (1997) refer to this as collective efficacy and reasons that a poorer neighborhood has less of this trait because disadvantage breeds cynicism and instability and undermines cohesion. A legacy of mistreatment, the day-to-day struggle to survive, and the instability associated with poverty leads to a sort of crabs in a barrel syndrome, where residents are distrustful of their neighbors. Poorer neighborhoods are therefore less able to enforce norms against vandalism, crime, or unruly teens. Middle-class households might enhance a neighborhood's collective efficacy to the extent their putatively exemplary behavior helps set norms and because they are in a better position to secure outside resources.

Finally, more affluent neighbors might also be a benefit because of their indirect influence on institutions that serve the neighborhood. I refer to this as institutional resources and consider the role of the gentry in shaping this important component of neighborhood life as well.

The influence of peers, collective efficacy/socialization, or social networks probably seems plausible to most. But what does that have to do with poverty concentration or gentrification for that matter? For example, why should we assume that one's peers will be more troubled if they are poor as opposed to middle class? Indeed, much of the literature on poverty concentration fails to address this connection explicitly. The implicit assumption here is that poverty is highly correlated with social pathology. Individuals who are poor lack social skills, lead disorganized lives, and are more likely to abuse drugs. Is this assumption correct?

Certainly if one reads firsthand accounts of life among the poor, one does get the sense that drama is more prevalent (see Deparle 2004; Leblanc 2003; Anderson 1999, for example). Wilson (1996) makes the case that when employment opportunities disappear, everyday routines and even long-range plans become disrupted and take on a transient quality. The act of having to get up, go to work, and socialize with one's boss and co-workers serve as regimenting force that gives one's life a sense of stability. Lane (1986) makes the same argument in describing the decline of violence at the end of the nineteenth century in Philadelphia. Those who were incorporated into the industrialized workforce (white immigrants) saw their rates of interpersonal violence decline dramatically, whereas suicide rates increased. Working in the modern world served to internalize the aggression of newly industrialized workers. Those who were excluded from the industrialized economy (blacks) experienced no such decline in rates of interpersonal violence.

Thus, perhaps it is exposure to the jobless rather than the poor specifically that is detrimental to one's life chances. More research surely needs to specify which aspect of the neighborhood is important. But for the neighborhood effects thesis as it is often presented to have any cogency, one must assume that poorer folks bring with them a host of social problems. This is a problematic assumption. Nevertheless correlations between poverty and social problems in urban America are high enough that it is probably safe to say that one is usually better off with neighbors who are not impoverished.

But even if it is typically the case that one is typically better off with middle-class neighbors, that still raises the question of whether this truism is equally applicable to gentrifying neighborhoods. In turn I consider the mechanisms through which neighborhood effects likely operate—peer effects, collective socialization, social networks, collective efficacy, and institutional resources—in the context of the gentrifying neighborhoods of Clinton Hill and Harlem.

## Peer Effects

How likely is gentrification to result in peers that will lead to improved life chances? The gentry are likely to have higher incomes or at least more education and more upward mobility. But are they likely to become peers of the long-term residents of gentrifying neighborhoods? Will the gentry serve as peers to the residents of Harlem or Clinton Hill?

My conversations with residents of these areas suggest that spatial proximity does not necessarily equal social proximity, at least not of the type that would lead to peer influences. Although the folks I conversed with were well aware that a different type of person—gentry, if you will— was moving into the neighborhood, most people described their interactions with them as superficial at best. Consider the words of Ms. Tate and Tammi:

LANCE: Do you see in general how they [the gentry] interact with the rest of the community or—?

MS. TATE: Well, they don't. You know, they just whatever, might walk by, and, and, and the people that are moving in here are younger people. When I say younger, they might be in their late twenties, early thirties, in that range. Not much interaction at all. You know, you might see one "hi," walk by, that's it, but it's no real communication going on.

LANCE: So the people the people that you have noticed moving in that perhaps are not like, you know, those who grew up here, or, those who you say are moving in 'cause they think it's trendy or whatever, um, how do you and others get along, how much interaction do you think is there between them—?

TAMMI: None. No. I mean, it's just a place to live. Their lives are completely elsewhere but I'm sure, you know, when, when my friend moves into Harlem in our neighborhood on 146th, she's not gonna have anything to do with, you know, because, she's only here as a student, so, she's gonna go back to wherever she came from, you know, because she's from out-of-state, so she's gonna go back or, you know, like the people who actually stay there, it's just like come and go.

Anthony, introduced in chapter 3 as someone whose suburban upbringing and recent arrival in Clinton Hill might classify him as a gentrifier, shared the view of the more long-term residents, going on to elaborate about why there is so little interaction between the newcomers and longer term residents:

LANCE: All right, I'm going to ask you a few questions about the interaction between...I guess if you want to call them the gentrified and the longterm residents. How do you see—

ANTHONY: I don't think they're really interact much, uh, I guess that it is different cultural things. Like in that movie *Do the Right Thing* when like the white guy has the bag and a Boston Celtics T-shirt and he was biking and the people in the neighborhood felt like he was trying to take over, it's kind of, like there is lot of truth to that, you know, but it's, it's not just got the white, the upper class, it's a class thing, and it's, it's like, from different, they are like from different planets, you know. They just don't understand each other, they really have nothing to talk about.

These narratives are illustrative of the way many residents viewed interaction between the gentry and longer term residents. For the most part, these residents witnessed little in the way of interaction. Their own individual experiences mirrored the responses given here. Adrienne moved to Clinton Hill as an adult and thus has been living in the neighborhood for a little more than two decades. Over the years, she has developed a dense network of relationships in the neighborhood. She and her local friends often visit one another, celebrate family milestones together, and assist each other with day-to-day necessities like serving as an emergency babysitter. Adrienne noticed how gentrification was extending to her section of Clinton Hill and had this to say about her interactions with the newcomers into the neighborhood:

LANCE: But do you interact much with the new, newcomers?
ADRIENNE: I mean, I speak to everyone, on the elevator, hi, how are you doing, that's about, that's about it. Um, but I haven't forged any, um, relationships or anything like that.

Ms. James, described earlier as someone who lived in Clinton Hill for four decades and has always been active in the community, had this to say about interactions with the newer residents:

LANCE: Do you ever get to know some of the newcomers in the neighborhood, or—?
MS. JAMES: Yeah, you know, we don't know anything about them, if we had a block party I don't remember them being there, so I wouldn't know what they do. And you know, um, the blacks moving in are just as mysterious as the whites, they don't, they have a sense of community or connecting see I, because I've been here so long, I had made some connection with, with other people. You know my next door neighbor, I don't know who is neither. I just see them coming along, and they barely speak, and then I have one next to him, and you know she turned her head so that she won't have to speak.

As a lifelong community activist, Ms. James has her finger on the pulse of the neighborhood. She plays an integral role in organizing events, like the block party, that are designed to foster interaction among the residents. In her view, the newcomers, both white and black, are not making connections to the community. This of course is not a universal rule. As I will show, there were some instances of residents who could be classified as gentrifiers integrating themselves into the community. But even here, their interactions were merely instrumental, as I will discuss in more detail.

For the most part, the residents who had lived in the neighborhood for a while, who would not be considered gentrifiers, typically described the gentry as a people who were not interwoven into the social fabric of the community. The two groups were sharing residential space and were cordial, but it seems unlikely that the indigenous residents of the neighborhood would find themselves mimicking the behavior of their more affluent neighbors as the peer effects model would imply.

Peer effects suggest that people will mimic the behavior of those close to them because they value opinions of these people and the sanctions that they can provide. This is especially pertinent to adolescents who struggle with fitting in and finding their social niche in the world. One can easily imagine that in a neighborhood where many teens join gangs or drop out of high school, the pressure on a teenager to engage in these activities will be greater. Likewise, in a neighborhood where virtually all teens attend college, an adolescent may feel additional pressure to pursue a college degree. Although not as strong as with teens, peer effects may also apply to adults as well. Indeed, some of the participants in the MTO experiment who moved to low-poverty neighborhoods reported being motivated to find work because they didn't want to be the "only" ones not working (Popkin et al. 2002, p. 97). In sum, the greater the degree in which residents are engaged in activities leading to upward mobility, the greater the likelihood that peer effects will be positive.

The type of relationships that would generate these types of effects, however, would have to be fairly close. Furthermore, one would need to identify with the other person as someone who is like them, or by definition they would not be a peer. The gentrification process implies a higher-class group coming to supplant a lower-class group in a neighborhood. Because the gentry are of a different class, however, they make for unlikely peers and are therefore unlikely to influence the behavior of long-term residents of gentrifying neighborhoods. Moreover, peer effects are likely strongest among teenagers. But gentrification is typically spearheaded by young to middle-aged adults without children and certainly not teenagers. Typically, concerns about schools and the temptations of city life discourage those with teenage children from moving into gentrifying neighborhoods.

The quotes listed previously are illustrative of this. The gentry are identified as young adults, and although relationships between the gentry and other residents are generally cordial, neither group is likely to view the other as peers and the relationships between the two groups do not appear to be intimate enough for peer effects to manifest themselves. The following narrative is useful in highlighting both the importance of some intimacy for peer effects to manifest, and the unlikelihood of such effects taking place simply because of spatial proximity:

MARC: I saw my friend's sister go back to school. She was thirty and working and she would go at night. And anytime I would even mention going back, she wasn't pushy, but she would say "it's not too late." Then one day I see her comin' through the projects with her cap and gown. She got her degree then went to get a master's, now she's talkin' about a Ph.D. So that motivated me to go back. And once I went back some other people her brothers, I think 'cause I'm a dude they were more likely to follow me, they started going back. Matter of fact, I took one of them to the school to register.

LANCE: There's many colleges not too far from where you live, let me
ask you did seeing all of these students ever motivate you?

MARC: No.

LANCE: Why not?

MARC: They're strangers. I don't know them. Seeing them doesn't
mean anything to me.

Marc grew up and still resides in a public housing development not too
far from Columbia University. In recent years, Columbia's spatial presence in terms of where students live, eat, and shop has expanded and now
abuts the public housing development. It is not an uncommon sight to see
whites "walking through the projects when before they were scared they
would be mugged." But spatial proximity does not a community make. It
is those who one has some connection to who will likely exert peer influences for good or ill.

## Collective Efficacy/Socialization

The lack of social intimacy between the gentry and long-term residents
also casts a shadow over the likelihood that neighborhood behavior will
be influenced by collective socialization. For children and adolescents,
adults serve as role models whose behavior sets norms for youngsters to
follow. Moreover, adults acting as "old heads" provide wisdom and advice to youngsters in the neighborhood (Anderson 1999). For adults, one
would assume they have already been socialized. Nevertheless, the wider
community does play a role in setting behavioral norms and therefore still
shapes behavior to some degree. For example, many of us are familiar
with newcomers who are "socialized" into a neighborhood by being
advised about what type of lawn upkeep is acceptable or what types of
social gatherings are appropriate. Sometimes these norms are enforced
informally and sometimes through formal mechanisms such as neighborhood associations. It seems likely that the social standing of adults in
the neighborhood will affect the way people are collectively socialized
and norms are enforced.

For youths in a neighborhood where most adults have successfully
navigated the wider middle-class society, the socialization that takes place
will point to paths that lead one through school and into middle-class
careers. Conversely, in communities where the adults have been marginalized by the wider society, the only trailblazing adults can offer might
lead to dead-end jobs or "beating the system." In some cases, the youth,
sensing the marginalization of the adults, might decide to ignore their
advice, blazing their own paths. Anderson (1999) depicts this scenario in
an inner-city community in Philadelphia where the disappearance of jobs

deprived old heads of their status by diminishing their ability to connect young men to employment opportunities. Instead, many young men in this community sought out opportunities in the drug trade. Likewise for adults the types of norms they choose to follow will be influenced by who is living in that neighborhood. Indeed, in many neighborhoods with troubled households, there may be little agreement over what norms are acceptable, and more stable households may feel powerless to enforce the norms they deem appropriate (Anderson 1999).

This mechanism implies a certain degree of intimacy and perhaps most important mutual respect between the socializers and those being socialized. Many of the people I spoke with described their childhood neighborhoods as places where local adults would also enforce norms of community behavior. These were places where if one did something wrong, one would get a beating twice—once from the adult who witnessed the infraction and once from their parent when they got home. Nowadays, parents are very defensive about other adults disciplining their children, or so the story goes. This narrative is probably somewhat apocryphal, as I have heard versions of it in different places since I was a child some three decades ago. Nonetheless this story is a folkloric version of the collective socialization thesis.

Anderson's (1999) description of this process in an inner-city Philadelphia community entails old heads taking young adults under their wings and schooling them to the ways of the world. The older adult, perforce, must have an interest in his or her pupil, otherwise they would be less likely to want to invest the resources necessary to mentor someone. This would seem to be more likely when the mentor and pupil share some bond, a bond that suggests some similarity between them. Thus, in Anderson's formulation men mentored boys and women mentored girls, and both served as role models for those who could be perceived as younger versions of themselves.

The social distance between the gentry and indigenous residents renders unlikely that the socialization of the residents will change dramatically in the face of gentrification. But what of the broader concept of collective efficacy? To what extent will the gentry facilitate a neighborhood achieving "common goals" in the words of Sampson (1999)?

Here the picture is murky, foremost because whatever the effect gentrification has on mechanisms that strengthen or weaken collective efficacy, a first order assumption is that there are common goals. Although some goals are probably ubiquitous—like clean air—others are not. It is up to each neighborhood's residents to set and enforce norms. Where residents are relatively homogenous and in agreement on what those norms should be, it will be relatively easy to set and enforce norms. In contrast, a neighborhood where people have competing notions of what is acceptable will find it difficult to enforce norms. Indeed, these competing visions of what is acceptable can serve as a source of contention and undermine cohesion in a community. Tina, introduced in chapter 3 as a native and current resident of Clinton Hill, related how gentrification was disrupting some of her rituals because of what the gentry considered to be an acceptable use of public space:

LANCE: Yeah, what about Fort Greene Park? What's that like?

TINA: Oh, that, that park has changed a lot. Well, that park, now that's where you see a lot white people. They sit outside tanning in the summer and they walking their dogs. You can't barbecue in that park no more. That's the only thing I don't like about it.

LANCE: What happened, well, what happens if you barbecue?

TINA: I don't really don't know, 'cause we didn't try to this year, because my mother she was, but then she was traveling, so she didn't have time, but they said the smoke, them folks in the brownstones over there says the smoke bothers them. And that's, you know, the white people, complaining about the smoke and stuff, but they have a lotta stuff in that park in the summertime like jazz, concerts and stuff like that. That park has really changed a lot, though.

The dialogue shows how the uses of public spaces are contested. Whereas before, cooking out in the park was acceptable, newer residents have started to complain. Their complaints have led to a change in what is acceptable in the park. Those who enforce park regulations have apparently decided to take seriously the concerns of those residing in proximity to the park who do not like the smells and smoke associated with cooking out.

These conflicting norms were especially evident in my interviews in Clinton Hill. As described in chapter 2, many of the respondents lived in cooperative developments. These cooperatives have both renters who moved into the development before it went coop in the late 1980s, coop purchasers who bought when prices were in the low five figures, and more recent arrivals who purchased when prices were well into the six-figure range. As such, the mix of residents in the cooperative has led to clashes around what is acceptable and what is not. The following story related to me by James, introduced earlier as someone who moved into Clinton Hill in the late 1980s and is a member of the cooperative board, highlights this clash:

JAMES: It is somewhat of a concern because there are different standards. And trying to bring two or more types of groups to a small insular community is a challenge. So as an example everyone would presume that at ten or eleven o'clock everyone turns off their loud music and go to sleep and do whatever it is you need to do to go through the night quietly, there are some people who work on different schedules and have a different sense and many of those people who believe that it is okay to play music at eleven or twelve o'clock at night. I have been living here for a long time and we have a set of house rules that you have to not play loud or disturbing music after ten at night. So anybody looking to move in looks at those house rules and says this is wonderful. I know I can go to sleep. I know there will be urban noise but I know it won't be affecting me. And then they move in and they move next door to someone who has been living here twenty-five or thirty years and are used to having their stereo at a certain volume. And are used to having whatever lifestyle over a period of time. And then I get the calls: "What are you going to do about that? The house rules says you can't play your music loud after this." But how do you determine if the music is loud? I'm not in either apartment.

LANCE: So people have different expectations?

JAMES: Different expectations and different interpretations.

Gentrification mixes people from different socioeconomic strata and also mixes the differing norms and expectations associated with these respective stratum. In the example, these differences in expectations are contested through the coop board. Of course, coop conflicts are notorious across the city even among coops that are relatively homogenous class-wise. But the respondents here, perhaps recalling a time before the gentry started moving into their development and such complaints were not as common, clearly attribute some of the changes to newcomers of a different class or race.

Unlike public services, where long-term residents perhaps feel powerless to contest the new norms, the cooperative seems to be a place where long-term residents battle over the norms. For example, Tina was not so willing to abide by new norms proposed for a place closer to home. In the following conversation she describes those norms and related how she contested them.

TINA: They don't want the kids, in Clinton Hills, they don't even want their kids to play outside. That's how it has changed. They don't want the kids to ride their bike or scooter downstairs in the courtyard. They bawl.

LANCE: Before you used to be able to do that if you were a kid?

TINA: Yeah, well, we...had parties downstairs. We have birthday parties, bring out a little table...and we cooked. We can't do that now.

LANCE: You can't do that now? So why, why, why do you think that changed? I mean—

TINA: Because the people complain. People complain that, that's the bourgie [bourgeois] people.

LANCE: The bourgie people were complaining?

TINA: Yeah. They don't like kids. [Laughter]

LANCE: Oh, okay. So they don't have their own kids?

TINA: Some of them have kids, but some of them little kids is bourgie like the grown-ups. Little kids wanta come out and play and they don't let the kids come out and play.

LANCE: When did you notice that change starting to occur in terms of like the kids not being able to play downstairs and that sort of thing?

TINA: It happened when the different people started moving in the area.

LANCE: So how do you feel about that? Because you said like before you used to able to have parties, uh, downstairs and like, for example, you mentioned, and in the park you would be able to barbecue, but like, you said, some of the people that are moving in, they complain about those types of things. So how does that make you feel?

TINA: You have to understand that, you know, you have kids. Some people like to do things with their children. You know what I'm saying? They have to understand something. You can't take, uh, you don't want to go all the way to Prospect Park, carry a grill . . . and food all the way to Prospect Park, when you got a big park right there. Why, why you can't barbecue right there? You know what I'm saying? Why the kids can't come outside and play? Because you want peace and quiet, know. You want it to be, come on. The kids have to play. It's summer time. It'll get quiet in the winter 'cause they be upstairs. Summer time, you know, they school is out. It's time for them to enjoy they summer. Like that's, that's the only thing that I don't like, and when we have meetings I do speak up. They don't like me at the meetings. Our kids is allowed to play. We pay rent here, too. We should play, our kids should play outside, too. We pay rent just like everybody else. It's mostly the shareholders that's been complaining, the people that buys the apartments and this and that. When they have, they want to sit down when they come home from work and have peace and quiet. Close the door. Don't leave the door open. We still let our kids stay outside until it's ten o'clock. If it's real, real hot, eleven. Okay. Come on. We sit out there with them and we, you know, like "ssh." They just riding their bike.

Here Tina, a lifelong resident of Clinton Hill, clearly considers the new norms the gentry or "bourgie" folks are attempting to impose to be unrealistic. She contrasts what the bourgie newcomers are expecting with her childhood and thinks it is ridiculous. *Bourgie* is a short hand reference to the bourgeoisie, a term meant to denote those who put on airs, whose comportment is not that of down-to-earth or everyday people. Here she is willing to fight to preserve the norms she values and remains defiant despite the complaints of the bourgie people. So the bourgie folks, or gentry, are responsible for upsetting long-established norms that have been in place for decades.

The conflict over norms also informs several of the narratives over police harassment depicted in chapter 4. These narratives suggested that loitering on street corners was no longer acceptable now that the gentry and particularly whites were moving into the neighborhood. Regardless of whether these narratives reflect actual changes in police tactics due to gentrification, it seems certain that long-term residents would not view these changes in a beneficial light.

For indigenous residents of gentrifying neighborhoods to reap the benefits of neighborhood effects through collective socialization or efficacy, they would have to share common norms and mutual trust with the gentrifiers. Common norms are necessary so that a consensus might emerge over what type of behavior is acceptable. Trust is necessary so that residents would feel secure to enforce these norms without resort to outside institutions like the police. The narratives reported here suggest both are in short supply in the gentrifying neighborhoods of Clinton Hill and Harlem. As already noted, there were clashes over just what the acceptable norms were, undermining the ability of the neighborhood to enforce them. Moreover, many of the residents I spoke with felt the changes under way in the neighborhood were for the benefit of "them," a point elaborated on in chapter 4. These perceptions would hardly inspire feelings of trust and cohesiveness. Indeed, it is probably just as likely that gentrification serves to undermine cohesiveness and trust and therefore weakens the likelihood that the process of collective socialization will become stronger during gentrification. The perspective offered by Danielle, a resident of Harlem in her late thirties whose demographic characteristics makes her a part of the black gentry (black but with a graduate degree from an Ivy League institution, professional parents, and moved to Harlem five years ago), are instructive. Here she describes how she reacts to the harassment of some of her neighbors:

> I don't say anything. But I have not called the police on these cats across the street who harass me. But my impact has been nonimpact 'cause I don't want to mess with it, and I don't want to get hurt. I'm not trying to start conversations. Now if I see somebody out, um, taking his garbage out or, um, shoveling snow or something, that's different, but, um, just folks who don't seem to be attached to anything necessarily, sort of walking up and down or just standing around, it's not gonna happen.

This interviewee speaks directly to the street disorder that social scientists refer to when speaking of collective socialization or collective efficacy. In describing the importance of trust Sampson et al. (1997, p. 918) describe how collective efficacy manifests itself in "a willingness to intervene to prevent acts such as truancy and street corner hanging by teenage peer groups." Harassment of female pedestrians would surely be an example of the type of disorder that would be prevented in a neighborhood with a strong sense of collective efficacy. In this case, although gentrification has brought someone with a more privileged background into the neighborhood, this does not translate into the type of informal social control that would preclude this type of street disorder. This person only feels comfortable interacting with those who signify by their actions that they are safe—people engaged in everyday activities like shoveling snow. Those engaged in suspect activities like loitering or harassing female pedestrians, the very people presumably in need of collective socialization, are left alone by the gentry.

Contrast this woman's response to the possibility of confronting individuals engaged in disorderly acts with that of Ms. Jones, who grew up in the nearby Fort Greene public housing development and has been living in Clinton Hill for thirty-five years, or Marc, a native of Harlem in his late thirties.

LANCE: Well how active are you in the, um, tenant organization here? Are you active in that?

MS. JONES: Well, well, I try. I'm not basically, they try to keep me to try to keep the teenagers in line.

LANCE: Okay. You're in charge to keep the teenagers in line?

MS. JONES: I took that upon myself, because as I said, my children was born and raised right here in this apartment. This was it, you know. So I, most of the kids are my children's age. Most of them call me aunt Jenny, or ma or whatever and if I see them doing something wrong, I step to them. "Look, this is not gonna work." One time they was trying to hang in the lobby. Uh uh. No, no, no, no. We're not gonna have that.

LANCE: The teenagers were hanging out in the lobby?

MS. JONES: Um hum, they wanted to try, they wanted, they tried to but we kept, kept 'em moving and like, there's teen, there's young adults that smoke their little reefer and whatever, whatever and they had a habit, they was trying to sit back there on the benches. No. When you come out there, sit down, they're doing some, we sit down there, they get up and leave. We could never let them, our kids here, these are little kids. They're not going to be smelling this weed. Now, we can't make you stop, but we can make you leave. You have to, you have to go. We're not going to bring our kids out here, they smelling this reefer. So we kind of nipped that in the bud. You know, but, um, I ain't saying this was a perfect, but we work hard to try to keep it whichever way. I tell you that, if I see something going wrong, I, I speak on it. I'm not afraid to speak on it. So I'll say, well you know you all come on now, come on now. Don't even go there. Let's get to stepping. You know, you can't be hanging in these hallways. People come home from work, they tired. You know, you all have to get out. You have to go. I can't make you all go, I can make you leave this hallway.

You know, I said, you need to, "okay, ma, okay, Ms. J." or something like that and they go ahead about their business. Because it's the way you present yourself to them. You're going to get the so and so out, yack, yack, yack, yack, you know. Then they ain't gonna, they're not gonna respect me. But I respect them and they respect me in turn, you know. Like if they need for anything or, you know, of course that, just as I say these are my children's friends. My daughters is grown, but these are their friends. They grew up with them. And I mean, these kids, and me and them parents used to be close. So you know, like sitting in the park with our little kids and stuff. And so it's like, I, they, they all grew up together.

MARC: I used smoke crack, I smoked angel dust, I used to sniff cocaine, I was an alcoholic. I used to fight a lot, I'm talkin' about hand-to-hand combat right in the streets. I was arrested. But I've changed. But a lot of people haven't changed. . . . The neighborhood has changed so much. But there's still killings going on in these projects. People have gotten killed. Because I'm a Christian today, I'm like stay away from the murder. I never killed nobody and I never even owned a gun, but I had all those cats around me that scrambled and were notorious thugs. Now that I'm a Christian, I'm telling these same cats to "put that gun away. As a matter of fact you're not even supposed to own that cuz you settin' yourself to go to jail the rest of your life. Just let it go, give it up kid. . . . Who wants to be on the run for the rest of they life? Why you want to be on drugs and killing for some little hot money that's gonna evaporate with the speed?" So now I try to be a light, a shining light for everyone. So now I want to open up some kind of neighborhood center, you know day care, the after-school program, a drug program for addicts or even the old lady who can't clean her house. And all this came from one day coming out the building and seeing this kid I knew when he was in his mother's stomach and he was in front of the building selling drugs. And I'm trying to tell him to stop,

but I need something to offer him, a job to put money in his pocket
so he don't have to go back to the scramblin'.

The individuals in the narratives above have longtime ties to the neighborhood and to those engaged in disorderly or even criminal behavior.
Ms. Jones knew these teens since they were kids. Moreover, although she
would chastise them when they did wrong, she would also help them if
they "need for anything." The other narrative illustrates how Marc, an
individual who lived on the edge of the thug life, getting high and hanging
out with criminals, now tries to show them the error of their ways. Marc
also tries to counsel youngsters in the community to walk a straight line.
These two individuals differ from the woman who feared approaching
her harassers in that they have long-standing ties to the community, know
the perpetrators of disorder personally, and because of these ties have
their respect as well. Presumably, the perpetrators respect them because
they can be sure that even though they are being chastised, the chastisers
have their best interests at heart. In contrast, the woman who recently
moved to the neighborhood would probably be seen more as an interloper
and would unlikely have the social connectedness to informally monitor
their behavior.

The narrative that follows is just such an example of how someone
who is viewed as an outsider might be received by those engaged in
disorderly acts and how this perception can translate into conflict. Jennifer grew up in a public housing development in Queens and attended a
few years of college after high school. She purchased a city-owned coop in
Clinton Hill at a subsidized rate. As such, she does not fit the stereotypical
view of a gentrifier. Nonetheless, at least some residents view her as an
outsider despite being black.

LANCE: Do you get a sense of how the long-term residents feel about the
    changes under way in the neighborhood?
JENNIFER: I think there's resentment. There's resentment. I had an in-
    cident when I first moved into my building. Like I said my building
    was abandoned so people were accustomed to hangin' out on the
    corner, using the bathroom in the doorway. There was a man who
    drove a tractor trailer and he parked it right outside my window.
    And it had a refrigerator in it. And it was loud, and it was summer,
    so I didn't want to keep my window closed. So I went downstairs
    and asked him, you know asked him very politely "can you turn off
    the truck?" And he was belligerent. He was like "you people move
    in here think you could do this and do that." And there was some
    street woman who was with him, she was like, it was weird because
    clearly I'm black, and she's like "these white people moving in
    here, they want to take over the neighborhood, and they think they

better than us." And I'm like is she crazy? Is she out of her mind?
And she kept going on about "white people." So I was like if you're
not gonna turn it off, I'm gonna call the cops. And his reaction was,
"Bitch, you call the cops and see what happens." So I went right
to the phone booth and call 911. So the cops came, but this woman
kept threatening me. And for a while afterwards, she worked in
the liquor store across street, she would call me out "there goes
that bitch." I just ignored her.

Although it is humorous that Jennifer, who is clearly black, would be
referred to as white, this labeling her as white can also be interpreted as
shorthand for her outsider status. Gentrification and more upwardly mobile people moving people moving into a neighborhood and trying to
dictate new norms has come to be associated with whites in the minds of
some, so someone can use "white" as a shorthand for gentrifiers. Perhaps
lacking the vocabulary to identify a black gentrifier, "white" becomes a
quick way of identifying such a person. In this context, what it signals is
outsider status. This is someone who is moving into the neighborhood
and trying to take over as indicated by her trying to enforce new norms.
Ironically, Jennifer's background is not congruent with the profile of a
stereotypical gentrifier, as she is a single parent who grew up in public
housing and did not graduate from college. She has, however, achieved a
modicum of success, being able to purchase a cooperative apartment in
Clinton Hill, and as such is lumped in with the rest of the gentry.

What these examples suggest is that informal social control as a manifestation of collective socialization or efficacy is more likely when the
enforcers are known and viewed as part of the community. As Sampson,
Raudenbush, and Earls (1997, p. 919) write: "At the neighborhood level,
however, the willingness of local residents to intervene for the common
good depends on large part on conditions of mutual trust and solidarity
among neighbors."

The gentry, although perhaps better educated, more affluent, and os-
tensibly better role models, would seem to lack the social intimacy necessary to influence behavior through informal social control. Indeed, their
attempts to do so are likely to breed resentment and spur conflict.

Although gentrification seems an unlikely candidate for strengthening
the mechanisms of informal social control, there may be other outcomes
whereby the process can strengthen collective action. More specifically,
when the target is internal to the neighborhood or there is no consensus
over what the objective should be, such as residents hanging out or deciding on community norms, gentrification may serve to exacerbate existing divisions and actually weaken community cohesion and efficacy. In
contrast, when target of collective action is external to the neighborhood

and/or there is a consensus about the objective, gentrification might indeed strengthen the collective efficacy of a neighborhood and enable it to demand and receive better services and amenities. As noted in chapters 3 and 4, many residents do indeed believe that the gentry (especially whites) are able to demand and receive better services and amenities. Although some saw this as the result of preferential treatment that the gentry receive, others attributed it to the savvy of the gentry to know how to get better services. Jennifer provided just such an example.

LANCE: What about in terms of the schools? Have they been changing recently?

JENNIFER: To give you an example of how it's changing, there's a group called Friends of PS 11, which is a group of parents whose children are not of school age yet who decided to do some fundraising for the school. So that when their children move to the school they have everything they need. My daughter started in the school in the fourth grade. They didn't have a library. They were able to get $60,000 for a science lab. I was on the PTA on the fundraising committee and I was having a hard time dealing with the older parents, the ones that were here before.

The narrative is an example of neighborhood residents collectively raising resources for the benefit of the community. Parents with professional backgrounds and perhaps fundraising experience might be more adept at fundraising of the type described. In this way, gentrification, by introducing more affluent and perhaps more politically savvy residents to a neighborhood, could increase the collective efficacy of the neighborhood to achieve objectives around which there is a consensus and do not necessarily require the gentry and nongentry to work closely together. In this case, all of the children in the school will benefit, even those whose parents are not part of the gentry. In the case of collective efficacy as it pertains to external threat or objects around which a consensus can easily emerge, such as improvements for a school, the putative benefits of middle-class neighbors may indeed manifest themselves in the context of gentrification.

In sum, the relationship between gentrification and collective efficacy is likely to vary and be fluid depending on the goal in question. Where the gentry and indigenous residents share common goals, the gentry may be a help. Where the goals differ, they will be a hindrance.

It would seem in general that relations between the gentry and indigenous residents are not particularly close. To some degree it is not surprising that these ties are not particularly tight. With increasing modernization we are no longer bound to our immediate environs to establish relationships. The auto, rail, plane, phone, and Internet all make it easier to establish and maintain relations with people who do not live proximate to us. Furthermore, increasing modernization leads to increased specialization, and with that comes the potential for establishing ties through school or work and outside of the neighborhood. Communities of interest have come to supplant communities of place (Wellman 1979). Nevertheless, even the infrequent social interactions between the gentry and indigenous residents can be important, as shown next.

## Social Ties

Social ties are another mechanism through which having more affluent neighbors might be an advantage. More specifically, more affluent neighbors might be advantageous for a particular type of social ties. Briggs (1998) distinguishes between two types of social ties, or what he calls social capital. One type of ties refers to those that provide support, or help cope with day-to-day life. These are ties of the type that one might use for a small loan until payday, to watch the kids, and to confide in. We all make of use of such ties, but there some evidence to suggest that the poor are especially reliant on them to substitute for goods and services that the more fortunate among us typically buy. In *American Dream*, journalist Jason Deparle (2004) describes how three women on welfare relied on each other to provide temporary housing to each other's families and supervision for each other children's in addition to emotional support and how this support was necessary for them to survive.

For getting ahead or becoming upwardly mobile, however, these ties were of limited use. To be sure, the women shared with each other information about the superiority of welfare benefits in Milwaukee vis-à-vis Chicago and job information, such as opportunities as nursing assistants. But while gaining access to higher welfare benefits or a job as a nursing assistant did improve their lives, these improvements were marginal at best and did not put them on a secure trajectory out of poverty. Instead these ties helped them get by but not get ahead. Because the women were themselves poor with limited access to resources, knowing them did not lead to upward mobility.

The second type of ties Briggs describes does just that—help people get ahead. These are ties that can lead not only to a job but a good job, or ties that would help one navigate the wider middle-class world in a way that significantly affects one's life chances. These are where more affluent neighbors are presumably beneficial. Whereas a poor neighbor might provide information on how to qualify for housing assistance or obtain a job at a fast-food outlet, a middle-class neighbor might be able to advise a youth on how to prepare and apply to college or for a stable job with room for upward mobility. Moreover, although some might assume that the notion of social ties implies intimate contacts of the type that I argued were unlikely between the gentry and others, what social scientists refer to as *weak* ties are of import as well (Granovetter 1973). Neighbors and other casual acquaintances are examples of this type. Thus, it would not be necessary for someone to develop intimate relationships with their neighbors; ties of a more casual type will suffice to bring potential benefits. The neighborhood effects thesis therefore suggests that more affluent neighbors might lead to ties that are more leverageable, that is, ties that can lead to upward mobility.

How likely is gentrification to lead to these types of ties? As we saw with the case of peer effects and collective socialization, there is reason to be cautious about expecting neighborhood effects to manifest themselves in the context of gentrification. Relationships between the gentry and indigenous residents appear too fleeting. Is there reason to be cautious when thinking about social ties in the context of gentrification?

Gentrification certainly brings individuals with more leverageable connections into spatial proximity with indigenous residents. Moreover, the type of relationships necessary for leverageable social ties to be beneficial—weak ones—certainly seem plausible in the context of gentrification.

Indeed, my research in Clinton Hill and Harlem did reveal instances where individuals who might be considered part of the gentry played roles that were beneficial to indigenous residents. We were first introduced to Barbara in chapter 3 as she related her satisfaction in seeing the value of her home rise. With her suburban upbringing, degree from an Ivy League university, and current enrollment in graduate school, Barbara fits the profile of a pioneer, that is, a middle-class person who serves in the vanguard of gentrification. The neighborhood effects thesis suggests that someone like this living in a neighborhood like Harlem might serve as a role model to others in the community and could potentially serve as a bridge to the wider middle-class world. Below are snippets of some her interactions with the Harlem community that shed some light on these notions.

LANCE: I'll ask you about is community organizations or churches, or religious institutions, have you noticed—I don't know if you are involved or active with them, but have you noticed any changes in those since you've been there?

BARBARA: Well my sorority did a project at Frederick Douglass Academy [a local high school], and we worked with high school girls. We did a project on Saturdays. We worked with the girls. We took them on trips. We had workshops and we mentored them. And a lot of them started coming out. Maybe the first time we had like ten, fifteen. After a while we had like sixty girls coming out. And the principal was very thankful. He said, "Because you do me a favor by being there and having the kids come in to hang out there," because he said that statistics show that between those hours more kids get arrested on a Saturday—because the cops are looking for overtime. And so any little thing can get them. And I thought that was a scary thought, you know. So those type of projects go on unnoticed. You know, we never got an award or a thank you for doing these kind of things.

Barbara also described the process by which her building was converted from a rental to a cooperative. In New York City there are regulations governing this process that are designed to prevent preconversion residents from being displaced. According to Barbara, the landlord was deviating from these guidelines in a way that was disadvantageous to the tenants.

> Like, the owners barely advertised to the tenants that that they could purchase a coop. So me and a few owners at the time said, "You need to advertise this place. You need to put a sign up that says it's a coop, in case anybody is interested in buying." There was a time I became very adamant. I was very confrontational with the managing agency who was supposed to be taking these concerns back to the sponsor. Then I found out that the owner of the building has another coop on the Upper West Side. There he was following the rules to a T. And he wasn't getting away with any of the things there. I just found this out, and I went to the state office building and I got lots of information. And I threatened to take him to court and things like that. And they were becoming concerned because they were like, "Uh-oh, she's starting to do her research." And I asked everybody [in the building] to meet in. And I said, "We have to figure out a way to get these apartments. And maybe if we all come together and we ask to purchase, he'll give you a break, because twenty-five percent down is too much. But as a group, collectively, you can go and say to him, 'You know what? We've been here in this building.'"

These examples are instructive in illuminating how even weak ties between the gentry and indigenous residents can nonetheless have important effects. In this case Barbara served as a mentor in a formal capacity through her sorority at a local high school. Her proximity to a local high school no doubt played a role in her getting involved as a mentor, as she frequently mentioned her concern about and desire to assist the people in her community. Certainly her residence in a building with other residents put them in a situation of mutual interest. Her knowing where to turn to obtain information about tenant's rights under a coop conversion as well as her savvy negotiating with the landlord proved to be a valuable resource to her neighbors.

If her mentoring helped persuade a teen to select a college or choose a career or even avoid getting arrested as the principal suggested, her ties to these youths may indeed have helped them get ahead. Choosing a college or a career can be bewildering to any teen; for one who does not personally know adults who have tread in these paths before, the choices may seem not only bewildering but are probably truncated as well. In this way, her mentoring can make a real difference to some of the residents in the community. Likewise, by informing her neighbors about their rights as tenants and about opportunities to become homeowners, her presence in the neighborhood could make a real difference to at least some of the residents in the community.

From the perspective of some her neighbors, coming into contact with Barbara was potentially very important. Nonetheless, those neighbors who might have benefited from her presence (either through being mentored or being informed of opportunities to become homeowners) did not develop intimate, long-lasting relationships with her. Indeed, when asked to describe her relationships with her neighbors she used the common "hi and bye" refrain described earlier in this chapter. Despite the fleeting nature of these relationships, they still had the potential to connect these residents to important resources.

Barbara's story raises the question of how common are these types of casual but potentially leverageable social ties? To be sure, Barbara is exceptional—most people do not participate in mentoring programs or organize their neighbors. Moreover, active people like this are present in all classes. Nevertheless, Barbara is better situated to navigate the wider middle-class world and provide entry to someone attempting to break into that world. To the extent that gentrification brings into the neighborhood more individuals with access and savvy like her, there is the potential for indigenous residents to benefit.

Casual contact between the gentry and indigenous residents would seem more likely than the type of intimate relationships necessary for collective socialization or peer effects to manifest. But these casual relationships may indeed be important as Barbara's story and the example to follow attests.

Anthony was introduced earlier as a college-educated professional who moved to Clinton Hill four years ago and who grew up in suburban Maryland. As an armchair sociologist, he describes the potential benefits exposure to the gentry could bring to the indigenous residents of his neighborhood:

LANCE: Anything else, um, I guess as far as the neighborhood changing that I haven't touched upon, that, um—

ANTHONY: Not really, and I think it's a general positive because it's maintaining its racial diversity and like I said it's safer, above anything it's safe, the safeness. And I think that there's a certain, I think there's a certain male black crisis. But I think it's good because now you're seeing all types of black folks. You've got your artsy black person in Clinton Hill now, you know the job-like person or whatever it is, and you've got your gay couples, you got your, your suited black person out there, you've got the guys with the baggy pants, whatever, but that shouldn't be all you'll see. 'Cause the media, that's how they portray us in the media, they give you one version and, and you see it on TV, then that's all you see, well that must be all there is. Now you see the dad with the kid, that's a big strong message that these kids never see. On the downside there is some shadiness going on in terms of people trying to raise rent and get people kicked out and stuff, but I think there is a general positive to the people that can stay. But I talk to a lot of black kids from housing projects, lots of kids that never left their block, never even been to Manhattan, you know, never left the Bronx, never left Bed-Stuy, never left East New York, and like well what's out there, they don't really even know. I mean they think the whole world is like what they've seen and the males that they see aren't necessarily the best role models I don't think. And even if you see a white man walking around doing a certain thing, you know, may be he doesn't look just like you, but he's still a man doing something, that's still more positive than not seeing anything at all. So, I think that plays itself out as like a certain positive, I hope some of the kids can come up. Like, for instance, I make it a point to wear, not right now, to wear like suits or like khakis and stuff, not because I'm, I want to be your European, not because I want to simulate, just because I want people to see something different. So, I think that's the biggest positive of gentrification and it's definitely like that in Clinton Hill. And, I'm not saying you have to be white or you've got to simulate to European ways or American ways, but so at least you know, you can understand, kind of how society works in that, you can, you can have good health care, you can have good food, or you can have good services or like, the police is like another thing, too. But maybe the police is there to serve you, you know. A lot of people are just really scared of the police or they hate the police or all these things, its all stereotypical, I'm not saying the police are the best in New York, you know a lot of them probably are racists, but you know, you are paying taxes and they serve you, you know, and so instead of just being scared of the police, you're saying, a lot of people don't want us calling the police when we see things going wrong in the neighborhood, right, but we have a right to call just like everyone else. So, people need to see that you control the

police, they don't control you, you know, so like you demand
service in the neighborhood and no you're not going to harass our
kids and like, you've got to control the police, you can't just not call
them in and but, that people wreak havoc in your neighborhood
because you don't want the police to come in.

Anthony articulates in layman's terms the notion that weak social ties
can influence the indigenous residents of gentrifying neighborhoods. His
theory that the youths of Clinton Hill will be influenced by seeing him
and other blacks walking around in suits is speculation and dubious for
the reasons described. Without knowing what one does to become a suit,
Anthony's mere presence seems unlikely to significantly alter life chances.

Anthony's comments about the police, however, are illustrative of the
notion that the gentry can present an alternative way of thinking to indigenous residents. The longtime residents' fears of the police are probably
well founded. Nevertheless, Anthony's reasoning that the police should
be viewed as servants of the community rather than an occupying force
would seem more likely to result in better police protection in the long run.
In the larger middle-class world, the notion that the police work for the
community is generally accepted, and the police generally act accordingly.
In the 'hood, the police behave as an occupying army and are treated that
way. But holding the police accountable as servants of the community,
rather than ignoring them as appeared to be the inclination of many of the
indigenous residents probably holds more promise for getting better police
protection. This is not to deny that getting better police protection or any
other public service, especially in disadvantaged communities, is an uphill
battle. But if Anthony's perspective on how to view the police does rub off
on some of his neighbors, they may be more likely to demand and receive
better police protection. In this way, the presence of Anthony, who as
a gentrifier and a catalyst for demanding and receiving better services,
could be beneficial to the indigenous residents. Moreover, better services,
whatever their origin, are something that certainly benefit indigenous
residents.

## Institutional Resources

Anthony's narrative also brings into focus another potential mechanism
through which having more affluent neighbors may be beneficial—their
impact on institutional resources. As noted before, I use *institutional
resources* to refer to those institutions that provide services and amenities
to a neighborhood. These institutions might be externally based, such as
in the case of the chain stores, police, or public schools; draw their resources from within the community as in the case of community-based

organizations like the development corporations; or be some combination of both, as in the case of schools. The neighborhood effects thesis posits that relative to poorer residents, the middle class will bring more institutional resources to the neighborhood for the following reasons: (1) The middle class will be better positioned to create and support community-based organizations. Indeed, when Wilson (1987, p. 56) first wrote about "concentration effects" he described how "economically and stable and secure families" would keep churches, schools, stores, and recreational facilities and other institutions viable even during times of economic deprivation. He reasoned that it was the absence of these families during trying times that would cause these institutions to wither. (2) Because of their greater purchasing power, middle-class residents will be more attractive to commerce and hence stores will follow. (3) More affluent residents, perhaps because of being better connected to the wider society and/or their knowledge of how to manipulate bureaucracy, are able to command better resources for the community. By bringing such middle-class residents to the neighborhood, gentrification would be expected to impact the institutional resources present there. What did my research reveal regarding this thesis?

My conversations with neighborhood residents and observations all strongly suggest that the institutional resources in the form of better amenities and services were improving. Indeed much of chapters 4 and 5 were devoted to describing residents' perceptions of and reactions to these improvements, so I do not reiterate that here. What is less clear, based on my research, is the role the gentry are playing in this improvement. Many of the residents attributed the improvements to the powers that be favoring the gentry and providing them with preferential treatment. Others attributed the changes to the squeaky wheel syndrome—that is, the gentry were more likely to demand and consequently receive better amenities and services. And as was mentioned earlier, some respondents were eager to take credit for the improvements themselves, pointing to their efforts through community-based organizations. As I described in chapter 2, a number of community-based organizations were active in both Clinton Hill and Harlem both before and contemporaneously with the onset of gentrification. Some of their actions, such as building housing and improving storefronts were undeniably having an impact that all could see. In addition, as I noted in several places earlier in this chapter, the gentry sometimes became active in existing institutions, such as the local public school where parents began raising money for supplies or the example where Michael advocated for a new way of dealing with the police. Thus there are several competing and not necessarily exclusive explanations about the role of institutions and how they interacted with the process of gentrification to create better neighborhood conditions.

Given that the research presented in this book did not focus on the evolution of community-based organizations, only how they were perceived by residents, definitively ruling out specific explanations would be premature. It is fair to conclude, however, that the presence of the gentry did attract more commerce to these neighborhoods and that in at least some instances changed the dynamics of institutions serving the neighborhood. Barbara's efforts to organize a coop, Jennifer's experience in the local school where parents raised money, and Michael's attempts to change how his coop board dealt with the police are all such examples. In these instances, gentrification introduced individuals with different outlooks and resources that influenced the type of services residents received and their access to these services.

Thus one could argue that gentrification both strengthened internally based organizations, by bringing people with diverse backgrounds and talents into some groups and changed the way externally based institutions interacted with neighborhood, encouraging these latter institutions to provide more and better services. Whether the absence of the gentry would cause the internally based institutions to wither as Wilson implies is not clear. When I discussed local community-based organizations with residents these organizations were typically not described in a way that suggested dramatic changes were afoot as a result of gentrification. Thus I have no evidence that gentrification was leading to a widespread increase in community-based organizations that served the neighborhood. Indeed, there were examples of organizations whose raison d'être was to combat gentrification or the ills associated with it like the West Harlem Tenants Coalition and Harlem Operation Take Back.

The proliferation and maturation of the community development movement should also give one pause before expecting gentrification to substantially increase the number or visibility of indigenous community-based institutions. By the beginning of the twenty-first century when the research that informs this book commenced, an infrastructure of foundations, intermediaries, informal networks, and professional organizations had developed to support local organizations across urban America, and this infrastructure was especially strong in cities like New York with a long tradition of community organizing. It would therefore be surprising if gentrification greatly enriched the community institutions already in place in these neighborhoods. The gentry probably diversified many of these institutions to be sure, but beyond that one should be cautious before inferring much of the changes in amenities and services to them.

The role the gentry seem to have played is not one of creating or supplanting existing institutions. Rather it is one of augmenting these institutions. The narratives cited earlier in this chapter when gentrifiers volunteered at schools, raised funds, or suggested a different way of engaging the police are examples of such. The presence of the gentry could then lead to better services and amenities perhaps because the powers that be are more sympathetic to their needs. It is also perhaps because the gentry are more savvy about demanding better services, as in the story Anthony told about demanding better police service. It could be the gentry have the resources to contribute to improving some services themselves as the story Jennifer related about the local schools earlier in this chapter would seem to suggest. In the case of stores, it could also be that proprietors are attracted to the purchasing power of the gentry and open stores that might be of use to indigenous residents as well. Whatever the mechanism, it seems clear that many residents perceived the arrival of the gentry to be linked to improvements in services and amenities.

Although I would argue that gentrification has the potential to benefit indigenous residents through improving the institutional resources available to them, I would also advise caution in applying this interpretation to different contexts. The narratives I presented in earlier chapters suggested most people were appreciative of the improvements in amenities and services. It is easy to imagine, however, that certain services, such as those for the indigent or substance abusers, might decline with gentrification either because the gentry don't want these services around, the services providers cannot afford to stay, or the service provider's clientele base is shrinking. People making use of these services might associate gentrification with a decrease in amenities and services. People fitting this profile were not represented in my conversations (at least no one was obviously a substance abuser), so I cannot rule out the possibility that some residents already hold this sentiment. It should also be kept in mind that Harlem and the section of Clinton Hill that was the subject of this study suffered from a dearth of services and amenities that would be available in most middle-class neighborhoods. Whether residents of a poor or working-class neighborhood that nonetheless had ample services and amenities, such is common in many immigrant communities, would feel as positively about this aspect of gentrification is open to debate.

## Neighborhood Effects in Context

The concentration of poverty thesis put forth by Wilson (1987) has led to renewed interest in the importance of neighborhoods in determining life chances. Scholars have used Wilson's arguments to conceptualize how neighborhoods might matter to the residents within them. This chapter examines the theory of neighborhood effects in the context of gentrification, a context that has been for the most part overlooked but one that is likely to become increasingly important in the future as the forces leading to gentrification spread across more and more central city neighborhoods (Wyly and Hammel 1999).

The narratives presented in this book suggest that neighborhoods do indeed matter. Neighbors higher up on the socioeconomic ladder bring changes to a neighborhood that can benefit other residents as well. For planners and policy makers using the neighborhood effects thesis to inform their work, however, this conclusion should be interpreted with a heaping of caution and more than dash of nuance. Caution is warranted because although there may be benefits to having the gentry as neighbors, there are costs as well. These costs manifest themselves in clashes over neighborhood norms that were described in chapter 4 and earlier in this chapter. Increased police harassment is an example of what might be beneficial to some being a cost to others. Although some might appreciate the police cracking down on quality of life infractions, others (particularly young black and Latino men) will bear the brunt of often unwarranted increased police surveillance. Costs like these are real and must be placed on the other side of the ledger when considering the benefits of neighborhood effects that accrue due to gentrification.

Nuance is required because an understanding of how neighborhood effects operate can inform our expectations of what the likely impacts of having more affluent neighbors will be. In the common parlance, neighborhood effects have come to be interpreted as role modeling, that is, residents of poor neighborhoods would be better off if they had middle- and upper-class neighbors whose behaviors they could mimic. To serve as a role model, however, someone must identify with and trust that person. Simply having higher socioeconomic status and being visible are likely not enough. Indeed, differences in class background and ignorance of each other will not only make individuals skeptical of viewing the gentry as role models but may give pause to would be role models themselves. Without long-term organic connections to the community, the gentry are ill-positioned to serve as role models or counsel others about what is appropriate behavior.

Another common way neighborhoods are thought to be important is through collective efficacy. But the collective efficacy of a neighborhood may or may not be strengthened as a result of gentrification. When there is a consensus around goals or the object of action is external to the neighborhood, collective efficacy may indeed be strengthened. Because the gentry are by definition of a different background than many of the indigenous residents, however, agreeing on common objectives may sometimes be a challenge.

Weak social ties may be a more consistent and realistic mechanism through which gentrification may benefit indigent residents. Because only casual ties are necessary, the obstacle of class may not be insurmountable and enable indigenous residents to take advantage of the bridge to resources that the gentry can provide.

Perhaps most likely, at least in the early stages of gentrification and in neighborhood suffering from poor services in amenities is that gentrification will bring improvements to the institutional resources that benefit the gentry and indigenous folks alike.

As a qualitative study based on a nonrepresentative sample of individuals, this study cannot be a definitive word on neighborhoods effects. What it can do is guide future research when thinking about the potential impacts of this process and guide the actions of those who work in gentrifying and potentially gentrifying communities who are confronted with the dilemma of gentrification. Rather than accepting or rejecting the poverty deconcentration thesis whole cloth, this chapter hopefully points to those areas where benefits might be plausible and where harms may be possible. With that, their actions can be better informed and, it is hoped, more effective.

# 6    Implications for Planning and Policy

THIS WORK IS MOTIVATED BY more than just academic interest. The aim here is to inform efforts to build just, livable, and prosperous cities. With that aim in mind, the findings reported here should contribute to the ongoing debates about gentrification in several ways and can be used to suggest strategies to achieve the goals in the face of gentrification.

The following themes emerged from my study of gentrification in Clinton Hill and Harlem: that gentrification can bring neighborhood improvements that long-term residents are appreciative of; although the residents can be happy about some of the neighborhood improvements, a great deal of cynicism pervades thoughts about why these improvements are occurring; the specter of displacement hangs in the air, and the gentry are likely to be both an asset (but only in limited ways) and a drawback to indigenous residents. What actions should community activists, policy makers, scholars, and other concerned citizens take in light of these findings?

Answering this question implies two steps. The first addresses the confidence we are willing to place in these findings. Are my interpretations credible? To what extent are they idiosyncratic to those interviewed, these specific neighborhoods, or New York City for that matter? After all, a study based on several dozen interviews with nonrandomly selected residents can hardly be thought to representative in the statistical sense. That is, we have no way of knowing with any degree of precision if these findings would have been similar had a different group of residents been interviewed. Moreover, there was no control group, or pretest–posttest design with which we could assign causal relationships with any degree of certainty. From a purely methodological perspective, such criticisms are accurate. Yet the type of qualitative interpretive inquiry presented here can still inform efforts to address the challenges and opportunities posed by gentrification.

In both the introduction, where the veracity of the methods used was hinted at, and in the appendix, where this veracity is discussed in more detail, the argument is made in reference to abstract notions of qualitative findings. In this chapter, the actual results and their likely veracity are discussed. On establishing the likely veracity and contexts under which these findings probably hold true, this chapter addresses specific actions that might be taken.

Although these results cannot be interpreted as representative in any statistical sense, we can still use judgment, logic, and prior research to infer beyond the environs of Clinton Hill and Harlem and beyond those interviewed here. As I discuss in more detail in the appendix, the narratives and neighborhood descriptions are hopefully rich enough so that one can tease out aspects of these findings that are transferable to other settings. Thus, while Clinton Hill and Harlem are unique neighborhoods set within the unique global city of New York and the individuals represented are unique, they certainly share commonalities with other cities, neighborhoods, and people experiencing gentrification. With this in mind, let us consider the major themes emerging in the preceding chapters.

## CAN GENTRIFICATION BE GOOD FOR INDIGENOUS RESIDENTS?

The narratives presented here provide unambiguous evidence that some residents of gentrifying neighborhoods view some of the changes associated with the process in a positive light. Although some appreciated the trendy new stores and increased diversity, what stood out was the increased access to everyday stores and the improved physical appearance of the neighborhood. This is particularly true in Harlem, where disinvestment had been particularly bad. But even in Clinton Hill, where disinvestment did not reach the depths experienced by Harlem, there was a positive reception toward many of the improvements taking place. Among those who were fortunate enough to be homeowners, the appreciation of their property was welcome indeed. This was more common in Clinton Hill, where homeownership rates are higher. Should we interpret this as an indication that gentrification is a good thing or at least that it necessarily brings some positive benefits to indigenous residents?

Not necessarily. Context is vital to interpreting these findings. As was stressed in chapter 1, black inner-city neighborhoods have come to occupy a uniquely disadvantaged place in urban America. Ghettos are not just another type of ethnic enclave; rather, taken as a whole they are more isolated and experience greater disinvestment than perhaps any other type of neighborhood. They are much more racially isolated than either the contemporary ethnic enclaves inhabited by Asian and Latino immigrants or the enclaves of yesteryear that were home to European immigrants (Massey and Denton 1993).

This isolation, however, has not translated into robust economic enclaves in black neighborhoods. Indeed, it is a common sight and source of tension for the few commercial enterprises in many black inner-city neighborhoods to be dominated by other ethnic groups (Lee 2003). Even the notorious slums of the Lower East Side, which in an absolute sense had much worse physical conditions than ghettos of today, did not lack for merchants and jobs, albeit low-paying ones that provided the poor with their everyday needs and some opportunity for upward mobility. The same could be said for Harlem of the early twentieth century. The ghetto of late twentieth-century America, however, was bereft of many of the everyday amenities and services taken for granted elsewhere. Whereas many poorer immigrant communities lack chain stores and enterprises typically found in middle America, these communities are typically dotted with indigenous immigrant enterprises providing residents with goods and services targeted specifically for that community (Light and Rosenstein 1995). In contrast, many inner-city black neighborhoods have lacked both the prototypical chain stores and indigenous commercial enterprises. Except for hair care and funeral parlors, black neighborhoods for the most part have not served as a base for a black entrepreneurial class.

As a result, predominantly black inner-city neighborhoods like Harlem and to a lesser extent Clinton Hill were sorely lacking in retail options. Gentrification, though typically associated with trendy boutiques, also brings commerce that appeals to a broad range of people, including the residents indigenous to the neighborhoods. *This is especially true in those neighborhoods that experienced a great deal of disinvestment.* Other neighborhoods undergoing gentrification may have provided adequate options for residents in terms of stores and amenities. For example, in describing gentrification in the Philadelphia neighborhoods of Fairmount and Queen Village during the 1970s, Levy and Cybriwsky point out that these neighborhoods, like many other older areas undergoing gentrification, were relatively stable before the gentrification process. They write:

> For despite the grim language of "decline," "disinvestment," "abandonment," and "decay," most older urban neighborhoods hardly ever became devoid of people and supportive social and economic institutions.... Frequently these were working class, European ethnic communities or long-standing black neighborhoods which withstood decline. They were commonly regarded as essentially "good" neighborhoods. (Levy and Cybriwsky 1980, p. 139)

Levy and Cybriwsky chronicled a number of reactions by indigenous residents, including the initial welcoming of "new blood," conflicts over the use of public space, and concerns about rising housing prices. An appreciation for new stores or amenities, however, was not among the reactions they recorded. Most likely this is because as predominantly white neighborhoods, these sections of Philadelphia did not experience disinvestment on the scale of black neighborhoods like Harlem and perhaps to a lesser extent Clinton Hill. As "good" neighborhoods, there probably was an array of shops and services that served the community quite nicely. Perhaps the incoming gentry would not have been satisfied with the existing stores, but for the indigenous residents they were satisfactory. This would explain why much of the literature on gentrification has been so negative. If neighborhoods of the type described by Levy and Cybriwsky are typical, there should be no surprise why little was written about the potential positives of gentrification from the vantage point of indigenous residents. In these cases residents already had access to the stores and amenities they deemed necessary, and gentrification, though bringing more affluence and investment, did not necessarily enhance their quality of life in any way.

Thus, the conclusion that gentrification can bring benefits to indigenous residents has to be tempered with the caveat that this finding is likely to be true in those neighborhoods that have experienced a great deal of disinvestment and that lack basic services and amenities. In the past, such neighborhoods were often bypassed by the gentry, but as noted earlier a number of forces—including the increased availability of capital, policies like HOPE VI that encourage mixed income housing, declining crime rates, an increase in the size of the black middle class, and increased tolerance for residential integration—suggest depressed inner city-black communities are likely targets for gentrification in the future. One potential benefit here will be the increased access to commercial activities.

## ARE RESIDENTS OF OTHER GENTRIFYING NEIGHBORHOODS LIKELY TO BE CYNICAL TOWARD GENTRIFICATION?

One of the strongest reactions reported earlier in this book was cynicism toward the process of gentrification. Though appreciative of some of the neighborhood improvements, some residents had a great deal of bitterness and cynicism about why these improvements were taking place. Some equated this with class differences, but more often the perceived privileged status of whites ignited the cynicism residents felt toward the gentrification process. Put another way, there is a perception that the neighborhood is improving and that the improvement is linked causally to the inmigration of whites. Even more galling, conscious decisions are being made to treat whites more favorably and remake the neighborhood to whites' liking. In sum, much of the cynicism expressed by residents I spoke with was premised on the notion of white privilege. That is, perforce whites receive preferential treatment in all walks of life, including neighborhood services and amenities. Should we always expect gentrification to breed such cynicism?

Context is again key in shedding light on the likelihood of this phenomenon accompanying gentrification. Of course Clinton Hill and Harlem are unique neighborhoods in their own right. For example, Harlem is unique in its role as the capital of black America and home to the Harlem

Renaissance. Nevertheless there are many other black neighborhoods in urban America with rich histories and beautiful architecture that are experiencing gentrification, and therefore the findings may be relevant there. For example, much of the resentment toward gentrification in Clinton Hill had racial overtones, presumably due to residents' collective memory of racial oppression and current-day racism they have experienced. Neither the collective memory of racial oppression nor modern racism is exclusive to Harlem. Consequently, if my interpretation of this cynicism as stemming in part from the legacy of racial discrimination is accurate, then we can expect to find such cynicism in many other black neighborhoods as well.

There is ample evidence that this cynicism is the accepted wisdom in many parts of the black community. Numerous examples support this contention. One could point to the matter of fact way that residents related their suspicion about preferential white treatment to me in a way that assumed that by being black, I would be familiar with this narrative—which indeed I was. The long history of racial oppression in the Unites States has created a collective memory among blacks that is deeply suspicious and ready to believe the worse where whites are concerned.

Where gentrification is associated with an influx of whites—even a relatively modest influx, as was the case of Clinton Hill and Harlem—it seems likely that much of the resentment that gentrification inspires will be racially tinged. It remains an open question if the expressions of cynicism discussed here would be parallel to those found in other nonwhite neighborhoods undergoing gentrification. Certainly racial/ethnic oppression is not unique to blacks in the United States. The unique experience of slavery and Jim Crow and the position of blacks at the bottom of the racial order, however, should give one pause before assuming this type of reaction to gentrification will be universal across nonwhite neighborhoods.

Resentment and ill will toward the gentry may indeed be common occurrence among indigenous residents. A number of authors have chronicled clashes between the gentry and indigenous residents over the competing visions for their neighborhoods. For example, Auger (1979) described how in the South End of Boston long-term residents clashed with the incoming gentry over the role of affordable housing in their community. As was discussed earlier, this resentment was common among residents I interviewed as well. But a resentment based on the notion that the gentry are a preferred class whom the powers that be consciously favor is probably less well developed outside of black neighborhoods. This assertion is premised on the fact that a class-based politics is much less well developed in the United States than in many other industrialized nations and certainly than race-based politics in the United States (Lipset and Marks 2000). It thus seems likely that the cynicism expressed in Clinton Hill and Harlem is more likely to parallel that found in other black neighborhoods than in other nonblack and especially white working-class neighborhoods undergoing gentrification. Put another way, it is certainly possible that the cynicism expressed earlier in this book will be found in other gentrifying neighborhoods that are black, white, and other alike. But in keeping with the aim to develop criteria for applying these results beyond those interviewed here, one should keep in mind the unique history of blacks in the United States and how this history has informed perceptions before expecting to find similar findings elsewhere.

## THE SPECTER OF DISPLACEMENT

Of all the themes discussed in this book, that residents are fearful of displacement is probably the easiest sell and something one can probably feel confident is likely to be found in other gentrifying neighborhoods. After all, gentrification is almost synonymous with increasing housing prices, and such increases may not be tolerable to indigenous residents. Moreover, the problem of displacement has been an overarching concern in much of the gentrification literature, a point made in chapter 1. Given the logic behind fears of displacement and the widespread concern about it reported from a multitude of sources, the notion that displacement haunts residents of gentrifying neighborhoods is probably something that can be expected to be found beyond my interviews and observations in Clinton Hill and Harlem.

Those who have closely followed the displacement debates over the years, however, may be skeptical. As noted at the beginning of this book some of the most rigorous research on displacement has failed to find much evidence of this occurring in a widespread fashion (Freeman 2005; Freeman and Braconi 2004; Vigdor 2002). In addition, the research that has attempted to gauge the impact of displacement on the displaced has been mixed. A number of studies have found that although displacees typically bore the burden of greater housing costs, their satisfaction levels most frequently remained the same or increased postdisplacement (Gale 1986). Even Legates and Hartman, two scholars who have frequently been sympathetic to the concerns of displacees. wrote:

> In summary, evidence of what happens to outmovers paints a picture of mixed hardship. Some outmovers appear to find satisfactory, even superior, housing without harm. Many others judge their units to be the same, and a substantial number judge them to be worse. Cost almost always rise, sometimes severely . . . those with the lowest incomes tend to fare worst in the process. (Legates and Hartman 1986, p. 194)

If, as the quantitative evidence suggests, displacement is a relatively rare event, and displacees are often more satisfied with their housing than before, surely some might ask what the fuss is about displacement.

The narratives discussed in chapter 4, however, are suggestive of a more nuanced view of displacement and deserve some further elaboration. As noted there, although some people had personal experience with displacement pressure, this was certainly not the case for all of the residents I spoke with. Many people—whether due to rent regulation, housing assistance, homeownership, or a landlord who valued a relationship with a long-standing tenant as opposed to charging what the market will bear—were in housing situations that insulated them from displacement pressures. This is a finding echoed by Newman and Wyly (2004) who in studying displacement in New York City neighborhoods also found that many residents of modest means were able to withstand displacement pressures for the reasons cited already. Nevertheless, a specter of displacement still hung in the air.

I attribute this fear of displacement despite not necessarily facing the immediate threat to two things—a meaning of displacement beyond personal movement and the potentially catastrophic nature of the moving experience. A common definition of *displacement* by Grier and Grier (1978) is:

> When any household is forced to move from its residence by conditions which affect the dwelling or its immediate surroundings, and:
> 1. Are beyond the household's reasonable ability to control or prevent;
> 2. Occur despite the household's having met all previously imposed conditions of occupancy; and
> 3. Make continued occupancy by that household impossible, hazardous, or unaffordable.

To some of the residents of Clinton Hill and Harlem that I spoke with, however, displacement also has the broader connotation of being "pushed out" and losing one's community. Thus, when someone who is securely housed in their parents' public housing apartment cannot find an apartment in the neighborhood that they can afford, this contributes to the feeling of being pushed out or displaced. According to the technical definition, they are not threatened with displacement. But they might still feel as though they were being pushed out of their community because in the past children who grew up in the neighborhood could expect to get a place of their own as they reached adulthood. Now that they no longer can afford to do so they are being displaced from the neighborhood. In this way, displacement can be thought of as affecting a much wider swath of the community beyond those personally threatened with having to move in the near future.

It is also important to emphasize the potentially catastrophic nature of displacement. Having to leave one's residence is likely to be perceived as a scary experience. Even if many residents who are displaced eventually rebound from such an event (as much of the empirical evidence suggests), anticipating the possibility of being displaced is likely unnerving. There is a strand of research in social psychology that suggests people routinely underestimate their resilience in the face of adverse life events like the loss of a limb or a loved one (Gladwell 2004; Gilbert et al. 1998, 2004). Displacement could possibly be similar in this way. Hence, studies that purport to show that displacees fare relatively well does not necessarily discount the real dread with which displacement is held by residents of gentrifying neighborhoods. Taken together, the reality of increasing housing prices, limited housing options for those of limited means, and the actual pushing out of some residents combine to make the specter of displacement a likely fear across gentrifying neighborhoods.

## NEIGHBORHOOD EFFECTS IN THE CONTEXT OF GENTRIFICATION

By bringing the gentry into inner-city neighborhoods, gentrification has the potential to achieve the mixing of classes that has been heralded as an elixir for ailing poor areas. In the previous chapter I cast a skeptical eye on this notion, arguing that to the extent indigenous residents benefit from gentrification, it is likely to be mostly through improved amenities and services and to a lesser extent more diverse social ties and not some of the other mechanisms cited in the neighborhood effects literature, including peer effects and collective socialization. This is based on my reasoning of the type of relationships between the gentry and indigenous residents that would be necessary for these mechanisms to manifest. These relationships were not very apparent to the residents I interviewed and seemed unlikely in the context of gentrification. Would neighborhood effects appear more robust in other gentrifying neighborhoods outside of Clinton Hill and Harlem? Would the gentry be more likely to serve as role models who socialized wayward youth and taught by example?

I see little reason to expect this to be the case. The gentry would seem just as likely to be viewed as interlopers and to lack social intimacy with residents in other gentrifying neighborhoods as well. Indeed, several other studies set in gentrifying areas have also described relations between the gentry and residents as superficial and certainly not intimate (Anderson 1991; Levy and Cybriwsky 1980). Class differences between the gentry and indigenous residents and the continuing declination of space as a determinant of community (Wellman and Leighton 1979) should give one pause before expecting the gentry to move in and serve as role models for indigenous residents. Moreover, the prototypical gentrifier as a young childless adult is not especially oriented toward their immediate neighborhood for social ties. When gentrification does occur, newer residents are probably more likely to have ties elsewhere as a result of school, work, or other interests, thus limiting their opportunity to develop the type of relationships necessary to serve as role models.

When gentrification is planned and involves an entire community, such as the case of many HOPE VI developments, however, it is possible that more intimate relations might manifest. Typically HOPE VI demolishes a low-income public housing development and replaces it with a mixed-income development that rehouses only some of the original residents. Under this scenario, a new gentrified community is created virtually from scratch. Hence, the gentry may be less likely to be viewed as interlopers and perhaps might develop close ties with indigenous residents. To date, the research on HOPE VI has not addressed this question, so we can only speculate (Popkin et al. 2004; U.S. General Accounting Office 2003). I bring it up here to highlight a circumstance where the gentry might mix with poorer residents differentially than already described.

It does seem likely, however, that gentrification will generate casual or weak social ties between the gentry and residents. These are the types of casual relationships that are likely to occur simply from sharing the same neighborhood. To the extent that these weaker ties produce benefits to indigenous residents, and the discussion in the previous chapter suggests this is possible, gentrification may induce neighborhood effects in this way.

As mentioned previously, the presence of the gentry seems quite likely to bring about improved services and amenities. Moreover, where gentrifying neighborhoods previously lacked basic amenities and services, these improvements will likely benefit indigenous residents as well. This is a finding that I would expect to see in other gentrifying neighborhoods, assuming there was indeed a lack of amenities and services.

In some circumstances, gentrification seems likely to weaken the cohesiveness of a neighborhood. Because the gentry may have a different class and cultural background, there are times when their presence may spark conflict over neighborhood norms. It seems likely that clashes of the type chronicled earlier in this book would be present in neighborhoods in other settings. Wherever there are differences in class and culture, such clashes seem highly likely. This potential downside should be kept in mind in any calculus that considers the benefits of gentrification.

Having summarized the key findings and discussed their applicability, I now turn to considering both action and reflection on gentrification. *Action* refers to those who confront the reality of gentrification as community activists, planners, and policy makers. *Reflection* refers to the way we think about the meaning of gentrification. The remainder of this chapter addresses the policy implications of the findings related earlier in this book. In the concluding chapter I rethink the meaning of gentrification in light of the findings discussed here.

## POLICIES FOR GENTRIFICATION

Before recommending how to get there, we must consider exactly where we wish to go. More specifically, what should be the goals of policies addressing gentrification? I start out with the assumption that we should have a concern with equity as well as efficiency. An equitable outcome is preferable, as well as one that achieves the most for a given amount of resources. Notions of equity discussed here operate on the assumption that the least among us deserve special concern. Some redistribution of wealth to the disadvantaged is desirable and necessary.

A reasonable goal of a neighborhood policy is that all Americans should have access to decent and safe neighborhoods. Indeed the Housing Act of 1949 specifically states a "suitable living environment" for all Americans as one of its goals. A decent neighborhood is one that is adequate physically and provides a modicum of opportunity for upward mobility. With these assumptions and goals in mind, one can consider whether policy makers would want to discourage, encourage, or be neutral toward gentrification.

I argue that particularly in the case of black inner-city neighborhoods that have experienced disinvestment, gentrification can bring benefits, and efforts should aim to reduce the negative side effects of the process. The positives associated with gentrification include increases in wealth for those fortunate enough to be homeowners, more diverse social ties for indigenous residents, and improved amenities and services to a neighborhood—improvements that residents will benefit from.

The socioeconomically diverse neighborhoods that gentrification has the potential to produce is a stated goal of much housing policy. At a time when inequality is rising, we should be hesitant before dismissing any force that serves to bring individuals of differing socioeconomic strata together. In recent decades the truly disadvantaged have increasingly been isolated from the rest of society, divorced from employment, and residing in neighborhoods where their chances of encountering a middle-class person grow ever slimmer (Jargowsky 1997; although see Jargowsky 2003 for countervailing trends during the 1990s). With American society increasingly cleaving along class lines, the notion that some individuals would relocate into relatively poor neighborhoods is a glimmer of hope. This fracturing of American society, aside from limiting opportunities for the less fortunate, also bodes ill for the nature of our democracy. It limits interaction between classes and the forging of collective interests and political accommodation between classes that are necessary in a healthy democracy (Swanstrom, Dreier, and Mollenkopf 2002).

The mixing of socioeconomic classes is not only beneficial to our larger society but brings benefits to indigenous residents as well, as discussed at length in the previous chapter. Although we should have realistic expectations of just how much can be accomplished by simply mixing the gentry with indigenous residents, it does appear likely that the presence of the gentry can serve to enhance the local quality of life.

Although gentrification does have its beneficial aspects, it nevertheless beckons us to collection action. For one thing, as chapter 4 and 5 illustrated, many residents of gentrifying neighborhoods fear the possibility of being displaced and are unsettled by the feeling of being pushed out. One might question, however, whether the fear of displacement warrants a policy response. This counterargument is buttressed considerably by the ambiguity of the empirical evidence that has attempted to measure displacement due to gentrification (Freeman 2005; Freeman and Braconi 2004; Vigdor 2002). Much of this literature has not found a strong link between gentrification and displacement. Even if it is unambiguous that indigenous residents are displaced by gentrification, one might ask whether this is a societal concern. If gentrification reflects a shift in tastes for certain neighborhoods, this means that the original residents are being outbid for this space. But virtually all housing is allocated in this way. Although it is unfortunate that some residents may no longer be able to afford to live in neighborhoods they grew up in, this doesn't necessarily cry out for a policy response. Neighborhoods are constantly changing, sometimes to the chagrin of the original residents. Furthermore, given the ugly history of federal and local government intervening to maintain neighborhood character, typically to keep minorities and the poor out, we might be hesitant before adapting a policy that specifically aims to allow neighborhoods to maintain their existing socioeconomic status. The more affluent occupy the choicest real estate (i.e., on the coast, scenic views, etc.), and gentrification-induced displacement is just a manifestation of this allocation process. The poor can't afford to live on the Upper East Side of Manhattan; why should society be so concerned if they can no longer afford to live in Harlem? Unless one is ready to jettison the entire system, this doesn't seem to be a justification for policy intervention.

From the perspective of concerns for equity, there are at least three reasons why we may wish to intervene in the case of gentrification even though access to housing and neighborhoods are allocated primarily through the market. One reason is the notion of security. The thought of some households having to move against their wishes contradicts the nation's conceptions of home, where one can be secure. This is a concern that appears to resonate across American society. This is also clearly evidenced by the rhetoric surrounding homeownership. "Owning a home provides a sense of security" is one of the key benefits cited by the Bush administration (Whitehouse Web page 2005). Gentrification, by raising housing prices, might threaten the security of some households, and this would seem to be a concern worth taking into consideration. This is the insecurity that many residents expressed in the narratives presented in chapters 4 and 5. Thus, to the extent that we feel that citizens should feel secure in their homes, gentrification calls out for a collective response.

A second rationale for collective action in response to gentrification is motivated by concerns for social justice. It would be a supreme irony (and patently unfair) if those who were once confined to neighborhoods like Harlem could no longer afford to live there. For much of the twentieth century, racial minorities were confined to ghetto neighborhoods that were treated with systematic disdain. The actions of policy makers, private actors, and private individuals through red lining, disinvestment, and housing discrimination (to name a few tactics) conspired to create the desperate conditions described in chapter 2 and elsewhere (Jackson 1985; Massey and Denton 1993; Sugrue 1996). Given this history, remedial measures such as the Community Reinvestment Act and Empowerment Zones are surely warranted. But so, too, are initiatives that would ensure that low-income households continue to have access to these neighborhoods after they improve through gentrification. It should also be remembered that it was the actions of residents who stayed in the community fighting to improve deteriorated neighborhoods through various development initiatives that demonstrated to the market that it could be profitable to invest in places like Harlem or Clinton Hill. For these reasons, it seems only fair that some type of collective response is taken to ensure that those who were formerly confined to these neighborhoods when they were at their nadir continue to have access to these neighborhoods when they improve.

Even if one is skeptical about notions of redress for past wrongs or feels that concerns about displacement are exaggerated, it does seem likely that these neighborhoods, however gradually, are destined to become gentrified. That is, whether the original residents are displaced or replaced through normal processes of succession, gentrifying neighborhoods often become upscale enclaves with few poor or working-class residents. One can think of neighborhoods like Park Slope in Brooklyn or the Upper West Side of Manhattan that are almost completely gentrified. If this is the case, the benefits that indigenous and poorer residents derive from having the gentry as neighbors and the benefits of a more integrated society would be short-lived as they were displaced or replaced by more affluent residents. For this reason, too, gentrification calls out for some type of policy response if we wish make the socioeconomic diversity that it can bring more than a temporary phase.

Finally, the cynicism and resentment expressed by many residents toward gentrification cries out for a rethinking of the way we plan and allocate resources across space. Here the policy response may not be toward gentrification so much as to empowering people to feel they are valued in the wider society. Gentrification, however, lays bare the stark differences in treatment received by differing classes and thus calls out for special attention for alleviating this problem.

Gentrification, then, provides the opportunity to improve the quality of life of deteriorated neighborhoods and mix residents from differing socioeconomic strata with benefits for both the indigenous residents and the larger society. Against these benefits must be weighed the insecurity that gentrification instills in residents, the choking off of affordable housing that renders any benefits from socioeconomic integration fleeting, the injustice of those who were confined to these neighborhoods now being excluded from them, and the cynicism and resentment that gentrification breeds. Next I outline specific strategies for allaying some of these concerns about gentrification.

PHOTO 10. The site of a planned luxury development in Harlem. This is an area that was formerly plagued by abandonment.

## Improving Security and Accessibility

What can be done to improve the security of residents who happen to reside in neighborhoods undergoing gentrification? An obvious solution is home-ownership. Homeowners are less vulnerable to the whims of a landlord and do not have to worry about rent increases or their lease not being renewed. The control over one's domicile that homeownership confers has been posited to enhance a person's self-efficacy or an individual's belief that he or she can control the trajectory of his or her own life (Rohe, Van Zandt, and McCarthy 2000). Indeed Saunders (1978) posits that "[homeownership] does function in important ways as a means of maintaining control over one's personal world" (p. 220). This sense of control was sorely missing from the narratives discussed in chapter 4, where respondents described their fears of displacement and being pushed out. Recall that the difference between owners and renters was especially stark on this matter. Whereas renters had to rely on the goodwill of their landlords or Byzantine rent regulations for security, owners rarely expressed the fear that they would be pushed out or, if they did, knew this was a threat they could manage because they owned their homes.

Aside from increasing residents' sense of security, homeownership has the added benefit of increasing owners' wealth in a time of rising housing prices—as is typically the case in gentrifying neighborhoods. Those who were fortunate enough to own their homes witnessed their equity increasing by several multiples in ten or fifteen years. As discussed in chapter 4, this is a benefit that should not be overlooked in any assessment of gentrification.

The benefits of homeownership have been analyzed and debated at length elsewhere, so I do not rehash this discussion here. Moreover, the 1990s were a period where access to homeownership was expanded considerably—to the point that many observers question the wisdom of further encouraging homeownership. I would stress, however, that homeownership is rarely viewed as a tool that would protect indigenous residents from the threat of gentrification. This is probably because once gentrification occurs, ownership in the affected neighborhood is no longer feasible for residents. In addition, to many residents of distressed neighborhoods like pregentrification Clinton Hill or Harlem, homeownership means a single-family house in the suburbs or as close an approximation to that ideal as possible. Consequently, potential home buyers in pregentrification Clinton Hill or Harlem often left for greener pastures in Queens, Long Island, or the South.

In communities that have not yet experienced gentrification, the threat in the form of housing inflation and opportunity in the form increased wealth that gentrification represents is another reason to promote home-ownership. Thus, in thinking about ways to address the negative costs of gentrification, a forward-thinking approach would take into consideration the expansion of homeownership within neighborhoods before they gentrify. This could help the upwardly mobile residents of the neighborhood stay and dampen feelings of being pushed out.

Homeownership will increase the security of those in a position to become homeowners. But what of those with severe credit blemishes, unstable incomes, or for other reasons are not suitable candidates for homeownership? Are they destined to live in fear of being pushed out? Moreover, homeownership does little to ensure that housing will remain affordable in the future or preserve access for low-income households and thereby help maintain the much desired socioeconomic diversity that gentrification can bring. Increases in housing prices thus confront us with two choices: attempting to restrain the increase or subsidizing residents who can no longer afford such increases.

Stopping price increases would entail some sort of price control mechanism such as New York City's rent regulation. Indeed, a number of the residents I spoke to benefited from rent regulation. By limiting the pace at which rents can rise, rent regulation can be an effective means of dampening displacement pressures. The major criticism of rent regulation is that it is an extremely blunt tool for accomplishing the task of keeping housing affordable. More specifically, rent regulation is not necessarily equitable because it effectively transfers wealth from landlords, of whom not all are rich, to tenants, not all of whom are poor. Moreover, by not allowing the market to set prices, it prevents price from playing the role of rationing housing. Instead housing is rationed on a first come, first served basis. Those lucky enough to obtain a controlled unit benefit, whereas others are left out. The removal of price as a signal also means there is less incentive to supply more housing when there is upward pressure on housing prices, resulting in housing shortages. Initiatives that dampen the market distortions associated with rent control, such as vacancy decontrol or exempting newly constructed housing, also weaken rent control's effectiveness as a tool to keep housing affordable and in the case of the latter give landlords an incentive to encourage their tenants to move. Witness the stratospheric rents in Manhattan despite the presence of rent control—courtesy of the watering down of New York City's rent regulations. Vacancy decontrol also means that lower-income households attempting to move into a gentrifying neighborhood will have a difficult time locating a rent-regulated apartment. Thus, under vacancy decontrol, only the current residents will benefit. Although rent regulation can keep rents low, there are a number of inequities and inefficiencies that suggest other affordable housing strategies are worth considering.

What would be preferable is a mechanism that transfers resources from those more fortunate and targets the poor. Voucher programs like Section 8 meet these criteria because it is funded through a generally progressive tax system and allocated through means testing. And although this system distorts the market, too, by increasing demand among low-income households, it does so in a way that is intended by augmenting the demand of these households. As a tool for increasing security in gentrifying neighborhoods, however, a voucher program has serious handicaps. One major handicap is that Section 8 sets the fair market rent at the fortieth percentile of all units available for rent in a given metropolitan area. Tenants can pay more than the fair market rent as long as it does not exceed more than 40 percent of their income. In gentrifying neighborhoods this may or may not be competitive.

The biggest problem with Section 8 as a tool for addressing gentrification is that it falls far short of serving all of those eligible and does not target subsidies specifically to gentrifying neighborhoods. So even if the payment standard were sufficient to serve those in gentrifying neighborhoods, there is not an adequate supply of vouchers to meet the need. A program that targeted housing subsidies to needy households in gentrifying neighborhoods would go a long way in allaying concerns of displacement or being pushed out. The current funding mechanisms of most affordable housing programs, including Section 8, however, would make such a program politically difficult to implement. Affordable housing programs are generally funded through general tax revenues, wherein income is transferred from the more affluent to the needy. Detractors would argue that targeting residents of gentrifying neighborhoods would be inequitable because those not residing in these neighborhoods could be just as needy. More specifically, why should people outside affected neighborhoods be asked to sacrifice to benefit only those within gentrifying neighborhoods when there are needy persons outside of the neighborhoods as well? One could argue that displacement is more problematic in gentrifying areas. The displacement fears chronicled in this book notwithstanding, much of the empirical literature, however, fails to support this contention (Freeman and Braconi 2004; Freeman 2005; Vigdor 2002). It would therefore be a difficult sell to convince the polity that housing assistance should be targeted to gentrifying neighborhoods.

Savvy specialists, however, have developed a number of innovative techniques for producing affordable housing in targeted areas without imposing costs on the wider society. Inclusionary zoning is an example of this approach. Under inclusionary zoning schemes, new housing developments are required to set aside a number of units to be affordable to low- or moderate-income households. The developer and/or nonsubsidized occupants of the development subsidize the affordable units. The subsidy is paid by the developer when he or she accepts lower profits to subsidize the affordable units and by the nonsubsidized occupants when the developer passes the costs of the affordable units onto them. Under some schemes the developer receives a density bonus in return for providing affordable housing. With a bonus the developer offsets the cost of providing affordable housing with the profits obtained from building additional units. An inclusionary zoning scheme can therefore increase the supply of affordable housing within a targeted area. In terms of equity, a criticism of inclusionary zoning programs is that new developers or residents are asked to bear the cost of the subsidy while other long-term affluent residents escape unscathed (Hughes and Vandoren 1990). A counterargument could be that new developments impose a cost on current residents in terms of increased congestion and hence the developer or occupants should provide some benefit to the community in the form of affordable housing. Moreover, this critique is dampened somewhat if a density bonus scheme is used. From a political perspective, moreover, shifting the cost of the housing subsidy onto future residents has obvious advantages. Residents who have not moved into an unbuilt building will not organize or protest the higher prices they may pay.

Although inclusionary zoning may be politically attractive and can be designed in ways to dampen some of the inequities in such a scheme, there are inherent limitations to such an approach. For one thing, it assumes that developers and residents of new developments who pay market rate prices will not be deterred by the higher prices inherent in a scheme that uses market rate units to subsidize affordable units. This may or may not be a reasonable assumption. Finally, the effectiveness of inclusionary zoning is limited to the extent that new housing is being built. In gentrifying neighborhoods, where there is substantial new development on vacant land or gutted buildings taking place, like in Harlem, such an approach would be feasible. In other areas, where the housing stock may be deteriorated but little in the way of vacant land or buildings is available, such inclusionary zoning may not have much of an impact. Thus, although inclusionary zoning can be a tool to address the displacement concerns of indigenous residents as well as providing a supply of affordable housing, it may not be feasible in neighborhoods that are already built out or where new development is sensitive to the price increases necessitated by this type of subsidy scheme.

An alternative mechanism for targeting affordable housing to specific areas that also imposes the costs of producing such housing on the targeted area is tax increment financing (TIF). TIF has typically been used as an economic development strategy. Local governments designate an area as a TIF district and assess the value of the real property for purposes of taxation. Bonds are used to finance improvements to the district, usually in the form of infrastructure improvements. These improvements encourage private investment in a TIF district that otherwise would not have occurred. The new investment makes the area more attractive, raising property values and the concomitant property taxes. The increment in the property tax base is used to retire the bonds that paid for the public investment in the first place. The beauty of TIF is that it is self-financing. Local government leaders need not go to state capitals or Washington, DC, with their hat in hand, nor incur the wrath of angry voters by raising taxes. Perhaps because of these advantages, TIF has become a popular tool for financing economic development (Weber 2003).

Although TIF is typically used to fund infrastructure for commercial or industrial development, there is no a priori reason that this tool could not be adapted to produce affordable housing and thereby alleviate displacement concerns and ensure that gentrifying neighborhoods maintain socioeconomic diversity. Neighborhoods that appeared to be posed to undergo gentrification could be designated as TIF districts. If gentrification began, the resultant increase in property tax revenues stemming from rising property values could be directed to affordable housing.

A TIF would be especially timely when government redevelopment projects spur gentrification. These projects could include a tax increment component whereby increases in property values are translated into increased property tax revenues that are directed to provide housing assistance to those in the affected area. It is by no means rare for residents of many neighborhoods to oppose redevelopment projects because of the fear that the resulting improvements will raise property values and render their neighborhoods unaffordable to them. If the increased tax revenues that accompany property value increases were used for affordable housing, these fears might be allayed.

To be effective as a tool to address the affordable housing problems associated with gentrification, policy makers would have to anticipate the neighborhood change and implement TIF before gentrification was well under way. Expecting accurate prognostications from public officials is probably not realistic, and hence some type of triggering mechanism might be more practical. TIF districts could be targeted toward low-income neighborhoods and would kick in only if housing prices rose by some preordained amount, say one-third or 40 percent. The increment in property tax revenues from when the TIF district was first designated and when the properties were reassessed would be set aside for housing assistance in the gentrifying neighborhood. This housing assistance could be used to build new developments or take the more cost-efficient route and provide assistance to residents directly in the form of vouchers. Although the gentrifying neighborhood could be targeted for housing assistance, it would not be necessary to limit housing assistance to those who currently reside there.

With many policy prescriptions, the devil is often in the details. How long would the subsidies last? Should all of the tax increment go for housing assistance? If the housing assistance is not limited to current residents (and even if it is), the demand for such assistance is likely to exceed supply. How will this assistance be rationed? Although these are potentially thorny problems, they do not appear to be prima facie deal breakers. The long, varied, and for the most part successful implementation of TIF to fund economic development gives reason for optimism. Most of these and other technical details have been addressed in the numerous TIF programs that have been implemented in the United States. In addition one of the biggest risks in TIF schemes—that property values will not rise enough to offset the initial public sector investment—is not an issue here. If property values don't rise, the need for housing assistance will presumably not increase either, and there will be no need for additional revenues. A strong case can therefore be made in favor of TIF on equity grounds. To the extent that gentrification increases housing prices, those who are receiving the greatest economic benefits, property owners, are being asked to assist those who are most vulnerable: needy residents in gentrifying neighborhoods. Moreover, the transfer only entails the increment in rising property values and hence would less likely be seen as a new tax to benefit the needy—an important political consideration.

The Low Income Housing Tax Credit (LIHTC), which is virtually the only source of new project–based housing assistance at the federal level, could also be modified to take account of conditions specific to gentrifying neighborhoods. Currently the LIHTC provides an incentive to develop in census tracts where at least 50 percent of households have incomes below 60 percent of the metropolitan area median family income, where the poverty rate is at least 25 percent, or where development costs are high relative to the area median income. Although many neighborhoods that are in the early stages of gentrification would meet this criteria, as the areas continued to gentrify perhaps they no longer would qualify. Moreover, as land became more expensive, it would be increasingly difficult to develop LIHTC projects in these neighborhoods. As a means of keeping these neighborhoods accessible to a diverse range of persons and fostering greater socioeconomic mixing, LIHTC developments in gentrifying neighborhoods should be the encouraged. This could be done by providing an incentive to develop in formerly depressed neighborhoods where housing prices had increased rapidly. For example, an incentive might be given to develop in tracts where at least 50 percent of households have incomes below 60 percent of the metropolitan area median family income at the time of the last census but where rents now exceeded the metropolitan area median.

## Would It Make a Difference?

Imagine that housing policies of the type just described were in place in Clinton Hill and Harlem before gentrification commenced. If such policies were in place, would that have changed the nature of my findings in these neighborhoods and consequently what I interpreted as the most troubling aspects of gentrification—namely, the fear of being pushed out and the cynicism toward the whole process? These were feelings that were especially salient in Harlem as rates of homeownership there were lower, but the policies would be applicable to Clinton Hill if the goal is to promote economically diverse neighborhoods. If these policies had been implemented in Clinton Hill or Harlem fifteen or twenty years ago, how much difference would it have made? In other words, would residents still cite fears of being pushed out or displaced? Because the dynamics of change in Clinton Hill and Harlem have been different, I discuss this possibility for each of these neighborhoods separately.

As it stands, much of Clinton Hill is already gentrified. This study focused on some of the few remaining pockets that have not become the playground of the elite. There are few opportunities for someone not of substantial means to now move into Clinton Hill. As more of the older and less wealthy residents die or move away, Clinton Hill seems posed to become an upscale neighborhood and follow the paths of other gentrifying Brooklyn neighborhoods like Park Slope or Boerum Hill. Thus the fear expressed by many residents is of losing the community they know—one that is accessible (or at least part of it) to a broad range of classes.

Although those fortunate enough to own their homes, have rent-regulated apartments, or a relationship with a landlord who does not charge what the market will bear can take advantage of the improvements under way in Clinton Hill, poorer residents not in one of these fortunate scenarios are out of luck. Furthermore, for Clinton Hill to remain economically diverse, the flow of in-migrants must be diverse as well. But the available housing in Clinton Hill is typically not very affordable. Homeownership, rent regulation, and relationships with landlords who will provide a break on the rent are usually not available to people who want to move into the neighborhood. It is therefore not surprising that many residents of Clinton Hill, including those not personally threatened with displacement, described the changes taking place with a tinge of anxiety. As Clinton Hill becomes more expensive, its character will surely change.

Had programs been in place like inclusionary zoning or TIF, resources would be available to subsidize housing in Clinton Hill. These funds would have been available to produce affordable housing or provide subsidies to residents in the form of a voucher. The risk of Clinton Hill becoming a completely gentrified neighborhood would therefore be lower. Moreover, current residents would see the neighborhood changing and new residents moving in, but a significant portion of those residents would not be part of the gentry.

I would have probably found even greater anxiety toward gentrification in Clinton Hill had the multifamily developments that were the site of many of my interviews not converted to cooperatives in the 1980s. By becoming homeowners before their section of Clinton Hill became hot, at least some of the residents were protected from housing inflation and reaped a great deal of economic benefits from gentrification. Many of the renters regretted not purchasing their apartments when prices were much cheaper. The benefits of gentrification that homeowners described in chapter 3 are a testament to the potential benefits that homeownership can bring in the face of gentrification. Thus community initiatives to encourage homeownership through the conversion of multifamily buildings to coops paid off for those who took advantage and became homeowners. Homeownership opportunities that were affordable in the 1980s and 1990s, however, do nothing to assist those who might wish to move into Clinton Hill now. To assist these households, housing subsidies that are directed to this area specifically, for instance, an inclusionary zoning or TIF program, would be necessary.

We can conclude that homeownership in Clinton Hill perhaps dampened some of the anxiety and antagonism toward gentrification. Had more affordable housing policies been in place, presumably these feelings would have been dampened even further. But would housing policy alone be enough to significantly alter how residents felt about the process of gentrification? I return to this question later, but first consider how housing policy might have made a difference in Harlem.

Given the widespread fears of displacement in being pushed out, it is ironic that much of the development that had been occurring in Harlem for several decades after World War II targeted a disadvantaged clientele. Harlem has one of the largest concentrations of public housing in New York City, much of it built in the post–World War II era. With the cessation new public housing in the 1990s the LIHTC moved to the fore as the primary mechanism through which affordable housing is built. Here, too, Harlem was certainly the site of much activity. Indeed some 37 percent of all housing constructed in Harlem during the 1990s received some financing through the LIHTC (author's calculation). And as described in chapter 2, much of the redevelopment of abandoned and vacant properties was used for affordable housing, and typically residents of Harlem were given preferences for obtaining units. Thus although the mechanisms may have been slightly different from what was recommended before, it is not as though the housing needs of the poor were being ignored in Harlem.

Historically, the development of affordable and supportive housing there was so pervasive that by the 1980s many residents felt the neighborhood was being dumped on. Partially in response to this feeling, many residents advocated for attracting more homeowners and middle-class residents. An official at the New York City Department of Housing Preservation and Development (HPD) related to me that the community's desire for more mixed-income housing was taken into consideration when formulating plans for redevelopment.

Thus in Harlem it could be argued that assisted housing programs were already in place before and during the process of gentrification. If homeownership had been more widespread, however, more of the indigenous residents could have benefited from the onset of gentrification. At the beginning of the 1990s Harlem's homeownership rate was in the single digits. Although this rate has increased in recent years, it is much more difficult for someone of modest means to become a homeowner now because prices are so high. Had efforts to increase homeownership been implemented earlier and with more success, it seems likely that fewer residents would have fears of being pushed out and would also see personal financial benefits resulting from gentrification. My findings in Harlem would have more closely paralleled what I found in Clinton Hill, where homeownership rates are higher. But were more Harlemites homeowners, not only would they have less to fear from rising housing prices they would themselves benefit from the increasing prices. Housing policies that allow disadvantaged residents to benefit from the wealth being created by gentrification, such as homeownership, inclusionary zoning, or TIF, would seem to have the potential to give residents a stake in the process and perhaps would engender less negative feelings toward gentrification.

Realistically, it would have been a challenge to substantially increase homeownership in Harlem in the 1970s or 1980s, even if the affordable homeownership programs of later decades were in place. As noted earlier, the American dream is associated with the single-family home and suburban surroundings, an amenity package that Harlem, experiencing the ravages of abandonment and drugs, would be hard-pressed to compete with. Nonetheless the experience in the past few decades does offer the lesson that in a society where housing is commodified, owning one's home is one way to ensure against the vagaries of the market.

But the lack of homeownership alone is surely not enough to explain the levels of cynicism in Harlem or especially Clinton Hill, where homeownership rates were higher. Moreover, to the extent that feelings of being pushed out serve as a metaphor for lack of control over one's community, assisted housing programs alone may not be enough. Put another way, increased homeownership would certainly have made the gentrification under way in Clinton Hill and Harlem less threatening, as would additional affordable housing programs of the type I suggested earlier in this chapter. These additional affordable housing programs (inclusionary zoning, TIF, modifying the LIHTC) would also ensure that portions of Clinton Hill and Harlem remained affordable into the future. But affordable housing alone may not change the feelings of cynicism and impotence that some people expressed in the face of the forces of gentrification. To address that, the process of neighborhood planning too may need change. More specifically, if residents felt they had the power to countenance the forces impinging on their neighborhood, they would perhaps be less likely to attribute local improvements to the arrival of whites.

This is not to say that the indigenous residents of Clinton Hill or Harlem were mere bystanders to gentrification. Taylor (2002) describes how when Harlem reached its nadir in the 1980s, many residents had a vision of redeveloping the neighborhood for Harlemites or blacks at least. They battled with the city to make sure that the city did not dictate the redevelopment of the area. Taylor attributes Harlem's community activists with some success quoting a New York City official as saying, "No one is going to stop whites from moving in, but it is not our goal to bring them in" (Taylor 2002, p. 35). Another is quoted as saying, "We have very deliberately tried to make it clear what is going to be done with city-owned property in Harlem will be a joint decision of the city and the community. That has meant we've had to go slowly" (Taylor 2002, p. 35). Practically, what this meant was that the community's desire for a more middle-class yet black community was taken into consideration by the city when disposing of city-owned brownstones that were acquired through foreclosure.

My conversations with a representative of the HPD were consistent with Taylor's interpretations. HPD officials met with and took into consideration the desires of the Community Board before taking any significant action. Although the city could not use racial preferences to dispose of abandoned properties they had taken title to, they could (and still do) provide preferences to residents of Harlem. And though much of the city's redeveloped properties were targeted to low-income households, significant portions were targeted to moderate and middle-income households. Moreover, the template for city–community collaboration in the disposal of city-owned properties had already been developed in the South Bronx and Brownsville/East New York in Brooklyn, two other New York City neighborhoods that had experienced widespread abandonment and where the city consequently had a large number of properties to dispose of (Von Hoffman 2003).

So if the community provided input, the city was at least somewhat responsive, and substantial amounts of affordable housing was built in recent years, why is there so much cynicism and fear of displacement?

To some extent, the redevelopment of Harlem was more successful than anticipated. None of the city representatives or community development activists I spoke with expected the dramatic change in Harlem's fortunes. But the fears of displacement also speak to some of the limitations inherent in relying on abandoned city-owned property to develop affordable housing in Harlem. What once seemed like an inexhaustible supply is now drying up. Without cheap city-owned property, it is not so obvious how affordable housing will be built in the future. Residents who are not currently in subsidized units are rightfully concerned about their ability to stay in the community. Further infusions of money from the federal or state governments seem unlikely, given the budgetary constraints likely to haunt us as the Baby Boomers begin retiring. In contrast, if Harlem were able to tap some of the wealth being created through rising property values, the future for affordable housing would not be as ominous. Inclusionary zoning or TIF would allow such wealth to be tapped. Even without vacant city-owned properties to be developed, funds raised through TIF could be used to subsidize tenants through vouchers.

There are also some specific aspects of city policy that rankle Harlem residents. For example, the housing being sponsored by HPD targets both low-income and moderate-income households. These designations are based on the median area for the entire metropolitan area, where incomes are substantially higher than those found in Harlem. The median income for the New York City metropolitan area, $63,000, is more than twice that for the residents of Harlem. Consequently, housing built to be moderately priced for someone with the median income might as well be luxury housing for the residents of Harlem because most of them cannot afford it. This policy contributes to the perception that gentrification is for outsiders and makes a cruel joke of the notion of moderately priced housing. To be fair, the HPD does develop housing targeting very low-income households, and as a representative of HPD correctly pointed out, making the units more affordable would require deeper subsidies and limit the amount of redevelopment taking place. Furthermore, at least some residents of the community pushed for more middle class housing in earlier years, as I pointed out earlier.

This difference in thoughts about how the program should be structured points to some of the pitfalls of community involvement and the limitations of housing policy alone. In the wake of the many disasters associated with urban renewal, where entire neighborhoods were bulldozed for ill-conceived schemes without nary a concern for those displaced and the upheavals of the 1960s, the notion of community involvement became almost paradigmatic. Virtually all of the federal neighborhood initiatives implemented since the 1960s required community input. Moreover, neighborhood-based organizations are virtually ubiquitous across the urban landscape. It is now rare to find an inner-city neighborhood without at least one community development corporation operating. Abyssinian Development Corporation and Harlem Congregations for Community Improvement in Harlem and the Pratt Area Community Council in Clinton Hill are examples of such organizations. Thus, the cynicism expressed by so many residents toward the gentrification process might seem paradoxical. If community-based organizations are developing in the name of the community and the government is seeking input from the community, why the cynicism?

Because this was not a study of community participation nor the political economy of neighborhood change, I can only offer tentative hypotheses for this seeming paradox and consequently very tentative prescriptions for solving it. One potentially bedeviling pitfall that confronts all community-based organizations is to remain firmly rooted in the community. At a conference in Harlem on gentrification that I attended, a representative of a community-based organization was peppered with questions about some of the initiatives her organization was undertaking. The general tone was almost inquisition-like, and the implicit accusation being made was that the organization was in bed with big, downtown (read: white) developers. As to the veracity of this accusation I must plead agnosticism, but the feeling and perception is real for at least some community members. If some residents felt the community-based organizations were not acting in the community's interest, this would explain the apparent paradox between community involvement in the redevelopment underway in Harlem and the cynicism described earlier in the book.

Remaining firmly rooted in the community while trying to truly empower and represent the community is a daunting challenge. Some observers describe it as a difficult but necessary task:

> Most CDCs are based in communities but they are not community based.... Blending the realities of housing development—cost effectiveness, technical expertise and cooperative deal-making—with the requirements of successful organizing—inclusiveness, great independence in thought and action—has proved a daunting challenge for many a neighborhood. Yet it is a challenge that must be met. (Medoff and Sklar 1994, p. 260)

This school of thought recognizes the inherent tension between trying to manage and develop housing or commercial enterprises, partnering with government and outside institutions to raise funds, and representing and empowering the community.

Some go a step further and see this tension as unmanageable:

> It is this insecure and unpredictable middle location that CDCs occupy. CDCs manage capital like capitalists, but do not invest it for a profit. They manage projects but within the constraints set by their funders. They try to be community oriented while their purse strings are held by outsiders. They are pressured by capital to produce exchange values in the form of capitalist business spaces and rental housing. They are pressured by communities to produce use values in the form of services, home ownership, and green spaces. This is more than a "double bottom-line." It is the internalization of the capital-community contradiction and it leads to trouble. . . . The problem of maintaining community control is rooted in the fact that poor communities do not have enough community controlled capital and must woo outside capital whose tendency is to transform use values into exchange values. The role of funders in subverting social change efforts has been well established generally and in regard to CDCs. The Local Initiatives Support Corporation (LISC), the single most lauded funder of CDCs at the local level, is controlled by elites who often view redevelopment from an exchange value perspective rather than a use value perspective. (Stoecker 1997, p. 16)

Stoecker not only recognizes the tension but sees it as untenable, calling for a separation of development and organizing activities. Community-based development organizations would build and manage housing and commercial enterprises, whereas a separate group would focus on mobilizing and organizing residents to demand a fundamental restructuring of the political economy. Moreover, residents of poor neighborhoods would be better served by focusing their energies on mobilizing and organizing first, rather than the bricks-and-mortar development typical of many CDCs.

Whatever the merits of either approach, trying to balance community development with organizing (or focusing on organizing) first, the tension between community mobilization to address the disenfranchisement of poor communities and community development is highlighted by these commentators. To some extent these critics are suggesting that a focus on development puts the cart before the horse. That is, the goal should be to mobilize and empower residents to demand and receive better treatment. This may or may not include affordable housing development and other activities that CDCs typically engage in. But the emphasis should be on empowering communities to articulate, demand, and receive what they need. According to Stoecker (1997), the mobilization among residents participation in neighborhood organizations "increases confidence, efficacy, power, identification with the community, interaction, mutual aid, leadership development, and problem solving capacity among residents." When this is done residents would perhaps be less cynical about the redevelopment they witness. They would view themselves as equal players in the game and assume they could demand better treatment as anyone else could.

There is also the question of whether the development that does occur actually represents the needs and desires of the communities served. As Rohe (1998) points out, there is virtually no empirical evidence that suggest CDCs are carrying out the desires of community residents as opposed to responding to available funds or their own preconceived notions of what is best for the community. Presumably in neighborhoods where the focus is on community organizing, the development that does occur will better reflect the will of the residents. (This, too, is admittedly speculation as I am unaware of any evidence that suggests community organizing leads to initiatives that better represent the will of the community.)

Consider the city's policy of setting income criteria for some housing projects based on the median income for the entire metropolitan area. To what extent can this decision be said the result of choices made by residents of Clinton Hill or Harlem? It may very well be the case that from an efficiency or equity perspective, this is the optimal way to determine eligibility for affordable housing. The larger point to be made here is that community residents do not feel they made the decision. Had the community made this decision they would perhaps be less resentful about it. The challenge is to empower residents of the community so that they have a real voice in what happens in their neighborhood. Empowerment is, of course, a two-way street. Residents have to be willing to attend meetings, write letters, and participate in other activities. But to the extent that the aim is to lessen the cynicism many residents expressed in earlier sections of this book, it seems that greater community empowerment would be in order.

The fact that those actively engaged in the community development process were less cynical about the gentrification process points to a possible way of addressing this problem. If as Stoecker (1997) posits, residents' mobilization leads to greater "confidence, efficacy, power, identification with the community, interaction, mutual aid, leadership development, and problem solving capacity," then it seems plausible to infer that such mobilization might also lead to less cynicism as well. The cynicism illustrated earlier in this book was of the type that perceived exogenous forces, the notorious "they," as dictating the trajectory of neighborhoods and doling out amenities and services to preferred groups.

In contrast, individuals who were actively engaged in community-based organizations were more likely to attributes changes in neighborhood conditions to the greater political savvy and social capital of the gentry. They appeared to feel that with proper education and mobilization, indigenous residents could receive the same or at least better amenities and services than they had in the past.

Community mobilization might also help dampen some of the conflicts over norms between the gentry and longer term residents that I chronicled elsewhere in this book. In chapter 4 I described a block association meeting where newcomers complained to the police about young adults and adolescents congregating on the corner. The block association was just getting off the ground, and there appeared to be no one representing the teenaged loiterers, not even their parents. If the police do "encourage" these teenagers to move along, this will likely inspire feelings of resentment and perhaps cynicism about gentrification. In contrast, if the community were already mobilized, rather than starting a block association from scratch, newer residents would likely be joining an existing organization. The extant organization would presumably have some representation of those youths congregating on the corners whether the youths' parents or the youths themselves. This would have given the newcomers and the older residents an opportunity to meet. Rather than viewing the teens as threatening hoodlums to be shooed away, perhaps the teens would then be viewed as youths simply in need of some guidance. As it is, the newcomers were stepping into a vacuum and hence could fashion the block association to fit their needs. In a well-organized community, the newcomers would have to mesh their desires with those of older residents.

Effective community mobilization thus might be the surest antidote to expressions of cynicism expressed herein. This tact generally entails focusing on community organizing first. Rather than first developing specific solutions to the problems confronting the neighborhood the goal is to get residents organized and thinking about what they can and want to do to improve the quality of life in their neighborhood. Starting out with small winnable projects, the community takes on institutions with in-your-face tactics if necessary (Stoecker 2003, pp. 51–52). ACORN and the Industrial Areas Foundation are examples of community-based organizations that stress this type of grassroots organizing. Although some subscribers to the organize first school of thought emphasize Alinsky-style confrontational tactics, others prefer more conciliatory approaches. One such approach still aims to mobilize the community and develop neighborhood leadership but rather than seeing outside institutions as enemies that must be confronted, sees them as partners that can be swayed. Confrontational tactics like picketing are avoided, as are highly divisive issues affecting the community (Gittell and Vidal 1998). The common theme is that community mobilization and organizing becomes an end in itself rather than the means to achieve a particular end like affordable housing.

These arguments could also be framed in terms of social capital. The need to mobilize and organize residents is a way of building community cohesion and ties that help people get by. Those who argue for more conciliatory rather than combative relations with institutions external to the neighborhood are recognizing the importance of "bridging social capital" that by building connections to those with access to more resources help people "get ahead" (Briggs 1998). Many proponents of social capital dwell on its importance for civic engagement and economic development (Putnam 2000), whereas others have highlighted social capital's importance for enabling a community to articulate and achieve its own ends (Sampson 1999). By being effectively mobilized and organized, a community's cohesion is enhanced and the community's ability to make demands and/or collaborate with exogenous institutions enhanced as well.

My arguments should not be interpreted as meaning that community mobilizing tactics of this type have been absent in gentrifying neighborhoods like Clinton Hill and Harlem. Grassroots organizing has been present in both neighborhoods, particularly in Harlem. Indeed, the flyer depicted in figure 3.1 comes from such a grassroots organizing effort. But such organizing is only effective to the extent that individuals are actively engaged. Therefore, when I speak to people who are not engaged, it is not surprising that they attribute neighborhood improvements to the conscious choice of the powers that be. If we wish to lessen such feelings—and I argue that is a worthy goal—it may be necessary to better and more extensively organize and mobilize the residents of communities like Clinton Hill and Harlem that are threatened with gentrification. The cynicism I encountered while interviewing residents of these areas likely represents those elements of the community who have not been effectively organized or mobilized. If the theory underlying the community organizing thesis is correct, residents of disadvantaged areas would come to believe that the way their neighborhood is treated is the result of their effectively demanding and receiving better services and not the arbitrary whims of unknown powers. Mobilization might not make residents any more enamored with outside institutions, but they would be aware that these institutions can be influenced by residents of the community. Had more residents of Clinton Hill and Harlem been organized for community improvement, rather than explaining neighborhood change in terms of cynicism toward the powers that be that were shaping the gentrification process, they would have more likely attributed it to their own efforts to remake the community—as many of those active in the community did indeed do.

As a policy recommendation the call for more mobilization is, of course, a daunting one. Most of those in community development are cognizant of the need to organize and mobilize residents. But not everyone, including those who are cynical wants to be mobilized. Only 60 percent of eligible voters voted in the last presidential election despite hundreds of millions spent advertising candidates, despite untold hours of media coverage, despite the presidential election being among the most important in the world, despite there being a day set aside for people to vote. Given this level of civic disengagement, it should not be surprising that many people are not actively engaged in improving their community. But as a means of addressing the cynical feelings described in chapters 3 and 4, effective community organizing and mobilizing would appear to hold the most promise. Bricks-and-mortar redevelopment, even if planned with community input or with set asides for affordable housing, will not by itself alleviate some of the antagonistic feelings residents have toward the process of gentrification.

## A POLICY FOR GENTRIFICATION

If, as Smith (1986) and Wyly and Hammel (1999) argued, gentrification is becoming a widespread trend that represents the future of many cities, we should be thinking about how to manage the process to help us achieve a more equitable and just society. Like Stoecker (1997) and others from the organize first school as well as those who trump the importance of social capital, I argue that effective and sustained community organizing and mobilizing is necessary to dampen the feelings of cynicism and alienation that many residents express toward the process of gentrification. This will amplify residents' voices, contribute to their sense of empowerment, and complement bricks-and-mortar redevelopment strategies.

Mobilization and organization alone, however, are unlikely to be enough to confront the challenges that gentrification engenders. Not surprisingly, my research shows that many residents are leery of the inflationary effects gentrification can have on housing markets. To counter these threats, mechanisms must be put in place that tap the wealth created by gentrification for the benefit of indigenous and poorer residents who may wish to move to the neighborhood in the future. Inclusionary zoning by using new development in gentrifying neighborhoods to cross-subsidize affordable housing does tap the market to benefit disadvantaged residents. TIF that targets affordable housing also taps the wealth created by gentrification to benefit disadvantaged residents by using the increment in tax revenues resulting from gentrification for affordable housing.

Affordable homeownership programs will provide a modicum of security and also help build wealth among homeowners.

Taken together, these policies offer a strategy for meeting the challenges and opportunities that gentrification presents, and they do this in a way that that is cognizant of the political obstacles that redistributive policies face in these increasingly reactionary times.

# 7  Conclusion

THE NARRATIVES IN this book, which address the process of gentrification in two predominantly black inner-city neighborhoods, speak forcefully to the ongoing debates among urban scholars. I addressed one of these debates in chapter 5 in the discussion of neighborhood effects in the context of gentrification. Here I address three additional themes that are germane to the findings depicted in this book—the meaning of the ghetto, our conceptualizations of gentrification, and the implications for neoliberal urban policy. I begin by invoking images of black inner city neighborhoods and considering whether for at least some of the neighborhoods, gentrification renders these images obsolete. The second part of this chapter addresses the extent to which two of the more common conceptions of gentrification as the scene of a new middle class and as the embodiment of middle-class vengeance on the urban poor are apt in light of the research presented here. The third debate given a reconsideration here is that over neoliberal urban policy. The narratives presented herein speak to any assessment of the neoliberal urban policy regime. The chapter and book conclude with a summary of the implications of these findings for gentrification scholarship.

## RETHINKING THE GHETTO

Ever since the ghetto crystallized into an enduring feature of American cities in the wake of the Great Migration, black inner city neighborhoods have been a place apart. These were neighborhoods that were excluded from the mainstream of American life. The civil unrest during the long hot summers of the 1960s only served to hasten the exodus of not only white residents who had always fled black encroachment, but business and commerce as well. In the wake of the 1960s turbulence, abandonment became the defining feature of many a ghetto. Many of those with means left for greener pastures. Businesses fled leaving behind an underserved and unemployed populace. Crack cocaine became the major employer for young black men.

The conditions in the ghetto nourished an entire musical genre known as Hip Hop, where lyricists spun tales of life that can be nasty, brutish, and potentially short. In it is a place pregnant with violence, a place lacking role models, and finally, a place of gloom where "the trees don't grow." The bravado inherent in the hip hop genre notwithstanding, the lyrics convey an image of the ghetto that is etched in the popular imagination. Rappers here serve as cultural ambassadors for the ghetto, bringing putatively authentic ghetto culture to the wider world. But the fact that the ghetto needs ambassadors for the larger American society, despite being primarily populated by the descendants of those who have been in America for centuries, speaks to the degree in which the ghetto has been a world apart.

The otherness of the ghetto is more than just a manifestation of it being populated by persons of a different race. Indeed, ethnic racial clustering has been the norm in the history of cities. As I argued in chapter 1, however, the ghetto is thought to be unique in its degree of isolation. Massey and Denton (1993) have emphasized the spatial isolation of blacks in the ghetto, the extent to which blacks are segregated residentially from others. For them, blacks have been and continue to be uniquely spatially isolated from wider society. Moreover, this spatial isolation is a reflection of and contributor to blacks' unique pariah status in American society. Wilson (1987) emphasized the social isolation of the modern-day ghetto, seeing as key the absence of employment opportunities and the middle class in today's ghetto neighborhoods and the concomitant lack of interaction between residents and those outside of the ghetto. In this way, the ghetto of today is different from that of the past or contemporary poor immigrant neighborhoods. Marcuse goes further, arguing that the ghetto is isolated on a number of dimensions. He goes so far as to state that "The black ghetto of today is a substantially different ghetto from the classic ghetto: It is an outcast ghetto, and those within it are subject to exclusion from the mainstream of the economic, social, and political life of the city" (Marcuse 1997, p. 228). For Marcuse, a key distinction between the ghetto of today and that of yesteryear is that today's ghetto serves no economic function for the larger society. Whereas in the past one might argue that the ghetto served as a source of cheap labor, today's idle residents no longer even serve that purpose. The picture painted by scholars, then, is also of a place apart.

The material presented in this book also highlights the extent to which many black inner-city communities were cut off from the larger society. Chapters 3 and 4 relate residents' reactions to the changes taking place in their neighborhood. They described their surprise at witnessing whites walking through the neighborhood, new housing being built, or chain stores moving in. In most places a new supermarket or drugstore is rather mundane. But for these residents, such changes to the neighborhood were truly startling. Marcuse's (1997) argument about economic isolation can be amplified here. Marcuse points to the low levels of employment among ghetto residents as evidence of their economic isolation.

But the absence of commerce is also evidence of their marginalization as well. It is certainly true that capital has always extracted profits from the ghetto. But the large multinational corporation that has come to dominate much of the global economy was virtually absent from the ghetto—further evidence that compels us to conclude that the black inner city was divorced from the larger society. Thus, the ghetto of today is a *qualitatively different* type of neighborhood than virtually any other type in American history.

## ENTER GENTRIFICATION: NO LONGER THE "OUTCAST GHETTO?"

Does gentrification challenge our conception of the ghetto? Is the ghetto still a place set apart, isolated economically, politically, and socially from the wider society? If we consider the specific criteria outlined by various writers, one would have to conclude in the negative. In describing the area as an "outcast ghetto" Marcuse (1997, p. 237) stated that "Harlem is no longer a magnet" for middle-class blacks. This is no longer true. As described by Taylor (2002), and in chapter 2 and elsewhere in this book, the black middle class is playing a major role in the gentrification of black inner-city neighborhoods like Harlem, Clinton Hill, or Bronzeville in Chicago (Boyd 2004). The presence of the "new black middle class" in Clinton Hill and Harlem that I described in chapter 2 would also seem to contradict Wilson's (1987) depiction of the modern ghetto as devoid of a stable middle class. Indeed it is debatable that the middle class had ever left, but certainly in light of gentrification this characterization is no longer apt.

Moreover, although Clinton Hill and especially Harlem are still overwhelmingly black neighborhoods, whites are increasingly considering these areas as a place to live. This is certainly counter to historic trends. Typically, integration was due to blacks entering white neighborhoods. Only in rare circumstances did the white population increase in predominantly black neighborhoods (Lee and Wood 1991). So although the absolute magnitude of the white population may be small in Harlem, for example, there is indisputable evidence that it is increasing. In Clinton Hill the white population is large enough that some would cite it as an example of a new paradigm—a predominantly black neighborhood with a sizable yet stable white presence (Rosenberg 1998). Harlem may be posed to follow this paradigm and become a neighborhood with a sizable white presence but is still overwhelmingly black. This, too, would be a reality that differs from existing images of the ghetto as a place where whites only tread as agents of the dominant white society—police officers, fire fighters, teachers, landlords.

PHOTO 11. New trendy restaurant in Harlem.

Arguments that with gentrification black inner-city neighborhoods are taking on a new reality do not deny the persistence of some forms of isolation. To date, gentrification appears to be having little impact on the employment woes that blacks face, thus doing little to lessen the type of economic isolation that Marcuse (1997) emphasized. This is perhaps to be expected, at least in the short term, for blacks, like most people live in predominantly residential neighborhoods. In today's specialized economy, most people work outside of the neighborhood in which they live. Hence, the prospects for gentrification improving employment opportunities would seem to be slight at best. Furthermore, even with the trickling of whites into black strongholds like Clinton Hill or Harlem, New York City remains one of the most segregated metropolises in the United States (Lewis Mumford Center 2003). Yet I would argue that gentrification is qualitatively changing the nature of ghetto neighborhoods like Harlem. In some ways Clinton Hill is much further along on this path, having never declined as much as Harlem and having experienced gentrification much earlier. Still, as gentrification spreads to portions of the neighborhood that were formerly untouched by gentrification and as the process pushes the boundaries of Clinton Hill further east into "do or die Bed-Stuy" this argument is applicable to this section of Brooklyn as well.

That gentrification is fundamentally changing the nature of a neighborhood like Harlem is in some ways obvious. By definition that's what gentrification is—a fundamental change in the character of the neighborhood. Specific neighborhoods change all the time. A larger and to some perhaps more interesting question is whether gentrification represents a fundamental shift in the stratification of neighborhoods or if it is merely reshuffling this stratification. Put another way, if Harlem's residents and institutions moved en masse to say, the northwest Bronx, and Harlem simply became an extension of the Upper West Side, it would be farcical to argue that gentrification altered the nature of the ghetto. It would have changed the nature of *a* ghetto, but the ghetto of isolation that was described earlier would still exist, only somewhere else. A better question then is does gentrification change the nature of *the ghetto* in addition to a *specific ghetto?*

Although the research presented in this book does not allow this question to be answered definitively, it does contribute to the steady accumulation of evidence that the indeed the nature of the ghetto is changing. Schaffer and Smith (1986) danced around this question some two decades ago with their analysis of the beginnings of gentrification in Harlem. While drawing conclusions about the significance of gentrification in

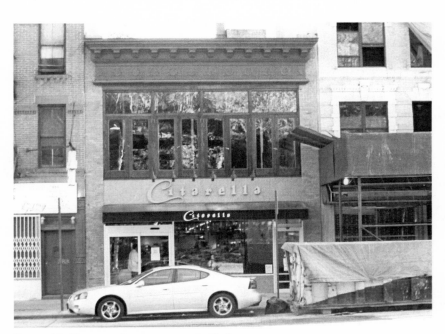

PHOTO 12. New upscale grocery store in Harlem.

Harlem for theories about urban space in general, they were for the most part silent about the meaning of gentrification for the ghetto. They wrote:

> The fact that the process has begun at all, that gentrification is even on the agenda in Harlem, lends support to the claim that we are witnessing not a curious anomaly but the trenchant restructuring of urban space and that this if the process of gentrification continued this would ultimately mean that large numbers of community residents would face displacement. (Schaffer and Smith 1986, p. 362)

With the luxury of twenty years of hindsight, we can clearly see that the picture is more complicated than their interpretation would suggest. Schaffer and Smith appear to be correct in diagnosing the restructuring of urban space, and the ghetto is obviously a part of urban space. It seems that a specific statement about the restructuring of Harlem might have been in order as well. From their vantage point, gentrification was an inherently unstable process that would lead to the displacement of indigenous residents in short order. Nevertheless, although displacement is and will continue to be a threat, several decades of gentrification would seem to reinforce the notion that gentrification is changing the relationship of the ghetto to the wider society. If the process of Harlem becoming a gentrified neighborhood takes twenty years, thirty years, or longer, this "transitional" period would seem to be worthy of consideration in its own right, which is what this book does indeed do.

Wyly and Hammel's (1999) work is also suggests that the nature of the relationship between capital and the inner city is indeed changing. They document the increasing flows of capital to inner-city neighborhoods, something they attribute to the deregulation of capital and changes in affordable housing policy—what some refer to as neoliberal urban policy (Newman and Ashton 2004). Like Schaffer and Smith, they interpret this as evidence of a fundamental restructuring of urban space, but they are relatively silent on the meaning of this restructuring for the ghetto specifically. Still, Wyly and Hammel's work suggests that the phenomena of ghetto gentrification that was described in this book is not anomalous to Clinton Hill and Harlem but is part of a wider trend.

The dramatic decrease in concentrated poverty in the 1990s is also further circumstantial evidence that the nature of the ghetto may be changing (Jargowsky 2003). It was the increase in concentrated poverty during the 1970–1990 period that was a major impetus behind notions of a new type of ghetto that was the home to an underclass (Wilson 1987). The link between declines in concentrated poverty and gentrification, if there is indeed one, has yet to be documented. But some of Jargowsky's evidence, notably the fact that declines in concentrated poverty were greater in central cities than in the suburbs, is consistent with what would be expected if there were a link between the decline of concentrated poverty and the rise of gentrification in ghetto neighborhoods during the 1990s. Moreover, Crowder and South (2005) also found that the rate at which middle and high income whites moved into poor central city neighborhoods increased over the 1970–1997 period, a finding they interpret as being consistent with increasing gentrification.

Finally, consider that in spring 2005 the NeighborWorks America (NWA) sponsored a one-day symposium, When Gentrification Comes Knocking—Navigating Social Dynamics in Changing Neighborhoods, at one of their training institutes. The purpose of the symposium was to provide community development practitioners with tools for dealing with the challenges and opportunities their communities will face under gentrification. NWA serves a national clientele, suggesting that the threat of gentrification is widespread and not anomalous to a few cities.

The focus of this symposium is noteworthy because the NWA training institutes typically focus on topics like developing affordable housing, community organizing, or community economic development. These are topics one would expect for an organization whose roots lay in the efforts of community activists to revitalize depressed inner-city neighborhoods. The NWA was formally created by the Neighborhood Reinvestment Corporation Act of 1978. The rationale for its creation was that without public intervention, private capital would continue to overlook poor inner-city neighborhoods because of the perceived risks there. A quarter of a century later, private capital has returned to the inner city with a vengeance, so much so that communities that once fought to access capital find their communities as they know them threatened with transformation by private capital.

The evidence cited suggests that from a temporal perspective gentrification is clearly changing the nature of the ghetto to the wider society. Neighborhoods like Harlem may one day become completely gentrified and devoid of poor blacks and Latinos. Until that time comes, which if we date the beginning of gentrification in Harlem to the mid-1980s might be at least thirty years in total, the relationship of Harlem to the outside world will be substantially different than it was prior to gentrification. Moreover, this relationship is different from the images and vocabulary of isolation and outcast would suggest.

The narratives of residents depicted in this book therefore suggest that at least in some ghetto neighborhoods, relations to the outside world are changing to such an extent that the "outcast" metaphor no longer adequately captures these relationships. But if gentrification can potentially change the relational dynamics between the ghetto and the larger economy, does this suggest a reimaging of gentrification is also in order?

Photo 13. New rowhouse development in Harlem. Developments of this type are cropping up on formerly vacant lots throughout the area.

## Emancipatory or Revanchist City?

When thinking about how the narratives herein may point toward a reconsideration of the meaning of gentrification, one runs up against the fact that there is no single image of gentrification. Rather, the literature has been the scene of fierce debates over its interpretation. Most well known are the differences between Ley (1996) and Caulfield (1994), who focus on the role of the gentry, and Smith (1996), who focuses on the role of capital in seeking causal explanations for the origins of gentrification. Yet the most unbridgeable chasm between these two camps might be the broader meaning of gentrification. Ley and others in the demand-side school who focus on the role of the gentry in the process tend to characterize gentrification as a spatial manifestation of an increasingly diverse middle class. More specifically, gentrification is a means of this new middle class expressing its identity outside of the mainstream suburban subdivision that had come to dominate much of middle-class North American life in the post–World War II era. In this way, gentrification is a potentially liberating experience that allows for new forms of expression and allows some marginalized groups, such as gays and lesbians, to carve out their own residential enclaves.

Not surprisingly, given that their vantage point is the gentry, this conception of gentrification does not describe the experience of long-term residents or the "gentrified," if you will. For them, there appears to be little in the process that could be described as emancipatory or liberating. Instead, the narratives repeatedly described how certain behaviors were now proscribed. Congregating on the corner, barbecuing in the park, and drinking alcohol in public are example of behaviors that are no longer acceptable. If anything, gentrification might be more aptly described as repressive and restrictive in the way that it narrowed the range of acceptable behaviors for some long term residents—a point I return to later.

In some ways, however, the gentrification of black neighborhoods is liberating in ways not imagined by Ley and others. That is, the process may be liberating for eclectic-minded segments of the black middle class as well who see in gentrification an opportunity to carve out their own the space without having to conform to the precepts of white America or the conservative social ethos that dominates much of black America. Gentrifying black neighborhoods like the ones examined here represent spaces where the black identity is celebrated, the norm and not considered the "other." These are spaces where blacks can feel at home and where they don't have to feel threatened by racial slights at the hands of whites. Several observers have noted that for some middle-class blacks, the legacy of the civil rights era was not integrating into white neighborhoods but having the wherewithal to create desirable black neighborhoods (Cashin 2004). For much of the post–civil rights era, desirable black neighborhoods were assumed to be found in the suburbs. Indeed, many such black suburban enclaves have sprung up around urban America. It is no longer surprising to find suburban neighborhoods with cul-de-sacs and tree-lined streets that are predominantly black. For many middle-class blacks these suburban enclaves represent the epitome of the American dream— single-family homes, owned by blacks, in safe, secure, tranquil neighborhoods (Cashin 2004; Dent 1992).

But suburbia, even if predominantly black, is not what a growing segment of the black middle class aspires to. Single adults, the elderly, and couples without children in particular may not find suburban amenity packages that attractive. This demographic might prefer proximity to the city and its attractions like clubs, dining, and the art scene or simply a shorter commute to the downtown business district. These are the same forces that have drawn the white gentry to the inner city in the closing decades of the twentieth century.

As was described in chapter 2 there is also a cultural force that draws blacks to the inner city. Blacks who subscribe to what I called a neosoul aesthetic might also find little in suburbia calling for them. Indeed, suburbia as the site of the hegemonic white-bread American culture might seem anathema to them. Thus, this component of black America might also be drawn to the inner city.

With the decline of many black inner-city neighborhoods in the post–civil rights era, however, the search for suitable living space left three options, broadly speaking. There was the deteriorating ghetto, where crime and other social dislocations were rising and the housing stock was often crumbling. Black suburban enclaves whose amenity packages were often inferior to those in white suburbs may not have been particularly attractive to some for the reasons described. Finally, neighborhoods without a black identity were increasingly an option. Access to this last option was by no means a forgone conclusion as a number of studies have demonstrated the persistence of housing discrimination against blacks (Yinger 1995).

For the black poor the choices were the same as always—they remained in the ghetto. Those blacks who found the suburbs amenable left for these new environs. A small but steadily increasing proportion of black America found homes in nonblack neighborhoods (Glaeser and Vigdor 2001). But for those with means who did not want to live in the suburbs, the choices may have seemed less than satisfactory—either the substandard ghetto or nonblack neighborhoods. For blacks whom the civil rights struggle meant the destruction of the racial caste system *and* the freedom to *be black* these were not attractive options. Living in the ghetto, with rising crime and substandard services hardly seemed to be the promise of a new day. Not only that, but the quality of life in the ghetto was actually declining in the post–civil rights era. What was the point of the struggle to be recognized as a full American if one still had to live in the ghetto? Living in a nonblack neighborhood was certainly a welcome option for some. But again, for many blacks the civil rights revolution meant having the option to integrate but not necessarily wanting to integrate.

This desire has clearly manifested itself in many suburban enclaves like Prince George's County outside of Washington, DC. In New York City, neighborhoods like St. Albans, Mount Vernon, and Roosevelt have served as suburban enclaves for upwardly mobile blacks (St. Albans is actually part of Queens and therefore is technically part of the central city. But with its single-family homes and distance from Manhattan it offers a suburban lifestyle). These suburban enclaves have developed, in part, by the conscious desire of middle class blacks to live among their own. To some these communities represent the ideal of what blacks can achieve—"nice" suburban neighborhoods that are predominantly black. Much as Harlem in the early twentieth century inspired pride among blacks, these neighborhoods do the same. I can personally attest to being driven around in some of the more affluent enclaves of Prince George's by a friend who wanted to illustrate what we as black people could achieve. But for those who do not march to the beat of the suburban drum, these suburban enclaves might inspire pride but nevertheless not be particularly attractive or affordable as places to live.

The gentrification occurring in predominantly black neighborhoods like Clinton Hill and Harlem would seem to be in part an expression of some segments of the black community to forgo the suburbs and an opportunity for other blacks to do so. As was described in chapter 2, blacks are an integral component of the gentrification process in these neighborhoods. Consequently, for those who wish to remain in the inner city, a gentrifying black neighborhood provides an alternative not available in a depressed ghetto, suburban black enclaves, or nonblack neighborhoods. Pregentrification, neighborhoods like Harlem certainly had their charms. They were predominantly black and could provide a haven of sorts, the culture of black America could be readily enjoyed, and the housing was affordable. Yet these charms were not enough to stem the flight of those who sought greener pastures elsewhere and left behind depopulated inner cities. Recall that Harlem lost 60 percent of its population between 1950 and 1980. Gentrification, to the extent it results in an improvement in amenities, services, and the physical landscape does provide a space for blacks to be black yet at the same time enjoy an improved quality of life. Moreover, this is a blackness that need not conform to the suburban ideal. In this way, it can be argued that the gentrification of the 'hood does allow for a form of expression that would not otherwise be available. What I referred to as the neosoul aesthetic in chapter 2 might be more at home in Clinton Hill than Laurelton, Queens (another suburban-like black enclave).

For at least some residents of Clinton Hill and Harlem, the gentrification of their neighborhoods might indeed be an incentive for them to stay, to live the type of lifestyle that might not have otherwise been available. Indeed this was a sentiment that some of the residents I spoke with described, as presented in chapter 3. Many of them were single adults, and hence suburbia may not have beckoned. Yet they may not have been able or willing to reside in nonblack neighborhoods. A nonblack neighborhood may not offer the sense of belonging that a black person would feel in a black neighborhood. But if one wants access to amenities and services, a nonblack neighborhood was often the only choice. The gentrification occurring in Clinton Hill and Harlem by no means erases the resource disparities between these neighborhoods and white neighborhoods. In relative terms, the gaps may be as large as ever. Nevertheless, the arrival of improved amenities and services does make these neighborhoods more livable, as the testimonies in chapters 3 and 4 attest.

Of course, if gentrification leads to these neighborhoods becoming all white, the notion that another form of blackness can find its expression

Photo 14. Upscale section of Harlem.

there is laughable. To the extent that rising housing costs price blacks out, neither Harlem nor Clinton Hill will be a haven for blackness. At best, they may maintain vestiges of their black past, much as Little Italy, which has been swallowed up by Chinatown, now does. One can still dine in Italian restaurants in Little Italy, but the bulk of the Italian population is long gone. In a whitened Harlem perhaps one will still be able to attend the fabled Apollo Theater, but the black masses will be long gone.

I make no pretensions about being able to predict the future, however, a completely whitened Clinton Hill or Harlem seems unlikely in the near future. As was discussed in chapter 2, the pace of gentrification in these predominantly black neighborhoods appears to be gradual. Perhaps most whites' unwillingness to move into predominantly black neighborhoods will in the long run preserve these neighborhoods' black identity. Moreover, a number of community-based organizations in both neighborhoods have acted to ensure that there will continue to be at least a modicum of affordable housing in these communities. For the next couple of decades at least, Clinton Hill and Harlem seem likely to maintain their black identity. As such, they will continue to be spaces where more eclectic forms of the black identity can manifest itself. In this way, Ley's argument about the eclectic sensibilities of a new middle class expressing itself through gentrification can be refracted through the prism of race. The gentrification of the hood, in these circumstances at least, can represent a spatial manifestation of an urbane black middle class. This is a view is absent from much of the discourse on gentrification.

## The Revenge of the Middle Class?

Lest the reader think I am too optimistic about gentrification and blind to its negative aspects, let me consider the other and in some ways more prevalent view of gentrification, as part of a class struggle whereby the middle class wreaks havoc on the lives of the indigenous poor. Smith (1996) coined the phrase "revanchist city" to describe the revenge the middle class wreaked on the poor in retaliation for the poor destroying the city. Smith writes:

> The revanchist city is, to be sure, a dual and divided city of wealth and poverty, and it will continue to be so as seemingly apocalyptic visions of urban fissure, anticipated by Davis (1992) and realized in the Los Angeles uprising, appear more and more realistic. But it is more. It is a divided city where the victors are increasingly defensive of their privilege, such as it is, and increasingly vicious in defending it. The revanchist city is more than the dual city, in race and class terms. The benign neglect of "the other half" so dominant in the liberal rhetoric of the 1950s and 1960s, has been superseded by a more active viciousness that attempts to criminalize a whole range of "behavior," individually defined, and to blame the failure of post-1968 urban policy on the population it was supposed to benefit. (Smith 1996, p. 227)

Chapters 3, 4, and 5 suggest that from the perspective of some residents of gentrifying neighborhoods like Clinton Hill and Harlem, the revanchist city is alive and well. The narratives reported there are replete with stories about how formerly acceptable behaviors are no longer acceptable in the wake of gentrification. Standing on the corner, drinking on the corner, drinking in the park, cooking out in the park, playing music or children playing outside late at night, and simply being black and walking down the street are some of the behaviors that are now thought to be proscribed. When viewed through the eyes of residents of affected neighborhoods, Smith's characterization of gentrification as a manifestation of the revanchist city would appear to be on the mark. Gentrification does indeed have an oppressive element to it, limiting the range of behaviors available to residents of these neighborhoods. Moreover, these limitations are linked directly to the arrival of gentrifiers. The reason these behaviors are now proscribed is to ensure the safety and comfort of gentrifiers moving into the neighborhood.

Groups of black men congregating on the corner, loud music, or drinking outside are signs of disorder and in the view of the reigning "broken windows" thesis not to be tolerated. This thesis (which has been challenged; see Sampson, Raudenbush, and Earls 1997) posited that allowing small acts of disorder sent a signal to would be criminals that more violent and serious crimes would be tolerated. If no one cared about broken windows, perhaps they would not care about a little drug dealing either. To squash crime, all acts of disorder must be stamped out. From the viewpoint of residents of gentrifying neighborhoods, it is clearly external definitions of disorder that are to be controlled. This, too, is coincident with Smith's depiction of the class struggle that gentrification entails. Thus the gentrification of the 'hood when viewed through the eyes of indigenous residents does appear to be the middle class and especially whites protecting their encroachment into the neighborhood.

It might seem paradoxical to affirm both the emancipatory and revanchist view of gentrification. But as I have stressed elsewhere in this book, gentrification is a complex process that can mean different things depending on one's vantage point. Writing from a neo-Marxist perspective, Smith (1996) not surprisingly emphasized the class clashes inherent in gentrification and perforce be skeptical of the motives of capital and the classes it represents. The revanchist elements of gentrification are coincident with this viewpoint. For at least some residents of gentrifying neighborhoods the revanchist city is an apt description of how they see their area changing. But this is only one aspect of the process. As the narratives presented in this book make clear, residents are quite capable of resenting the changes in what is considered acceptable *and* appreciating the access to improved amenities and services.

Other writers, looking at gentrification through a cultural lens, have emphasized changes in cultural norms that lead to gentrification and the way the process allows different groups to express themselves (Caulfield 1994; Ley 1996). This has led them to examine the cultural forces that have led to changes in residential preferences, and how those making these choices differ from those pursuing the American dream of a single-family home in the suburbs. This had led to a perhaps more optimistic view of gentrification as emancipatory or a space for diversity. For residents of black neighborhoods, gentrification does have the potential to allow some to live in a type of area that might not otherwise be available. This, too, is an aspect of gentrification. As Hamnett (1991) described, gentrification when viewed from these differing vantage points is akin to the elephant being described by the blind men.

## THE MEANING FOR NEOLIBERAL URBAN POLICY

As discussed in chapter 2, the gentrification of inner-city black neighborhoods, particularly more depressed ones like Harlem, was abetted by what many refer to as the neoliberal policy regime of the 1990s that encouraged public–private partnership as a means of revitalizing urban centers. Although the term is somewhat misleading as it suggests a conscious policy choice by a single actor or set of actors, *neoliberalism* has nevertheless gained currency as a word that describes policies that give the market or middle class a significant role to play. Certainly the gentrification of Harlem (and to a lesser extent Clinton Hill) were abetted by policies that encouraged private institutions to invest or lend in these neighborhoods and policies that encourage the middle class to move into or stay in these neighborhoods. Consequently, I will consider how the narratives expressed in this book speak to the broader debates on neoliberal urban policy.

What lessons can be learned from the narratives presented here about the neoliberal policy regime as it pertains to the black inner city? One important lesson is that it can indeed effect change in depressed inner-city neighborhoods. In contrast to the "nothing works" pessimism that bedeviled inner-city revitalization efforts for the quarter century after the civil disturbances of the 1960s, community development organizations are now counseled to anticipate their success (Blackwell 2005). When Wilson (1987) brought the plight of the inner city back to the fore of national debates, he was skeptical of the feasibility of revitalizing these neighborhoods:

> The program of [tight labor markets, job training, child care subsidies, and family allowances] will help address the problems of social dislocation plaguing the ghetto underclass. I make no claims that such programs will lead to a revitalization of neighborhoods in the inner city.... This discussion raises a question about the ultimate effectiveness of the so-called self-help programs to revitalize the inner-city.... In many inner-city neighborhoods, problems such as joblessness are so overwhelming and require such a massive effort to restabilize institutions (e.g., the reintegration of the neighborhood with working- and middle-class blacks and black professionals) that it is surprising that [the revitalization strategy] has received so much serious attention. (Wilson 1987, pp. 157–58)

And as noted in chapter 2, as late as 1994 respected journalist Nicholas Lemann (1994) could write about the myth of community development. The narratives described in this book speak to the real-life changes this policy regime has had on these neighborhoods in a way that census data or charts could not. Residents spoke of changes in the physical landscape, the types of stores available, and the type of people moving into the neighborhood that almost strained their credulity. Harlem more so than Clinton Hill was emblematic of the failures of U.S. urban policy and therefore the changes there are more striking. Nevertheless, residents of Clinton Hill were also surprised by some of the improvements taking place around them. Any assessment of the neoliberal policy regime would have to first consider the extent to which it had any effect. The narratives presented in this book provide ample evidence that there were indeed substantial changes in depressed inner-city neighborhoods like Harlem. Again, given the pessimism with which some skeptics viewed community development, this evidence is an important component the argument that debunks the "myth" of the myth of community development—that it does not work.

Significantly changing poor neighborhoods, however, is hardly enough to consider a policy successful. The urban renewal program dramatically changed the physical and social landscape of many neighborhoods, yet hardly anyone would describe it as a successful program. We must also consider the distributional effects of the regime, particularly for the poor and the original residents of the neighborhood. This was the Achilles heel of urban renewal—the original residents seldom benefited and were often

PHOTO 15. New development planned across from public housing in Clinton Hill.

made worse off through displacement (Fullilove 2004). When viewed through a distributional prism the assessment of neoliberal urban policy is clouded considerably. The previous chapter spelled out in considerable detail the costs and benefits of gentrification and places where collective action is warranted, so I do not reiterate that discussion here. I do, however, consider the implications of the policy discussion for the broader neoliberal policy debate.

Clearly poor renters are the ones most at risk in the case of gentrification. A policy regime that improves inner-city neighborhoods by relying in part on private investment and the return of the middle class will inevitably raise housing prices and threaten to price them out of the neighborhood. There is nothing in the broad package of policies called neoliberal, however, that precludes setting aside resources for the poor. Indeed, some of the policy instruments characterized as neoliberal, such as community lending or the LIHTC, do just that. To be sure, significant modifications to the extant policy regime will be necessary to ensure that the poor continue to have access to gentrifying neighborhoods. Whether the political power or will is there to accomplish these policy modifications is debatable. But there is nothing inherent in a policy that encourages reinvestment and attracting the middle class that precludes setting aside resources for the poor. If the goal is to make the spaces that some of the poor inhabit more livable, it would seem the neoliberal policy regime has the potential to accomplish this goal.

If the goal is to reduce or eliminate poverty, however, there is little to suggest that neoliberal policy or the resultant gentrification is effective. Increased opportunities for upward mobility due to gentrification was not a theme that emerged during my conversations with residents of Clinton Hill or Harlem. Moreover, as I discussed in chapter 5, there seems to be little reason to expect gentrification to significantly affect the class trajectories of residents indigenous to gentrifying neighborhoods—at least in the short run. Residents may have access to better services and amenities, but this will do little to enhance upward mobility. It is possible that the local public schools will improve over time in gentrifying neighborhoods. This would be one way that gentrification could actually enhance the prospects for upward mobility among indigenous residents. But because many early gentrifiers are childless, schools seem to be a lagging indicator in the gentrification process. The extent to which a poor household would be able to stay in a neighborhood to reap the benefits of improving schools is debatable and therefore suggests caution before assuming that this will be an unequivocal benefit for indigenous residents. Gentrification may also lead to a modest increase in the local employment base. But neither the number pay level nor the number of these jobs is likely to lead to significant upward mobility for the mass of residents.

PHOTO 16. New supermarket and housing development in Harlem. For years, full-service supermarkets such as this one were rare in Harlem.

What gentrification can do is help minimize the extent to which various aspects of quality of life are dependent on one's class. Because so many things are dependent in part on where one lives—primary education, exposure to crime and environmental hazards, access to decent and healthful food—the quality of one's neighborhood can affect life outcomes. To the extent the poor share residential space with those more affluent they will benefit from at least some of the amenities the more affluent are able to command and the disamenities they are able to avoid.

This is a potentially important benefit of mixed-income neighborhoods. Critics of poverty deconcentration policy have pointed out that such an approach does not address the root causes of poverty inherent in our extant political economy (Crump 2002). This criticism is certainly valid. But to the extent poverty is truly deconcentrated and not just shuffled about, poverty deconcentration does have the potential to lessen the extent to which inequality matters. The market may distribute wealth in vastly unequal ways. But we can limit the importance of this inequality by lessening the extent to which access to decent neighborhoods is determined solely by one's class. Gentrification, by bringing middle-class residents to relatively poor neighborhoods, has the *potential* to help create more mixed-income neighborhoods. I stress *potential* because as discussed in the previous chapter, significant policy intervention is necessary to ensure that low-income households continue to have access to gentrifying neighborhoods.

Politically, it might be easier to create mixed-income neighborhoods through gentrification than via the dispersal of the poor. Indigenous residents of affected neighborhoods have a moral claim on the area, having been there first and having weathered the bad times. In addition, the gentry are presumably more amenable than the suburban middle class to having the poor as neighbors. Otherwise the gentry would have not moved into the neighborhood. Policies that promote affordable housing in the suburbs face resistance not only because of their redistributive nature but because many people do not want to live near subsidized housing, regardless of who pays for it. In gentrifying neighborhoods the challenge is to preserve what is there or ensure new development takes into consideration existing residents. Such policies are less likely to meet the vociferous opposition that affordable housing in the suburbs has often faced (Briggs, Darden, and Aidala 1998; Carson 1995; Cuomo 1974).

A second strand of criticism of the neoliberal urban policy regime stems from the notion that communities, by acquiescing to private investment and the return of the middle class, will find their efforts to agitate and organize for a redistribution of wealth hampered. Inviting the private sector to invest in one's community makes it difficult to then demand that these institutions and those like them accede to a fundamental reorienting of the political economy. The antagonistic stance necessary to affect a redistribution of wealth is inconsistent with seeking to partner with the private sector to invest in poor communities (Stoecker 1997). Likewise, the arrival of the gentry will change the focus of community based groups from challenging the existing political economy to quality of life issues such as loitering on the corner or the appearance of the housing stock (Newman 2004). The gentry, black or white, would presumably be content with the existing political economy.

A moderation in the political aims of community-based organizations in the face of gentrification is certainly a risk. These organizations may be so consumed by promoting development and managing the threats inherent in gentrification that they lose sights of the need to agitate for a fundamental change in the political economy. It is worth pointing out, however, that the politics of the poor are not always distinguishable from the neoliberal policies criticized by some. The redevelopment of Brownsville, Brooklyn, surely one of the most depressed and arson-ravaged communities in New York City in the 1970s and 1980s, hinged in large part on the development of affordable homeownership opportunities (Freedman 1994). That is, repopulating the neighborhood with stable homeowners, albeit relatively low income, was what residents thought was needed to stabilize the neighborhood. This was the choice that resulted from community organizing spearheaded by the Industrial Areas Foundation (IAF). The IAF is the progeny of the radical organizing advocated by Saul Alinsky—hardly a group known for its neoliberal politics. Yet their redevelopment strategy, affordable homeownership, is not dramatically different from the redevelopment strategies of some other community-based organizations that have been criticized as neoliberal (Newman 2004). So even if fully empowered, community residents will often pursue what some refer to as neoliberal policies. One could argue that this is due to a sort of "false consciousness" on the part of community residents, although such arguments have paternalistic air about them. All of this is not to deny that the poor might be better served by a reorienting of the political economy toward more redistribution and that neighborhood revitalization could distract them from that goal. But against this possibility must be weighed the fact some of the poor may not want such a reorientation, only their opportunity to get their share; that revitalization can improve the local quality of life; and that a reorientation of the political economy may not be politically feasible. Finally, redistributing wealth to create a more equal society while maximizing economic growth so that everyone's standard of living improves is not an easy task. Too much inequality can serve to dampen economic growth. Redistribute wealth in a too heavy-handed manner, and this can also shrink the size of the pie. Given these caveats, it would seem imprudent to argue against neighborhood revitalization whether through neoliberal policies that spur gentrification or other means, because it may distract communities from demanding a greater redistribution of resources. The path to a fundamental reorientation of the political economy is too fraught with uncertainty to put aside much-needed improvements in the quality of life in inner-city neighborhoods.

To the extent one wants to attribute the gentrification occurring in black inner-city neighborhoods to a neoliberal policy regime, the narratives described here suggest the following: Even the most depressed black inner-city communities can be revitalized and become targets for gentrification. Gentrification can bring benefits that the indigenous residents of these neighborhoods are appreciative of. There are, however, significant potential downsides to this revitalization, including the loss of affordable housing, conflict between newcomers and more established residents, and resentment stemming from feelings of irrelevance; the neighborhood improvements are for "them." Any assessment of the neoliberal urban policy regime can therefore be informed by the findings presented earlier in this book.

## GENTRIFICATION RECONSIDERED

Gentrification continues to be a flashpoint among scholars, community activists, policy makers, and those living in gentrifying neighborhoods themselves. As someone who has published research that goes against some of the common wisdom, I am no stranger to these debates. As a social scientist I am tempted to try to rise above the fray and simply present the facts. I have decided to resist that temptation and wade directly into the controversy.

On one side, many are vociferous in their opposition to gentrification for some of the reasons discussed here. This is a common and pervasive feeling both in the academy and on the street. At the NWA symposium I described earlier, one of the attendees stood up and proclaimed, "There's nothing at all positive about gentrification!" For this woman, that is her reality. Certainly after reading analyses presented in this book one can understand why someone might have this type of sentiment. Those that write disparagingly about gentrification are not simply misinformed. There is a strong negative undercurrent toward gentrification, some of which was brought to light in this book. In addition, many of the scholars writing on gentrification have done so from a neo-Marxist perspective (see Smith 1996 for example). When viewed through a prism that pits capital against labor or pits those interested in exchange values versus use values, it is not surprising that gentrification would emerge sullied. Exchange values don't always win, but they do frequently. Moreover, a speculator interested in the exchange value of a property is not likely to attract much sympathy vis-à-vis a poor household that is displaced. Finally, the market can allocate wealth in ways that appear unseemly—gargantuan sums to a few, little and sometimes nothing for others.

Those writing from the Marxist perspective have also often illustrated the ways policy makers act on behalf of capital or exchange interests. Certainly if the government is going to intervene, it shouldn't be to benefit those who are already in an advantaged position. To the extent policy makers act in ways that foster gentrification and the economic benefits of the process flow almost exclusively to property owners, such policies might be viewed as unfairly benefiting the propertied class.

To some extent then, the critique of gentrification is a critique of using the market to allocate real estate. Those who abhor the inequality that this system produces are likely to look askance at gentrification. Although there might be some acknowledgment of potential benefits, these benefits do not erase the fact that property owners stand to benefit most and that existing wealth inequalities are likely to be exacerbated by gentrification. Although someone might appreciate that there is now a Starbucks in Harlem, it is the Starbucks owner who reaps the financial rewards.

Gentrification, which can further widen wealth inequalities, is thus likely to be viewed suspiciously.

I bring up this perspective not to discredit or support the Marxist perspective but to make clear the differences between their perspective and the one employed here. The Marxist viewpoint does shine a valuable light on some of the mechanisms that exacerbate and perpetuate inequalities between classes. Although conceding that point, I argue that class conflict does not make a complete understanding of the urban scene. To suggest that the arguments in this book render the neo-Marxist perspective "wrong" would be misguided because that perspective has a different focus. I also argue that by considering the perceptions and reactions of the residents of affected neighborhoods themselves a more nuanced picture of gentrification emerges than the one painted by a class conflict focus. The positive sentiments that some residents expressed toward gentrification that were described earlier makes clear that a class conflict approach will miss important dimensions of the changes gentrification brings. The neo-Marxist perspective seems reluctant to allow that in some circumstances indigenous residents, even low-income ones, can benefit from gentrification.

On the flip side, some have been perhaps too eager to sing the praises of gentrification, although this bias is relatively rare in the academy. As Atkinson (2002) points out, much of the scholarly writing on gentrification is written from a neo-Marxist perspective, and as described this perspective seldom views gentrification in a flattering light. Nonetheless, boosterism for gentrification is not in short supply outside of the academy. For those favorably inclined toward gentrification, this book highlights some of the negatives associated with the process. Some, like the fear of displacement, have received considerable attention. But other ill feelings, like the cynicism toward the neighborhood improvements, have not been considered in depth. Nor has there been a critical view of the neighborhood effects thesis in the context of gentrification. This book provides ample reason to be wary of the negative impacts of gentrification beyond displacement and to be skeptical of the extent that poverty deconcentration will be an elixir for urban ills. Champions of gentrification should thus be chastened by some of the material presented in this book.

One doesn't have to be a Marxist, however, to recognize that whatever its efficiencies the market can produce outcomes that are not socially desirable. Conversely, one doesn't have to be a libertarian to realize that the market produces choice, dynamism, and wealth. The most pertinent debate seems to be how to strike a balance between allowing the market to do its thing while correcting for some of the undesirable outcomes inherent in market capitalism. This book attempts to do that from the perspective of the residents indigenous to neighborhoods undergoing gentrification. By pointing out ways to dampen gentrification's harms and identifying the circumstances under which the process can bring benefits, this book can serve both as a motivator for those conducting systematic quantitative inquiries and as a guidepost for those who struggle to build better communities in the inner city. As an interpretive inquiry this book is not meant to be the definitive word on these debates. But it will hopefully stimulate thinking about how to build a more just and livable city.

# Appendix: Methodology

THE RESEARCH presented in this book is based on qualitative research in two gentrifying New York City neighborhoods. Semi-structured interviews were the primary mechanism through which data were collected. All interviews, except one, were taped and transcribed. The transcriptions were analyzed and coded. The coding was conducted by the author and two research assistants and compared to ensure intercoder reliability. The codes were then analyzed to discern recurring themes. This book discusses in depth three themes—residents' perceptions of the changes under way in their neighborhoods, their meaning and interpretation of these changes, and social interactions between indigenous residents and the gentry and the implications thereof. Text from the transcribed interviews was used extensively to demonstrate the feelings and perceptions of respondents.

The approach described follows the interpretive qualitative approach that has emerged as an alternative to the positivist approaches that have dominated the social sciences (Mason 2002). Like any research, this project is faced with the task of convincing the audience that the conclusions should be accepted and are of value. The positivist paradigm in the social sciences has well-established criteria to judge the quality of research and hence make a convincing case to an audience. Those operating in a qualitative paradigm have a much less developed set of criteria to draw from and consequently a more challenging task in legitimating the quality of their research. In part, this is because this approach arose in conjunction with the postmodern critique, which saw positivist criteria for truth as overly restrictive and inappropriate in many settings in the social world (Seale 1999). Moreover, this critique often held that there was no one objective truth and that the power of research to emancipate the oppressed was what was really important (Lincoln and Denzin 1994). To impose criteria, even if modified for qualitative inductive research, is therefore inappropriate according to this school of thought. An anarchic, "anything goes" paradigm, however, is likely to leave many unsettled, whatever their dissatisfactions with positivist criteria. This author can be included in this last group.

Using a nonstandardized questionnaire drawn from a nonrandom sample, I make no pretense of representativeness or generalizability in the well-known positivist sense. Nevertheless this research sought to meet some of the criteria being put forth by qualitative researchers as a means of establishing standards that could be used to evaluate this type of research (Mason 2002). Broadly speaking, these include credibility, or the extent to which my conclusions are plausible and analogous to the notion of validity in the positivist paradigm; transferability, or the extent to which the description is thick enough that so that the context of the research is well understood; generalizability, or the ability to make inferences beyond the study participants; and reliability, which some qualitative researchers have termed dependability and confirmability (Lincoln and Guba 1985). Here *reliability* refers not to the extent another researcher would obtain the exact same results but to the accuracy of my method in describing what I purport to describe (Mason 2002). Providing transparency and limiting my idiosyncratic imprint can help convince the audience of the accuracy of my method.

As described, a number of the tactics were employed that aim to sway the skeptical reader. Chapter 2 provides an extended description of the evolution of the two neighborhoods that serve as the setting for this research (see figures A.1 and A.2). By providing a detailed description of the setting, one can judge whether other settings are similar enough that one could expect to find similar patterns. Put in concrete terms, one could look at the evolution of gentrification in these neighborhoods and judge whether the themes discussed in this book are applicable to other neighborhoods undergoing the same process. If one were to look at Bronzeville, Chicago, another black neighborhood with a rich history that experienced significant disinvestment that is now experiencing gentrification under similar circumstances, one might expect similar themes similar to those discussed here to emerge. In contrast, an immigrant community in London might experience gentrification in a way wholly different than that depicted here. Thus, chapter 2 highlights the extent to which the research presented in this book is transferable to other settings.

In-depth interviews are probably the most credible way to tap into people's feeling and perspectives across a wide spectrum of individuals and when some of these emotions are unanticipated. In contrast to an ethnography that typically entails intensive interaction with one group, in-depth interviewing allows a wider of range of individuals to be included in the study. But because groups tend to be segregated along gender, race, class, and so on, an ethnography would necessarily limit the type of participants included in the study. At the other extreme, the standardized survey is typically ill-suited to tapping into feelings that are not anticipated. Surveys are also poor tools for establishing the rapport often necessary to facilitate participants openly discussing their feelings.

Although establishing a rapport with the study participants is desirable, it is not without risks. There were several occasions during the

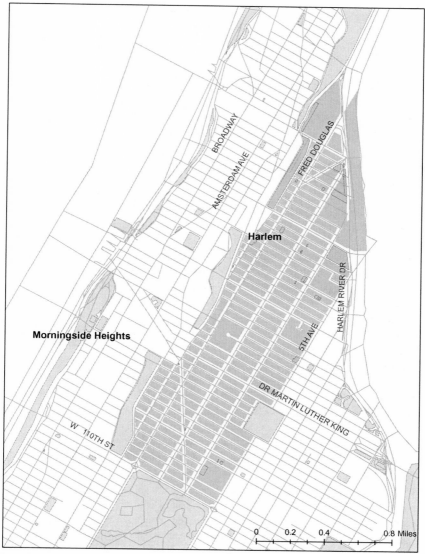

Figure A.1. Map of Harlem

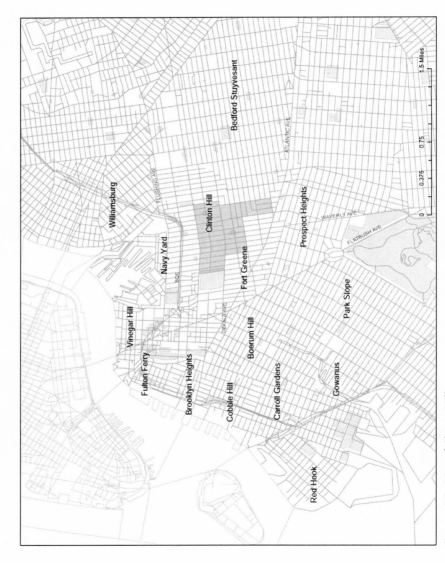

FIGURE A.2. Map of Clinton Hill

interview process when participants talked about "us" and "we," including me as an insider, most certainly because of our shared racial ancestry as African Americans. They would also mention things and describe situations assuming that I understood the nuances of what they were talking about as an insider. In most instances I did, or at least I think I did. The risk is the temptation to assume I did indeed understand the nuances of what they were referring to. For a social scientist, a major (some would say *the* major) objective of the research enterprise is to see things more clearly than would be by relying solely on our everyday observational skills. Further clarification would thus seem to be in order. Asking for such clarification, however, risks the very rapport that encourages such open discussion in the first place. After all, if I don't consider myself part of the "we," or I don't easily recognize the code words of the group, then perhaps I'm not really in the group and shouldn't be privy to this information in the first place. I generally took advantage of my insider status as an African American, acknowledging my membership in the group whenever a participant brought it up. I typically waited until the end of the interview to clarify when participants talked about "us" or "we" or made cryptic remarks that they assumed I understood because of membership in the group. This enabled me to take advantage of my in-group status and the rapport we may have developed but to also scrutinize our conversations as a social scientist. In-depth interviews should thus provide a credible account of residents' feelings about gentrification.

By transcribing the interviews, I limit the extent to which my perspective influences my analysis of them. Regardless of what I may choose to emphasize or recall, the transcribed interview is always there to serve as a check on my straying too far from the data. This helps speak to the credibility of my analysis. Moreover, coding the transcripts imposes some degree of neutrality on the researcher as the coding process forces one to deal with and analyze at least at a superficial level all of the data. Consequently, although one might be myopically focused on particular themes, the process of coding ensures that other themes in the data are recognized.

Having others both interview, code, and in some instances analyze the data can also speak to the dependability of this analysis. As already noted, my research assistants and I compared coding results and this process of striving for intercoder reliability forced us to confront any discrepancies in our interpretation of the data. This process instills a reflective self-discipline in the coding and subsequent analysis process, forcing me to consider why I was interpreting the data the way I did and whether this was reasonable. To the extent our coding diverged sharply, this would be a signal to further scrutinize my own analyses to ensure that my reading of the data was reasonable. In contrast, consistency among my coding team would suggest my conclusions were not idiosyncratic.

This also applies to the conclusions drawn from the analyses. One of my assistants conducted similar interviews and used these to write and defend her master's thesis (Patel 2003). Although my research was much more expansive, I compared her conclusions with mine, again as a way of testing the credibility and confirmability of my analysis, that is, whether they are plausible and not purely my idiosyncratic interpretation.

I use quotes from the interviews quite liberally throughout the book. The quotes illustrate the raw data I am using to draw conclusions. As such, the reader has the opportunity to judge for themselves whether my interpretation is reasonable. Consequently, the liberal use of quotes should enhance the credibility of my arguments.

In using purposive and snowball sampling I cannot, of course, generalize with any degree of precision. But as table 1.1 illustrates, the study participants represented a fairly broad class of individuals in terms of socioeconomic characteristics. I also attempt to weave some the individual's background into the narratives. This has the effect of highlighting how the individual's context colors their interpretations. For example, a homeowner would be expected to react differently than a renter to increasing housing prices. Moreover, by studying two distinct neighborhoods, I hoped to uncover patterns that might be relevant beyond a specific area. My discussions with neighborhood residents continued until the same themes continued to crop up over and over again. But it should be remembered that the ultimate aim here is not to prove that $X\%$ of residents feel a certain way or that certain particular variables are correlated in specific ways. Rather, the goal of an inductive exercise like this is to describe residents' perceptions and feelings and to use these to generate ideas about how gentrification impacts these neighborhoods. As stated earlier, systematic confirmation or refutation of these interpretations will have to await a later project.

As a further check on the reasonableness of my analyses, I had two participants read parts of my analyses and had two other participants sit in on a presentation of my research in a seminar at Columbia University. Presenting my arguments to the participants served as an additional check on the accuracy of my interpretations. These participants were for the most part in agreement with my conclusions. This, of course, is no guarantee that my conclusions are accurate. But it is another element that will hopefully help persuade the reader of the reasonableness of my arguments.

Finally, I squared my interpretations with the social science literature on gentrification, race, and the inner city. Seale (1999) points to this as an especially important step in ascertaining the plausibility of one's arguments. To the extent that my arguments deviate completely and cannot be synthesized with existing knowledge on gentrification, race, and other related topics, this should give the reader pause. Conversely, the extent to which I am able to fit these pieces in a congruent fashion into the larger puzzle of urban America should inspire confidence in the plausibility of my interpretations.

Some might argue that as an interpretive inquiry, this is ultimately my story and that tactics like striving for intercoder reliability are pointless, that the goal of interpretive inquiry is to convey a particular point of view that is as valid as any other. Though not wanting to impose the straitjacket of positivist criteria on this interpretive analysis, I am obviously tilting toward the school of thought that says criteria are needed if we wish to persuade people of the accuracy of our analysis and that explaining how one's conclusions were arrived at and self-consciously scrutinizing one's methods is a good way to do that.

The description of my original motives and goals in the introduction thus serves an important methodological purpose. Such reflexivity provides the reader with an intellectual narrative that describes how my thinking evolved as I encountered the data. It also illustrates some of the preconceived notions that I brought to this research project. Knowledge of these preconceptions and the evolution of my thinking are important for a reader who has to decide if my accounts are credible. Understanding my thinking will help readers decide if my interpretations are overly biased by my preconceptions or if my thinking is so idiosyncratic as to be of little value.

In the end, the book will hopefully provide a convincing account of some of the ways people perceive and interpret gentrification. The discussion in this appendix highlights the efforts undertaken to produce such an account.

# References

Abu-Lughod, Janet. 1994. *From Urban Village to East Village*. Oxford: Black-well.

Acheson, D. 1998. *Independent Inquiry into Inequalities in Health*. London: Stationery Office.

Amster, Linda. 1970. Brownstone Hunt Widens in Brooklyn. *New York Times,* January 30: p. 1.

Anderson, Elijah. 1999. *Code of the Street*. New York: Norton.

Anderson, Elijah. 1991. *Streetwise*. Chicago: University of Chicago Press.

Atkinson, Rowland. 2002. Does Gentrification Help or Harm Neighbourhoods? An Assessment of the Evidence-Base in the Context of the New Urban Agenda. ESRC Centre for Neighbourhood Research. Online document available at http://www.neighbourhoodcentre.org.uk/research/research.html.

Auger, Deborah. 1979. The Politics of Revitalization in Gentrifying Neighborhoods. *Journal of the American Planning Association* 45:515–22.

Basolo, Victoria. 1999. Passing the Housing Policy Baton in the US: Will Cities Take the Lead? *Housing Studies* 14(4):433–53.

Beauregard, Robert. 1986. The Chaos and Complexity of Gentrification. In Neil Smith and Paul Williams (Eds.), *Gentrification of the City*, pp. 35–55. Boston: Allen and Unwin.

Beveridge, Andrew. May 2004. Why Is There a Plunge in Crime? *Gotham Gazette.com,* www.gothamgazette.com/article/demographics/20040517/5/982; accessed May 20, 2004.

Blackwell, Angela. 2005. Radio interview. *The Tavis Smiley Show*. May 13, 2005.

Blumstein, Alfred, and Joel Wallman. 2000. *The Crime Drop in America*. Cambridge: Cambridge University Press.

Bourgois, Philippe. 1995. *In Search of Respect*. Cambridge: Cambridge University Press.

Bourne, L. 1993. The Demise of Gentrification? A Commentary and Prospective View. *Urban Geography* 14:95–107.

Boyd, Michelle. 2004. Who's Zoomin' Who? African Americans and Gentrification. Paper Presented at the annual meeting of the Urban Affairs Association. Washington, DC, March 31–April 3.

Briggs, Xavier. 1998. Brown Kids in White Suburbs: Housing Mobility and the Many Faces of Social Capital. *Housing Policy Debate* 9(4):177–221.

Briggs, Xavier de Souza, Joe Darden, and Angela Aidala. 1999. In the Wake of Desegregation: Early Impacts of Scattered Site Public Housing on Neighborhoods in Yonkers, New York. *Journal of the American Planning Association* 65:27–49.

Brown, Claude. 1965. *Manchild in the Promised Land*. New York: Macmillan.

Brown, Patricia Leigh. 1992. Artistic Mecca with a Brooklyn Flair. *New York Times*, September 20: p. 41.

Campbell, Bruce A. 1980. The Interaction of Race and Socioeconomic Status in the Development of Political Attitudes. *Social Science Quarterly* 60:651–58.

Carson, Larry. 1995. Baltimore County Wants More Say in Section 8. *Baltimore Sun* (Local) (March 6): p. 3B.

Cashin, Sherly. 2004. *The Failures of Integration: How Race and Class Are Undermining the American Dream*. New York: Public Affairs.

Caulfield, J. 1994. *City Form and Everyday Life: Toronto's Gentrification and Critical Social Practice*. Toronto: University of Toronto Press.

Chamberlain, Lisa. 2003. Exploding the Gentrification Myth: Columbia Prof's Surprising Findings. *New York Observer*. November 17: p. 13.

Chinelyu, Mamadou. 1999. *Harlem Ain't Nothin' but a Third World Country: The Global Economy, Empowerment Zones and the Colonial Status of Africans in America*. New York: Mustard Seed Press.

Cicin-Sain, Biliana. 1980. The Costs and Benefits of Neighborhood Revitalization. *Urban Affairs Annual Reviews* 18:49–76.

Clark, Kenneth B. 1965. *Dark Ghetto*. Hanover, NH: Wesleyan University Press.

Conley, Dalton. 1999. *Being Black, Living in the Red: Race, Wealth and Social Policy in America*. Berkeley: University of California Press.

Connolly, Harold X. 1977. *A Ghetto Grows in Brooklyn*. New York: New York University.

Cravatts, Richard L. 2004. Embracing Gentrification: A Case Study for Inner City Growth. *Intellectual Conservative*. Online document available at http://intellectualconservative.com/article3412.html; accessed November 23, 2005.

Crowder, Kyle, and Scott J. Smith. 2005. Race, Class, and Changing Patterns of Migration between Poor and Nonpoor Neighborhoods. *American Journal of Sociology* 110(6): 1715–63.

Crowell, Chester T. 1925. The World's Largest Negro City. *Saturday Evening Post* 198 (August 8, 1925): p. 8.

Crump, Jeff. 2002. Deconcentration by Demolition: Public Housing, Poverty, and Urban Policy. *Environment and Planning D: Society and Space* 20: 581–96.

Cuomo, Mario. 1974. *Forest Hills Diary: The Crisis of Low-Income Housing*. New York: Vintage.

Currie, Elliot. 1993. *Reckoning: Drugs, the Cities, and the American Future*. New York: Hill and Wang.

Davis, Mike. 1992. *City of Quartz*. New York: Vintage.

Davis, Perry. 1986. Partners for Downtown Development: Creating a New Central Business District in Brooklyn. *Proceedings of the Academy of Political Science* 36(2):87–99.

DeGiovanni, Frank. 1984. Neighborhood Revitalization in Fort Greene and Clinton Hill. *New York Affairs* 8(2).

Demaris, Alfred, and Renxin Yang. 1994. Race, Alienation, and Interpersonal Mistrust. *Sociological Spectrum* 14:327–49.

Dent, David J. 1992. The New Black Suburbs. *New York Times Magazine,* June 14: p. 199.

Deparle, Jason. 2004. *American Dream: Three Women, Ten Kids, and a Nation's Drive to End Welfare.* New York: Viking Books.

Dixon, Bruce. 1998. On Gentrification in Chicago. Online document available at www.mdcbowen.org/p5/np/on_gentrification_in_chicago.htm. Accessed May 19, 2004.

Duneier, Mitchell. 1999. *Sidewalk.* New York: Farrar, Straus and Giroux.

Dycoff, E. F. 1914. "A Negro City in New York." *Outlook* 108 (December 23): 949–54.

Ellis, Trey. 1989. The New Black Aesthetic. *Callaloo* 12(1):233–46.

Etzkowitz, Henry, and Gerald M. Schaflander. 1969. *Ghetto Crisis: Riots or Reconciliation.* Boston: Little, Brown.

Farley, R., Steeh, C. S., Jackson, T. et al. 1994. The Causes of Continued Racial Residential Segregation: Chocolate City, Vanilla Suburbs Revisited. *Journal of Housing Research* 4:1–38.

Fein, Albert, Lois Gilman, and Donald Simon. 1973. The Neighborhood of Fort Greene in the City of New York: A Historical Perspective. Urban Studies Program, Long Island University.

Fitzgerald, Simon. 2002. Public Housing and a New Plans of HOPE. Online document available at http://dc.indymedia.org/newswire/display/18336; accessed October 21, 2004.

Fort Greene Landmarks Preservation Committee. 1973. *A Proposal for the Designation of Fort Greene as an Historic District.* New York: Fort Greene Landmarks Preservation Committee.

Frazier, E. Franklin. 1957. *The Black Bourgeoisie.* New York: Collier Books.

Freedman, Samuel G. 1994. *Upon This Rock: The Miracles of a Black Church.* New York: Harper Perennial.

Freeman, Henry. 1958. "Brooklyn Slums Shock Officials." *New York Times,* November 19: p. 31.

Freeman, Lance. 2005. Displacement or Succession? Residential Mobility in Gentrifying Neighborhoods. *Urban Affairs Review* 40(4):463–91.

Freeman, Lance. 2004. *Sifting Affordable Housing: Location and Neighborhood Trends of Low Income Housing Tax Credit Developments in the 1990s.* Living Cities Census Series, Center on Urban and Metropolitan Studies. Washington, DC: Brookings Institution.

Freeman, Lance, and Frank Braconi. 2004. Gentrification and Displacement in New York City. *Journal of the American Planning Association* 70(1): 39–52.

Fullilove, Mindy Thompson. 2004. *Root Shock: How Tearing up City Neighborhoods Hurts America, and What We Can Do about It.* New York: One World/Ballantine Books.

Gale, Dennis E. 1986. Demographic Research on Gentrification and Displacement. *Journal of Planning Literature* 1(1):14–29.

Gilbert, D. T., M. D. Lieberman, C. K. Morewedge, et al. 2004. The Peculiar Longevity of Things Not So Bad. *Psychological Science* 15(1):14–19.

Gilbert, D. T., E. C. Pinel, T. D. Wilson, et al. 1998. Immune Neglect: A Source of Durability Bias in Affective Forecasting. *Journal of Personality and Social Psychology* 75(3):617–38.

Gittell, Ross, and Avis Vidal. 1998. *Community Organizing: Building Social Capital as a Development Strategy*. Thousand Oaks, CA: Sage.

Gladwell, Malcolm. 2004. Getting Over It. *New Yorker* 80(34):75.

Glaeser, Edward L., and Jacob L. Vigdor. 2001. *Racial Segregation in the 2000 Census: Promising News*. Brookings' Living Cities Census Series. Washington, DC: Brookings Institution.

Goering, John, and Judith D. Feins. 2003. *Choosing a Better Life?: Evaluating the Moving to Opportunity Experiment*. Washingtin, DC: Urban Institute Press.

Gould Ellen, Ingrid. 2000. *Sharing America's Neighborhoods: The Prospects for Stable Racial Integration*. Cambridge, MA: Harvard University Press.

Gould Ellen, Ingrid, and Margery A. Turner. 2003. Do Neighborhoods Matter and Why? In John Goering and Judith Feins (Eds.), *Choosing a Better Life*. Washington, DC: Urban Institute Press.

Granovetter, Mark. 1973. The Strength of Weak Ties. *American Journal of Sociology* 78:1360–80.

Grant, Benjamin. 2003. "What is Gentrification?" World Wide Web page available at http://www.pbs.org/pov/pov2003/flagwars/special_gentrification.html; accessed May 19, 2004.

Greenberg, Cheryl. 1991. *Or Does It Explode? Harlem in the Great Depression*. New York: Oxford University Press.

Grier, G., and E. E. Grier. 1978. *Urban Displacement: A Reconnaissance*. Washington, DC: U.S. Department of Housing and Urban Development.

Hamnett, C. 1991. The Blind Men and the Elephant: The Explanation of Gentrification. *Transactions of the Institute of British Geographers* 16:259–79.

Hardin, Russell 2001. Conceptions and Explanations of Trust. In Karen Cooke (Ed.), *Trust in Society*. New York: Russell Sage.

Harris, David R. 2001. Why Are Whites and Blacks Averse to Black Neighbors? *Social Science Research* 30(1):100–116.

Hartt, Rollin Lynde. 1921. I'd Like to Show you Harlem! *Independent* 105 (April 2):334.

Helling, Amy, and David S. Sawicki. 2003. Race and Residential Accessibility to Shopping and Services. *Housing Policy Debate* 14(1–2):69–101.

Henig, Jeffrey R. 1982. *Gentrification in Adams Morgan: Political and Commercial Consequences of Neighborhood Change*. Washington, DC: Center for Washington Area Studies, George Washington University.

Hinds, Michael deCourcy. 1987. Gentrification: The Case of Clinton Hill. *New York Times*, February 8: p. R1.

Hughes, Mark Alan, and Peter M. Vandoren. 1990. Social Policy through Land Reform: New Jersey's Mount Laurel Controversy. *Political Science Quarterly* 105(1):97–111.

Infoshare. 2005. Community Studies of New York. Available online at www.infoshare.org; accessed April 28, 2005.

Jackson, Kenneth. 1985. *Crabgrass Frontier*. New York: Oxford University Press.

Jargowsky, Paul. 2003. Stunning Progress, Hidden Problems: The Dramatic Decline of Concentrated Poverty in the 1990s. *Living Census Series*. Washington, DC: Brookings Institution.

Jargowsky, Paul. 1997. *Poverty and Place: Ghettos, Barrios, and the American City*. New York: Russell Sage.

Jencks, Christopher. 1988. Deadly Neighborhoods. *New Republic*, June 13: p. 29.

Jencks, Christopher, and Susan Mayer. 1990. The Social Consequences of Growing in a Poor Neighborhood. In Laurence E. Lynn and Michael G. H. McGeary (Eds.), *Inner City Poverty in the United States*, pp. 111–86. Washington, DC: National Academy Press.

Johnson, James Weldon. 1925. The Making of Harlem. *Survey Graphic* 53:635–39.

Johnson, Rudy. 1971. Fort Greene's Brownstoneurbia: Where Color Lines Are Fuzzy. *New York Times,* July 11: p. 46.

Kennedy, Maureen, and Paul Leonard. 2001. *Dealing with Neighborhood Change: A Primer on Gentrification and Policy Choices*. Washington DC: Brookings Institution.

Kleit, Rachel Garshick. 2001. The Role of Neighborhood Networks in Scattered-Site Public Housing Residents' Search for Jobs. *Housing Policy Debate* 123:541–73.

Kusmer, Kenneth L. 1978. *A Ghetto Takes Shape, Black Cleveland, 1870–1930*. Chicago: University of Illinois Press.

Lamb, Yanick Rice. 1991. Buying Black. *Essence,* October: p. 102.

Lane, Roger. 1986. *The Roots of Violence in Black Philadelphia*. Cambridge, MA: Harvard University Press.

Leblanc, Adrian N. 2003. *Random Family*. New York: Scribner's.

Lee, Barrett A. 1985. Racially Mixed Neighborhoods during the 1970s: Change or Stability? *Social Science Quarterly* 66(2):346–64.

Lee, Barrett A., and Peter B. Wood. 1991. Is Neighborhood Racial Succession Place-Specific? *Demography* 28(1):21–40.

Lee, E. D. 1981. Will We Lose Harlem? *Black Enterprise*, June: pp. 191–200.

Lee, Felicia. 1994. On a Harlem Block, Hope Is Swallowed by Decay. *New York Times,* September 8: p. A1.

Lee, Jennifer. 2002. *Civility in the City*. Cambridge, MA: Harvard University Press.

Legates, Richard T., and Chester Hartman. 1986. The Anatomy of Displacement. In Neil Smith and Peter Williams (Eds.), *Gentrification of the City*, pp. 178–203. Boston: Unwin Hyman.

Lemann, Nicholas. 1994. The Myth of Community Development. *New York Times Magazine,* January 9: p. 27.

Lewis Mumford Center. 2003. Ethnic Diversity Grows, Neighborhood Integration Lags Behind. Online document available at http://mumford1.dyndns.org/cen2000/report.html.

Levy, David, and Roman Cybriwsky. 1980. The Hidden Dimensions of Culture and Class: Philadelphia. In Shirley B. Laska and Daphne Spain (Eds.), *Back to the City: Issues in Neighborhood Revitalization*, pp. 138–55. New York: Pergamon Press.

Ley, David. 1996. *The New Middle Class and the Central City*. Oxford: Oxford University Press.

Light, Ivan, and Carolyn Rosenstein. 1995. *Race, Ethnicity, and Entrepreneurship in Urban America*. New York: Aldine De Gruyter.

Lincoln, Y. S., and N. K. Denzin. 1994. The Fifth Moment. In N. K. Denzin, and Y. S. Lincoln (Eds.), *Handbook of Qualitative Research*, pp. 575–86. Thousand Oaks, CA: Sage.

Lincoln, Y. S., and E. Guba. 1985. *Naturalistic Enquiry*. Beverly Hills, CA: Sage.

Lipset, Seymour, and Gary Marks. 2000. *It Didn't Happen Here: Why Socialism Failed in the United States*. New York: Norton.

Locke, Alain. 1925. Enter the New Negro. *Survey* 53 (March 1): 632.

Logan, John R., and Richard Alba. 1993. Locational Returns to Human Capital: Minority Access to Suburban Community Resources. *Demography* 30(2): 243–68.

Logan, John R., Richard Alba, Tom McNulty, and Brian Fisher. 1996. Making a Place in the Metropolis: Locational Attainment in Cities and Suburbs. *Demography* 33(4):443–53.

Logan, John R., and Harvey Molotch. 1987. *Urban Fortunes*. Berkeley: University of California Press.

London, Bruce, and John Palen. 1984. *Gentrification, Displacement, and Neighborhood Revitalization*. Albany: SUNY Press.

Lydersen, Kari. 1999. Shame of the Cities: Gentrification in the New Urban America. World Wide Web page available online at http://www.lipmagazine .org/articles/featlydersen_7.shtml; accessed May 19, 2004.

Marcuse, Peter. 1997. The Enclave, the Citadel, and the Ghetto: What Has Changed in the Post-Fordist U.S.City. *Urban Affairs Review* 33(2):228–64.

Marcuse, P. 1986. Abandonment, Gentrification, and Displacement: The Linkages in New York City. In N. Smith & P. Williams, (Eds.), *Gentrification of the City*, pp. 153–77. Boston: Allen and Unwin.

Mason, Jennifer. 2002. *Qualitative Researching*. Thousand Oaks, CA: Sage.

Massey, Douglas S. 2001. Residential Segregation and Neighborhood Conditions in U.S. Metropolitan Areas. In Neil J. Smelser, William J. Wilson, and Faith Mitchell (Eds.), National Research Council, *America Becoming: Racial Trends and Their Consequences*. Volume 1. Commission on Behavioral and Social Sciences and Education. Washington, DC: National Academy Press.

Massey, Douglas S., and Brooks Bitterman. 1985. Explaining the Paradox of Puerto Rican Segregation. *Social Forces* 64(2):306–31.

Massey, Douglas S., and Nancy A. Denton. 1993. *American Apartheid*. Cambridge, MA: Harvard University Press.

Massey, Douglas S., Nancy A. Denton, and Gretchen A. Condran. 1987. The Effect of Residential Segregation on Black Social and Economic Well Being. *Social Forces* 66(1):29–56.

McCord, Colin, and Harold Freeman. 1990. Excess Mortality in Harlem. *New England Journal of Medicine* 322(3):173–77.

McGee, Henry W. 1991. Afro-American Resistance to Gentrification and the Demise of Integrationist Ideology in the United States. *Urban Lawyer* 23(1): 25–44.

Medoff, Peter, and Holly Sklar. 1994. *Streets of Hope.* Boston: South End Press.

Moore, Keith, 1999. From Red-Line to Renaissance. *Salon.* Article online at www.salon.com; accessed May 2, 2002.

Montgomery, Marvin. 2002. Ghetto Red Hot. *Smooth* 34–37.

National League on Urban Conditions among Negroes. 1915. *Housing Conditions among Negroes in Harlem New York City.* Vol. 4, no. 2. January.

Newkirk, Pamela. 1998. Movin' Up Not Out: Livin' Large in the 'Hood. *Essence* 28(10):152.

Newman, Kathe, and Philip Ashton. 2004. Neoliberal Urban Policy and New Paths of Neighborhood Change in the American Inner City. *Environment and Planning A* 36:1151–72.

Newman, Kathe, and Elvin Wyly. 2004. Residential Displacement in New York City's Gentrifying Neighborhoods. Paper presented at the annual meetings of the Association of Collegiate Schools in Planning. Portland, OR.

Newman, Katherine. 2004. Newark, Decline and Avoidance, Renaissance and Desire: From Disinvestment to Reinvestment. *The Annals of the American Academy of Political Science* 594:34–58.

News Syndicate Co., New York Times, Daily New Mirror, and Hearst Consolidated Publications. 1943. *New York City Market Analysis.*

*New York Age.* 1923. High Rents and Overcrowding Responsible for Many of the Ills Suffered by Harlemites. August 11, p. 1.

New York City Department of City Planning. 1969. *Plan for New York City.* New York: Author.

New York Landmarks Preservation Commission. 1981. Clinton Hill Historic District Designation Report. New York: Author.

*New York Times.* 1920. Harlem's Astor Row for Colored Tenants. November 21: p. 106.

*New York Times.* 1904. He Prefers Negro Tenants. October 4: p. 2.

Nichols, Franklin O. 1939. *Harlem Housing.* New York: Citizens Housing Council of New York.

Oliver, Melvin. L., and Thomas M. Shapiro. 1995. *Black Wealth/White Wealth.* New York Routledge.

Osofsky, Gilbert. 1971. Harlem: The Making of a Ghetto, 2nd ed. New York: Harper and Row.

Patel, Radhika. 2003. You Don't See What I See: Residents' Views of Gentrification. Master's thesis, Columbia University.

Patillo, Mary. 2003. Negotiating Blackness, for Richer or for Poorer. *Ethnography* 4(1):1–34.

Popkin, Susan, Laura E. Harris, and Mary K. Cunningham. 2002. Families in Transitions: A Qualitative Analysis of the MTO Experience. Washington, DC: U.S. Department of Housing and Urban Development.

Popkin, Susan, et al. 2004. *A Decade of HOPE VI.* Washington, DC: Urban Institute.

Powell, John A., and Marguerite L. Spencer. 2003. Giving Them the Old "One-Two": Gentrification and the K.O. of Impoverished Urban Dwellers of Color. *Howard Law Journal* 46(3):433–91.

Putnam, Robert. 2000. *Bowling Alone.* New York: Simon and Schuster.

Rejnis, Ruth. 1973. Off We Go a-Brownstoning in Brooklyn. *New York Times,* November 25: p. 1.

Robertson, Tatsha. 2005. Harlem on the Rise. *Crisis* (June 9).

Rohe, William M. 1998. Do Community Development Corporations Live up to Their Billing? A Review and Critique of the Research Findings. In T. Koebel, ed., *Shelter and Society: Theory, Research and Policy for Non-Profit Housing.* Albany: State University of New York Press.

Rohe, William M., Shannon Van Zandt, and George McCarthy. 2000. *The Social Benefits and Costs of Homeownership: A Critical Assessment of the Research.* Washington, DC: Research Institute for Housing America.

Rosenberg, Jan. 1998. Fort Greene, New York. *Cityscape* 4(2):179–96.

Ross, Catherine E., John Mirowsky, and Shana Pribesh. 2001. Powerlessness and the Amplification of Threat: Neighborhood Disadvantage Disorder, and Mistrust. *American Sociological Review* 66(4):568–91.

Sampson, Robert J. 1999. What Community Supplies. In *Urban Problems and Community Development.* Washington, DC: Brookings Institution Press.

Sampson, Robert J., Stephen W. Raudenbush, and Felton Earls. 1997. Neighborhoods and Violent Crime: A Multilevel Study of Collective Efficacy. *Science* 277 (August):918–24.

Sanchez, T. W. 1998. "Equity Analysis of Capital Improvement Plans Using Gis: Des Moines Urbanized Area." *Journal of Urban Planning and Development-Asce* 124:33–43.

Saunders, P. 1978. Beyond Housing Classes: The Sociological Significance of Property Rights in Means of Consumption. *International Journal of Urban and Regional Research* 18(2):202–27.

Schaffer, Richard, and Neil Smith. 1986. The Gentrification of Harlem. *Annals of the Association of American Geographers* 76(3):347–65.

Scheiner, Seth. 1965. *Negro Mecca: A History of the Negro in New York City, 1865–1920.* New York: New York University Press.

Schill, Michael H., and Richard P. Nathan. 1983. *Revitalizing America's Cities: Neighborhood Reinvestment and Displacement.* Albany: SUNY Press.

Seale, Clive. 1999. *The Quality of Qualitative Research.* Thousand Oaks, CA: Sage Publications.

Shiller, Robert J. 2005. *Irrational Exuberance,* 2nd ed. Princeton, NJ: Princeton University Press.

Shipp, E. R. 1990. Fort Greene's Black Renaissance. *American Visions* 5(1): 30–34.

Slater, Tom. 2004. North American Gentrification? Revanchist and Emancipatory Perspectives Explored. *Environment and Planning A* 36:1191–213.

Slater, Tom, Winfred Curran, and Loretta Lees. 2004. Gentrification Research: New Directions and Critical Scholarship. *Environment and Planning A* 36: 1141–50.

Smith, Chris. 2000. Real E$Tate 2000: Uptown Boomtown. *New York Magazine,* April 10.

Smith, Neil. 1996. *The New Urban Frontier: Gentrification and the Revanchist City.* London: Routledge Press.

Smith, Neil. 1979. Toward a Theory of Gentrification: A Back to the City Movement by Capital not People. *Journal of the American Planning Association* 45:538–48.

Smith, Neil, and Michele LeFaivre. 1984. A Class Analysis of Gentrification. In Bruce London and John Palen (Eds.), *Gentrification, Displacement and Neighborhood Revitalization.* Albany: State University of New York Press.

Smith, Sandra S. 2003. Exploring the Efficacy of African-Americans' Job Referral Networks: A Study of the Obligations of Exchange around Job Information and Influence. *Ethnic and Racial Studies* 26(6):1029–45.

Spear, Allan H. 1967. *Black Chicago, the Making of a Negro Ghetto.* Chicago: University of Chicago Press.

Stoecker, Randy. 2003. Comment on William M. Rohe and Rachel G. Bratt's "Failures, Downsizing, and Mergers among Community Development Corporations." *Housing Policy Debate* 14(1/2):47–56.

Stoecker, Randy. 1997. The CDC Model of Urban Redevelopment: A Critique and Alternative. *Journal of Urban Affairs* 19(1).

Sugrue, Thomas. 1996. *Origins of the Urban Crisis.* Princeton, NJ: Princeton University Press.

Sumka, Howard. 1979. Neighborhood Revitalization and Displacement: A Review of the Evidence. *Journal of the American Planning Association* 45: 480–87.

Swanstrom Todd, Peter Dreier, and John Mollenkopf. 2002. What Really Matters. *Dissent* 49(3):110–11.

Taylor, Monique. 2002. *Harlem between Heaven and Hell.* Minneapolis: University of Minnesota Press.

Temkin, K., R. Quercia, and G. Galster. 2000. The Impact of Secondary Mortgage Market Guidelines on Affordable and Fair Lending: A Reconnaissance from the Front Lines. *Review of Black Political Economy* 28(2):29–52.

Tiebout, Charles. 1956. A Pure Theory of Local Expenditures. *Journal of Political Economy* 64:416–24.

Tierney, John. 2002. The Gentry Misjudged as Neighbors. *New York Times,* March 26: p. B.1.

Trotter, Joe William Jr. 1985. *Black Milwaukee: The Making of an Industrial Proletariat.* Chicago: University of Illinois Press.

Turner, Margery Austin. 1998. Moving out of Poverty: Expanding Mobility and Choice through Tenant-Based Housing Assistance. *Housing Policy Debate* 9(2):373–94.

Turner, Patricia. 1993. *I Heard It through the Grapevine.* Berkeley: University of California Press.

U.S. Census Bureau. 1935. *Negroes in the United States 1920–1932.* Washington, DC: U.S. Government Printing Office, p. 239.

U.S. Department of Housing and Urban Development. 1981. *Residential Displacement—An Update.* Washington, DC: HUD.

U.S. General Accounting Office. 2003. Public Housing HOPE VI Resident Issues and Changes in Neighborhoods Surrounding Grant Sites, GAO-04-109. Washington, DC.

U.S. Department of Labor. 1973. *Social, Economic, and Labor Force Characteristics of Residents in New York City's Low Income Areas.*Bureau of Labor Statistics Regional Report No. 30. Washington, DC: Author.

Van Deburg, William L. 1992. *New Day in Babylon: The Black Power Movement and American Culture, 1965–1975.* Chicago: University of Chicago Press.

Van Vliet, William. 1998. *Encyclopedia of Housing.* Thousand Oaks, CA: Sage.

Vigdor, J. 2002. Does Gentrification Harm the Poor? *Brookings-Wharton Papers on Urban Affairs*: 133–73.

Von Hoffman, Alexander. 2003. *House by House, Block by Block.* New York: Oxford University Press.

Washington, Elsie B. 1991. Brooklyn: The New Black Mecca. *Essence*, October 22(6):96–98.

Waters, Anita M. 1997. Conspiracy Theories as Ethnosociologies: Explanation and Intention in African American Political Culture. *Journal of Black Studies* 28(1):112–25.

Watkins-Owens, Irma. 1996. *Blood Relations: Caribbean Immigrants and the Harlem Community, 1900–1930.* Bloomington: Indiana University Press.

Watson, Jamal E. 2003. The Whitening of Black Neighborhoods. The National Black Family Empowerment Agenda. Available online at www.nbfea.com/news/news03/economics/whitening.html; accessed January 24, 2005.

Weaver, Robert C. 1948. *Negro Ghetto.* New York: Harcourt Brace.

Weber, Rachel. 2003. Tax Incremental Financing in Theory and Practice. In Sammis B. White, Richard D. Bingham, and Edward W. Hill (Eds.), *Financing Economic Development in the 21st Century.* New York: M. E. Sharpe.

Weisman, Steven R. 1971. Banks Relaxing Brownstone Ban. *New York Times,* June 6: p. BQ82.

Wellman, B., and B. Leighton. 1979. Networks, Neighborhoods, and Communities—Approaches to the Study of the Community Question. *Urban Affairs Review* 14(3):363–90.

White House. 2005. Homeownership Policy Book. Online document available at www.whitehouse.gov/infocus/homeownership/homeownership-policy-book-background.html#goodfor; accessed January 30, 2005.

Williams, Peter, and Neil Smith. 1986. From "Renaissance" to Restructuring: The Dynamics of Contemporary Urban Development. In Peter Williams and Neil Smith (Eds.), *Gentrification of the City.* Boston: Unwin Hyman.

Wilson, David, and Dennis Grammenos. 2005. Gentrification, Discourse, and the Body: Chicago's Humboldt Park. *Environment and Planning D: Society and Space* 23:295–31.

Wilson, David, Jared Wouters, and Dennis Grammenos. 2004. Successful Protect-Community Discourse: Spatiality and Politics in Chicago's Pilsen Neighborhood. *Environment and Planning A* 36:1173–90.

Wilson, William J. 1996. *When Work Disappears.* New York: Knopf.

Wilson, William J. 1987. *The Truly Disadvantaged*. Chicago: University of Chicago Press.

Wittberg, Patricia. 1992. Perspectives on Gentrification: A Comparative Review of the Literature. *Research in Urban Sociology* 2:17–46.

Works Division, Emergency Relief Bureau. 1934. *Real Property Inventory*. Prepared by the Works Division, Emergency Relief Bureau under the direction of the New York City Housing Authority, U.S. Department of Commerce and Mayor's Advisory Committee on Real Property Inventory.

Wrigley, Neil. 2002. "Food Deserts": An Introduction. *Urban Studies* 39(11): 2029–40.

Wyly, E. L., and D. J. Hammel. 1999. Islands of Decay in Seas of Renewal: Housing Policy and the Resurgence of Gentrification. *Housing Policy Debate* 10(4):711–72.

Yinger, John. 1995. *Closed Doors: Opportunities Lost*. New York: Russell Sage.

# Index

*Page numbers in italics refer to figures and tables.*

125th street (in Harlem), 28, 29, 65, 67, 81, 108, 121

Abu-Lughod, Janet, 6
Abyssinian Development Corporation, 116, 181
ACORN, 184
Afro-American Realty Company, 19
Allen, Gerri, 56
Anderson, Elijah, 99, 135, 136
Auger, Deborah, 6

Badu, Erykah, 56
Bed-Stuy. *See* Beford Stuyvesant
Bedford Stuyvesant, 17, 24, 35, 38, 39, 43, 60, 68, 72, 83, 150, 191
Black inner city: black middle class in, 56, 57; commercial enterprises in, 62, 65, 71, 72, 116, 158, 159, 189; community organizations in, 181, 210; crime in, 39, 41; cynicism in, 118, 121; deterioration of, 17, 41, 48, 51, 95, 118, 166, 194, 197, 202; gentrification of, 2, 3, 15, 49, 55, 56, 94, 122, 160, 188, 196, 197, 198, 202, 203, 204, 207; investment in, 29, 36, 50, 115, 116, 193, 194; isolation of, 3, 16, 82, 189, 190; lifestyles in, 105; middle class flight from, 9, 24, 65, 125; neoliberal policy in, 16, 202, 207; Philadelphia, 135, 136; revitalization of, 49, 51; unique history of, 1, 3, 4, 158, 188. *See also* Clinton Hill; Ghetto; Harlem

Black middle class: cultural attitudes of, 55–57, 190, 196–98, 200; as gentrifiers, 51, 53, *54, 55*–57, 87–92, 97, 190, 198, 200; presence in inner city 8, 53, 55, 88, 89, 92, 114, 125, 160; suburbs, 51, 56, 197, 198 (*see also* DeKalb County; Mount Vernon; Roosevelt; Prince George's County). *See also* Gentry, black
Boerum Hill, 178
Braconi, Frank, 4, 5
Briggs, Xavier de Souza, 146
Brooklyn: Downtown, 42, 52, 59, 69, 96. *See also* Bedford Stuyvesant; Boerum Hill; Brownsville; Clinton Hill; Park Slope
Brooklyn Hill Improvement League, 37
Brooklyn Navy Yard, 35, 38, 101
Brown, Claude, 25, 122
Brownsville, 38, 83, 179, 206

Carter, Betty, 56
Caulfield, J., 195
CDCs. *See* Community Development Corporations. *See also* Community Based Organizations
Chicago, 19, 20, *23*
Cleveland, 20
Clinton Hill: apartments, 38, *70*; black gentry in, 87–92 (*see also* Gentry: black); black presence in, 38, 39, 48, 52, *54, 55*–57, 150; boundaries of, 17, *214*; commercial activity in, 62, 65, 69, 154, 158; community mobilizing in, 185; conflicting norms

Clinton Hill (*continued*)
in, 137–40; crack epidemic in, 41,
42, 63, 93; cynicism in, 140; decline
of, 36–42, 72, 158; demographic
changes in, 43–47; Fort Greene,
relationship to, 34, 35; gentrification
in, 40–48, 58, 80, 97, 190–93, 202;
gentrification policies impacts on,
176–78; historic districts in, 35, 39,
40, 41, 96; history of, 34–48; homeownership rate in, 93, 158; housing
costs in, *43*; map of, *214*; middle
class residents in, 8, 90; as setting
for book, 7, 8, 12, 13; white
presence in, 52, 81–83, 85, 87,
97–115, 161, 191
Collective efficacy, 130, 131, 135–46,
155
Columbia University, 50, 109, 112,
113, 115, 122, 135, 216
Common (rap artist), 56
Community Based Organizations, 50,
52, 76, 102, 116, 117, 152, 153,
155, 156, 181, 182, 202.
*See also* Community development; Community development
corporations; Community
mobilization
Community development, 124, 126,
153, 182, 183, 186, 203
Community development corporations, 50
Community mobilization, 182–86,
206, 207
Community Reinvestment Act,
49, 168
Crack epidemic, 27, 41, 42, 101, 103,
118, 188
Curran, Winfred, 6
Cybriwski, Roman, 159, 160

DeCarava, Roy, 56
DeKalb Avenue (in Clinton Hill), 41,
63, 74
DeKalb County (Georgia), 51
Denton, Nancy A., 189

Deparle, Jason, 146
Displacement: definition of, 163; fears
of, 72–80, 92–94, 112, 162–64, 167,
170–72, 176–78, 209; as focus of
gentrification research, 5, 6, 127;
policies to address, 170–75; potential for, 198, 199; resistance to, 76,
77; of smaller stores, 68, 69; studies
of, 4, 5, 127, 162, 163, 172
Duneier, Mitchell, 119

East New York, 38, 40, 60, 150,
179
Ellis, Trey, 55
Empowerment Zone, 49, 168
*Encyclopedia of Housing*, 29

Fairmont (Philadelphia), 159
Fishburne, Lawrence, 57
Fort Greene, 34–42, 48, 56, 57, 96;
Clinton Hill, relationship to, 34, 35;
public housing, 37, 39, 41, 42, 75,
90, 98, 141
Fort Greene Housing Office, 52
Fort Greene Park, 35, 99, 137

Garvey, Marcus, 21
Gentrification: blacks role in, 51–55
(*see also* Gentry: black); as a cause
of displacement, 5, 6, 72–80, 92–94,
127, 162–64; chaotic interpretations
of, 3; community based organizations role in, 50, 51; cynicism
about, 103–24, 160–62, 169,
207, 209; demand side explanations
of, 2, 49; emancipatory interpretation of, 195–201; housing abandonment in, 50; improved amenities as a
result of, 1, 2, 47, 61, 62, 94, 98,
114, 145, 151–54, 156, 159, 160,
165, 166, 169, 198, 204, 205, 207;
Marxist interpretation of, 201, 208,
209; neighborhood effects and, 2,
14, 125–56, 164, 165, 209; police
harassment as a result, 105–10,
150–51; political conflicts as a result

of, 6; popular wisdom on, 59, 95–97; positive reactions toward, 60–72, 92–94, 158–60; revanchist interpretation of, 195, 200, 201; role of race in, 47; social clashes as a result of, 105–7, 117, 136–44, 165, 184, 200, 201, 207; supply side explanations of, 2, 3

Gentry: antagonism toward, 6, 107, 161, 164, 165; black, 8, 11, 53, 54, 55, 87–92, 109, 122; housing choices of, 97, 114, 160, 196, 198; indicator of gentrification, 30, 31, 79; interaction with long-term residents, 125–56; and mixed income neighborhoods, 2, 14, 125–56, 157, 164, 167, 168, 206; political interests of, 7; purchasing patterns of, 31, 34, 62, 64, 159; role in neighborhood change, 98, 101, 102, 115, 117, 165, 184, 195, 196. See also Black middle class; Middle class

Ghetto: avoidance of, 16; Brooklyn, 39, 40; Clinton Hill as, 86; definition of, 27; gentrification in, 48–51; Harlem as, 53, 55, 190; meaning of, 15, 16; middle class flight from, 125; origins of, 20, 21, 114; outcast, 188–95; problems of, 25, 95, 197; second class treatment of, 122, 159; segregation of, 168. See also Black inner city; Harlem

Grammenos, Dennis, 2, 6

Great Depression, 22, 24

Hammel, Daniel, 186, 193

Hamnett, C., 201

Harlem: abandoned buildings in, 26, 177–80; black gentry in, 54, 87–92, 197 (see also Gentry: black; Black middle class); boundaries of, 17, 213; commercial activity in, 31, 32, 33, 34, 61, 62, 67, 69, 154, 159, 191, 192; community mobilizing in, 185; crack epidemic in, 27, 63, 72; cynicism in, 140; decline of, 23–28,

71, 93, 198; demographic changes in, 29–34, 67; gentrification in, x, 28–34, 35, 48–50, 53–55, 58, 93, 94, 97, 180, 190–94, 195, 197, 202; gentrification policies impacts on, 176–80; great migration to, 20, 21, 24, 38; heroin epidemic in, 25, 28, 63; historic districts in, 28; history of, 17–33; homeownership in, 178; map of, 213; median income in, 32, 180 (see also Harlem: demographic changes in); middle class residents in, 8, 9, 54, 55, 89–92, 190; renaissance, 21–23, 28, 55–57, 83, 161; as setting for book, 7, 8; symbolic importance of, 29, 55, 159, 160; white presence in, 67, 80–82, 85, 87, 97–115, 161, 179, 190, 191

Harlem Congregations for Community Development, 116, 181

Harlem Operation Take Back, 76, 153

Hartman, Chester, 162

Henig, Jeffrey R., 6

Hispanic. See Latinos

Homeowners: attitudes toward gentrification, 123; as beneficiaries of gentrification, 9, 60, 61, 158, 166, 177, 178, 187; low numbers of, 61; protected against displacement, 75, 76, 168, 170, 171, 177; role in neighborhood improvement, 101, 117, 178, 207

HOPE VI, 2, 126, 160, 165

Housing subsidies, 78, 171–80, 183, 206. See also Inclusionary zoning; HOPE VI; Low Income Housing Tax Credit (LIHTC); Public Housing; Section 8; Tax Increment Financing

HPD. See New York City Department of Housing Preservation and Development

HUD. See U.S. Department of Housing and Urban Development

Inclusionary zoning, 172, 173, 176–80, 187

Industrial Areas Foundation, 184, 207
Institutional resources, 130, 131,
     151–54, 156

Jargowsky, Paul, 27, 193

Kusmer, Kenneth, 20

Latinos, 29, 53, 82, 110, 155, 158
Lee, Spike, 56
Lees, Loretta, 6
Legates, Richard T., 162
Lemann, Nicholas, 48, 202
Levy, David, 159, 160
Ley, David, 57, 195, 196, 199
LIHTC. *See* Low Income Housing Tax
     Credit
Lower East Side, 3, 6, 7, 49, 71, 158
Low Income Housing Tax Credit
     (LIHTC), 51, 175, 176, 178, 179, 204

Manhattan, 17, 18, 22, 23, 30, 36, 40,
     42, 49, 95, 96, 113, 120, 150, 167,
     168, 171, 197; Community Board 10
     of, 17. *See also* Harlem; Lower East
     Side; Upper West Side
Marcuse, Peter, 189, 190
Marsalis, Branford, 56
Massey, Douglas S., 114, 189
Methodology, 9–13, 15, 79, 156, 157,
     211–17; sample, *11*
Middle class: exodus of, 26, 71;
     housing choices of, 49; in mixed
     income neighborhoods, 205, 206;
     neighborhoods, 197; preferential
     treatment of, 100; presence in
     Clinton Hill, 40; presence in Harlem,
     9, 23; as source of neighborhood
     stability, 130, 131, 135, 152. *See
     also* Black middle class; Gentry
Mount Vernon, New York, 197
Moving to Opportunity (MTO)
     program, 2, 128, 134
Myrtle Avenue (in Clinton Hill), 17,
     36, 39, 41, 43, 63, 64, 65, 74, 82, 86,
     98, 101, 102

NeighborWorks America (NWA),
     194, 208
Neoliberalism, 7, 16, 49, 188, 193,
     202–7
Neosoul aesthetic, 56, 57, 196,
     198
New black aesthetic, 55
Newman, Kathe, 163
"New Negro," 21
New York City: black population, in
     25, 53; black settlement patterns in,
     18, 20, 22; city government of, 50,
     179; crack epidemic in, 41; crime in,
     82, 115; discrimination in, 23, 24,
     67; household income in, 44; hous-
     ing costs in, *43*, 44, *79*, 97; housing
     patterns in, 43, 72, 97; housing
     programs in, 126; illiteracy rates in,
     23; incorporation of Brooklyn, 36;
     public housing in, 177; real estate
     market, in 40, 44; segregation in, 19,
     24, 191; studies of displacement
     in, 4, 7; suburbs of, 24
New York City Department of
     Housing Preservation and
     Development, 89, 178–80
New York City Housing Authority,
     115

Painter, Noel, 56
Patillo, Mary, 7
Park Slope (Brooklyn), 29, 98, 168,
     176
Payton, Philip A., Jr., 19
Peer effects, 129, 131–35, 147, 149,
     164
Planning, to address gentrification, 8,
     166–87
Policies for gentrification, 166–87
Poverty concentration, 2, 8, 24, 27,
     33, 44, 48, 49, 82, 114, 127–34,
     146, 154, 156, 193, 194, 205,
     209
Pratt Institute, 40, 51, 75, 82, 90
Prince George's County (Maryland),
     51, 56, 197

Public housing: cessation of new, 51, 126, 177; demolition of, 165; in Fort Greene, 29, 39, 41, 42; in Harlem, 26, 29, 177; purchase by Columbia University 115, 112; residents lived in, 60, 64, 89, 90, 98, 112, 135, 141, 143, 144, 163; role in segregation, 112. *See also* HOPE VI

Queens (New York), 24, 52, 55
Queen Village (Philadelphia), 159

Real Estate Board of New York, 59
Rent regulation, 5, 74, 76, 77, 79, 89, 163, 170, 171, 176
Research Methodology, 9–13
Rohe, William, 183
Roosevelt (New York), 197

Saint Albans (New York), 197
Saint Joseph's College, 40
Sampson, Robert, 130, 136, 141, 144
San Juan Hill (New York), 18, 20
Schaffer, Richard, 34
Section 8, 126, 171, 172
Slater, Tom, 4, 6, 7
Smith, Neil, 3, 34, 40, 53, 60, 119, 127, 187, 192, 193, 195, 200, 201
Snipes, Wesley, 56
Socialization, 130, 131, 135–47, 149, 164
Social Ties, 14, 129, 146–51, 155, 164–66
South Bronx, 26, 50, 179
Starbucks, 28, 62, 208
Stoecker, Randy, 182–84, 186
Sumka, Howard, 126

Tax Increment Financing (TIF), 173–80, 186

Taylor, Monique, 8, 23, 55, 179, 190
Tenderloin, 18, 20
TIF. *See* Tax Increment Financing
Turner, Patricia, 120, 123

Upper West Side (Manhattan), 29
Urban League, 24
Urban Renewal, 4, 37, 38, 51, 58, 63, 121, 180, 203
Urban Technical Assistance Project, 51
U.S. Department of Housing and Urban Development, 48, 126

West Harlem Tenants Organization, 76, 153
Whites: as agents of gentrification, 12, 14, 80–87, 97–108, 196; cultural dominance, 190, 196; cynicism toward, 115–24, 160; discriminating against blacks, 19, 20, 111; flight from central cities, 3, 14, 39, 90, 102, 188; interactions with blacks, 132, 133; neighborhoods occupied by, 1, 61, 65, 98, 159, 162, 190, 196–98; population growth in black neighborhoods, 53, 80, 87, 190, 198; preferential treatment of, 67, 102–24, 137, 145, 160, 161; resentment toward, 83–87, 104–7, 143, 144; as symbols of gentrification, 80; visibility in black neighborhoods, 12, 80–89, 92, 98, 137, 150. *See also* Gentry; Middle class
Wilson, David, 2, 6
Wilson, William, J., 27, 71, 89, 114, 117, 125, 128, 130, 152–54, 202
Wouters, Jared, 6
Wyly, E., 163, 186, 193

# About the Author

LANCE FREEMAN is Assistant Professor, Graduate School of Architecture, Planning and Preservation, Columbia University.